I0795760

IMAGES
of America

Barnwell County

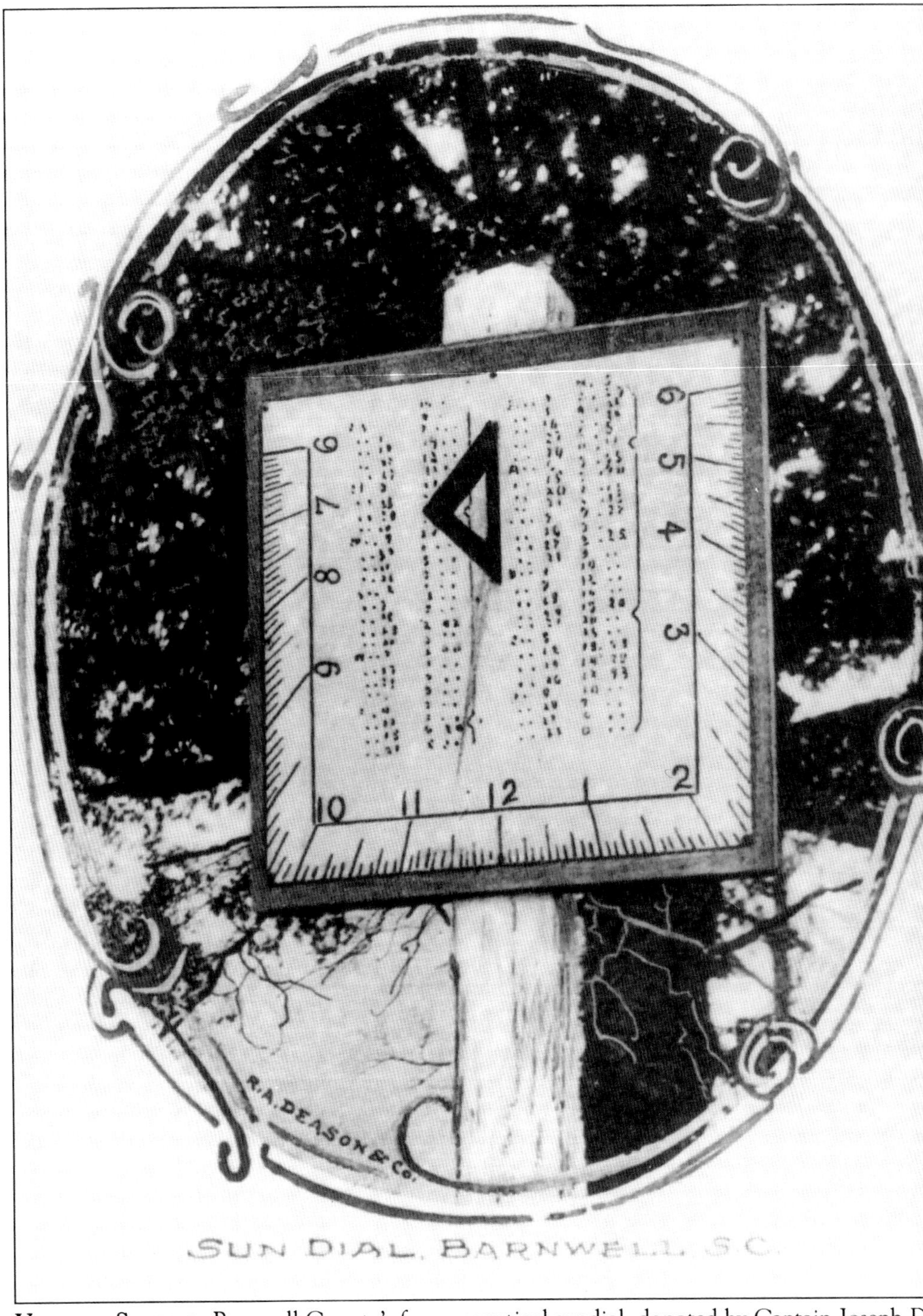

VERTICAL SUNDIAL. Barnwell County's famous vertical sundial, donated by Captain Joseph D. Allen, is a landmark that has endured since it was erected in 1858.

IMAGES
of America

BARNWELL COUNTY

H. Jerry Morris

ARCADIA
PUBLISHING

ISBN 978-0-7385-5417-4

Published by Arcadia Publishing
Charleston, South Carolina

Printed in the United States of America

Library of Congress Catalog Card Number: 99-60291

For all general information contact Arcadia Publishing at:
Telephone 843-853-2070
Fax 843-853-0044
E-Mail sales@arcadiapublishing.com
For customer service and orders:
Toll-Free 1-888-313-2556

Visit us on the Internet at www.arcadiapublishing.com

This volume is dedicated to the memory of my father, Harris Watson Morris, whose love of history inspired me. He is pictured here as a young man in the early 1930s, recently graduated from Barnwell High School and appearing ready to take on the world.

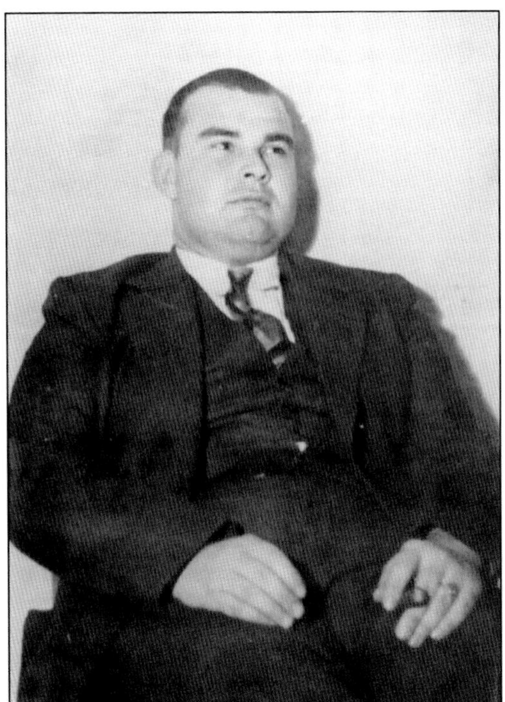

CONTENTS

Introduction

Barnwell, South Carolina

During the Colonial Period, South Carolina was divided into five counties, with what is presently Barnwell County being a part of the Colonial Colleton and Granville Counties. The settlers, predominantly English with a small contingent of German, were served by the Orangeburg Judicial District.

In 1800, Barnwell became an independent judicial district. The dividing line between this district and that of Colleton and Beaufort was the main fork of the Edisto River. Thus, a regional district 47 miles long and 30 miles wide was formed.

The present county was originally known as Winton County, with the first court being held in 1786. The first public buildings were established on land donated by Thomas Wyld and William Robinson near Cedar Branch. The last court for Winton County was held in 1791, and from that time on, the court was held for Barnwell District instead of Winton County.

In 1798, Orangeburg District was divided into Orangeburg and Barnwell Districts. The present Barnwell County was organized and named in honor of General John Barnwell, a Revolutionary War hero. In 1871, Barnwell County lost some territory to Aiken County, and in 1897, Bamberg became a separate county. Finally, in 1919, Allendale County was formed from a part of Hampton and Barnwell, and Barnwell County attained its present boundaries.

As the 18th century drew to a close, a small community was beginning to form on high ground just east of Turkey Creek, where the stagecoach road followed the old American Indian trail toward the coast. Named Barnwell after the same patriotic family that gave the county its name, the little village began to take shape. After the War of 1812, the town of Barnwell was laid out with many of the streets being given names to honor the patriots and warriors of the new country. Therefore, the names of Presidents Washington and Jefferson appear on the map, as well as luminaries of the time such as Burr and Franklin. General Andrew Jackson's name is immortalized in addition to other heroes such as Admirals McDonough and Perry, honored for their exploits on the waters of the Great Lakes during the War of 1812.

Williston, South Carolina

The first inhabitants of the Williston area were Native Americans, who made a living from the land, gathering food and hunting the abundant game in the forests. It is possible that the Spanish explorer Hernando de Sota was one of the white men that the American Indians encountered in the early years.

Williston is named in honor of the Willis family, who came to South Carolina from Virginia in 1750. John Willis, the patriarch of the family, fathered 14 children, including Robert, who prospered and became a well-known planter in the area before his death in 1844. Robert's son, Elijah, subsequently donated land to be used for a church, a depot, and a school. This gift became the nucleus for the town of Williston. The family cemetery is located 5 miles from town off the Springfield Road near the family's original home site.

As was the case in many small towns in South Carolina, the rapid spread of fire was a dreaded consequence of houses and businesses being located within close proximity. Williston has endured at least four major fires that have taken a major toll on the historical documentation of the area. Undoubtedly, many photographs, historical artifacts, and memorabilia went up in flames, never to be recovered.

Like many of the towns that were born along the railroad, Williston owes its very existence to the era of the steam locomotive. In 1827, the South Carolina Legislature issued a charter to the South Carolina Railroad and Canal Company, and by the early 1830s, it became operational. However, the fact that Williston was situated on an important railroad drew the small town into the bitter struggle between the North and South as the War Between the States came to a close. The destruction of the Charleston to Augusta Railroad was one of the major objectives of General W.T. Sherman's cavalry corps, led by General Judson Kilpatrick, and Williston was in the path of devastation.

By the turn of the century, Williston had recovered substantially from the effects of the War Between the States and was re-chartered on May 23, 1904. The area prospered agriculturally, and became a center for asparagus farming, with over 2,000 acres being devoted to the crop. This market dominance continued until the Depression years, when Southern California began to produce the popular vegetable in large quantities. By 1937, the production of asparagus had all but ceased in Barnwell County because California-grown asparagus could be more profitably marketed due to their longer growing season and more fertile soil. The farmers began to diversify and focus on other crops to make a living.

Blackville, South Carolina

One of the early settlers that came to the Blackville area was Nathaniel Walker, who started traveling along the Cherokee trail, which later became the Charleston/Augusta Highway. He settled at what was known as Walker Station, located just west of Healing Springs. Others gradually settled in the fertile area, which abounded with wildlife near the clear streams and springs. Walker served as a surveyor for the Commissioner of Locations, acquiring property along the Charleston/Augusta Road and building stagecoach stops. The *Mills Atlas of 1818 and 1825* shows several forks from this road leading south. Mr. Walker was a member of the Church of England and built a church near his home. After unsuccessfully attempting to get a minister from the Charleston Diocese, he formed his own church around 1770 and became the first pastor.

The growth continued, and by the 1830s a small village was established along the newly built railroad just south of Healing Springs. The village was named for John Alexander Black, sometimes referred to as Colonel Black, who was the chairman of the Intelligence Committee of the Southern Railroad and Canal Company. Mr. Black hailed from Charleston and was responsible for the placement of many of the communities' locations along the rail line from Charleston to Hamburg. Black built a house in the area and moved his family there. After his death, he was buried at the Methodist church in Blackville, and his grave is located under the present Methodist church.

In 1837, the village became incorporated, as the wording of the corporation papers indicated: "And be it further enacted, that the inhabitants of the village of Blackville be incorporated, under the name and style of 'The Village of Blackville,' with like powers and privileges as are granted to the village of Barnwell, except the power of granting license to retail spiritous liquors; and that the corporate limits of said village shall extend to the distance of one-half mile in every direction from the rail road depository." The document was signed by Patrick Noble, president of the Senate and D.L. Wardlaw, speaker of the House of Representatives. It was not until 1846, however, that the town was first mapped out and laid out on paper by Civil Engineer James Clark.

In the heyday of the railroads, Blackville was an important stop on the rail line. Its thriving farmer's market kept the town economically stable. Unfortunately, the demise of the railroads in recent years have left the inhabitants of Blackville struggling to maintain the economic levels of the past. However, the proud legacy of the area keeps the citizens ever vigilant and ready to reclaim the days of glory when the sound of steam whistles filled the air.

ACKNOWLEDGMENTS

I would like to express my thanks to the Barnwell County Museum Board for their willingness to share the museum's collection of photography. In addition, a very special thanks goes to Pauline Zidlick, curator of the Barnwell County Museum, for her assistance and encouragement in this project. I would also like to thank a number of others who contributed their personal photographs and knowledge: Mrs. Esther Williams, Stanley McDonald, Gerald Moore, Jack Gray, Jennings Rountree, Mrs. N.L. Mew, Miss Margaret Anderson, Ronnie Baxley, Nathan Cole, Mrs. Lawson Holland, Rev. Posey Belcher, and my wife, Marie, who supported me throughout the publication process.

One

Early History

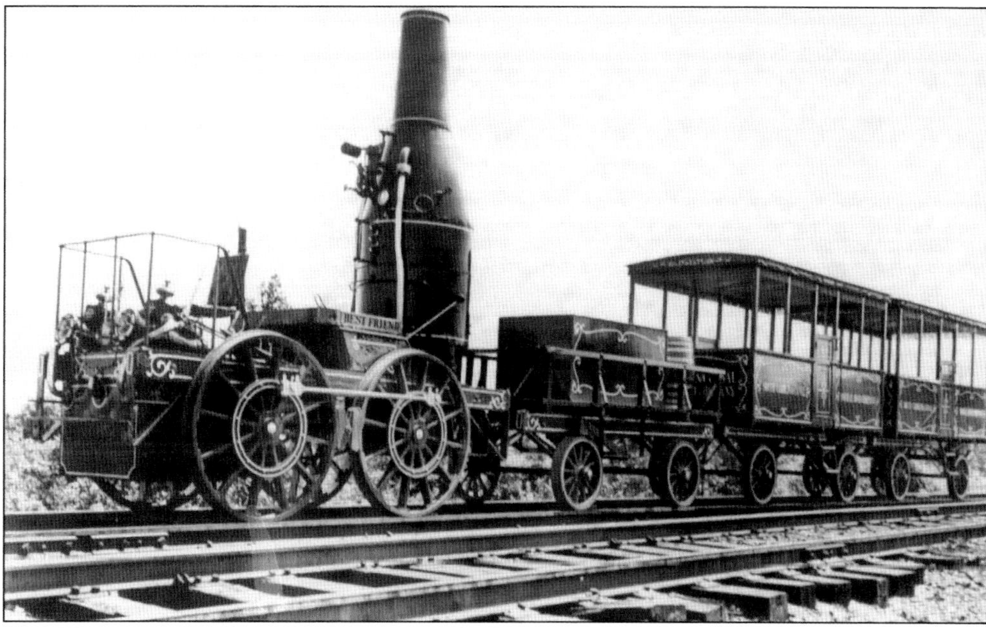

The Hamburg to Augusta Railroad. The locomotive *Best Friend* was constructed in New York and arrived in Charleston on the boat *Niagra* on October 23, 1830. After one of its regular runs, a fireman tied the pressure relief valve down and the 4.5-ton machine blew up. The fireman subsequently died from his injuries, and the engine was rebuilt and renamed the *Phoenix*. By 1833, the railroad from Charleston to Hamburg was ready to transport passengers, and on October 2, the president of the railroad company accompanied the *Phoenix* on its maiden trip. Passing through Barnwell County, the train was met by many well-wishers and curiosity-seekers. The car, with additional passengers and the Augusta mail, "was let down the inclined plane" at Aiken. After leaving Charleston at 5:45 that morning, the train arrived in Hamburg around 8 p.m. The fact that the area near what is now Blackville became an overnight stop on the line was instrumental in the formation of that town. A re-enactment of that original trip was held in the 1960s using a replica of the *Best Friend*.

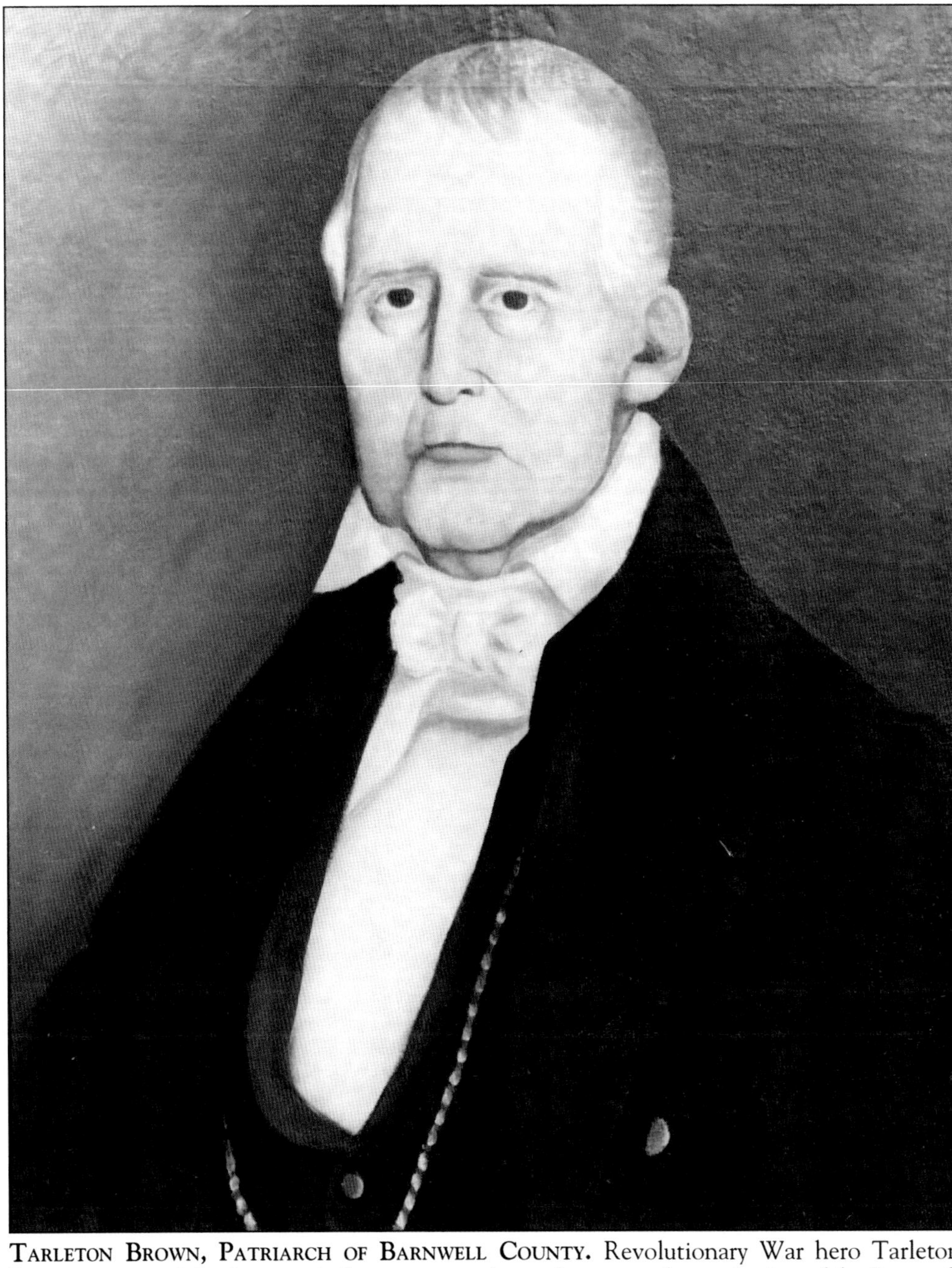

Tarleton Brown, Patriarch of Barnwell County. Revolutionary War hero Tarleton Brown was one of the foremost influences upon the settlement and organization of the Barnwell District. From 1788 to 1790, he served as coroner and high sheriff of Winton County, and in 1791, was a member of the General Assembly of South Carolina. Brown was also the first sheriff of Barnwell District, serving from 1800 until 1804. In the mid-19th century, General Johnson Hagood pronounced, "No man of his day has more of his blood in the present population of Barnwell County than Tarleton Brown." Indeed, his descendants can be found around the county and all proudly proclaim his heritage of service. The publication of his memoirs in 1862 attracted national attention.

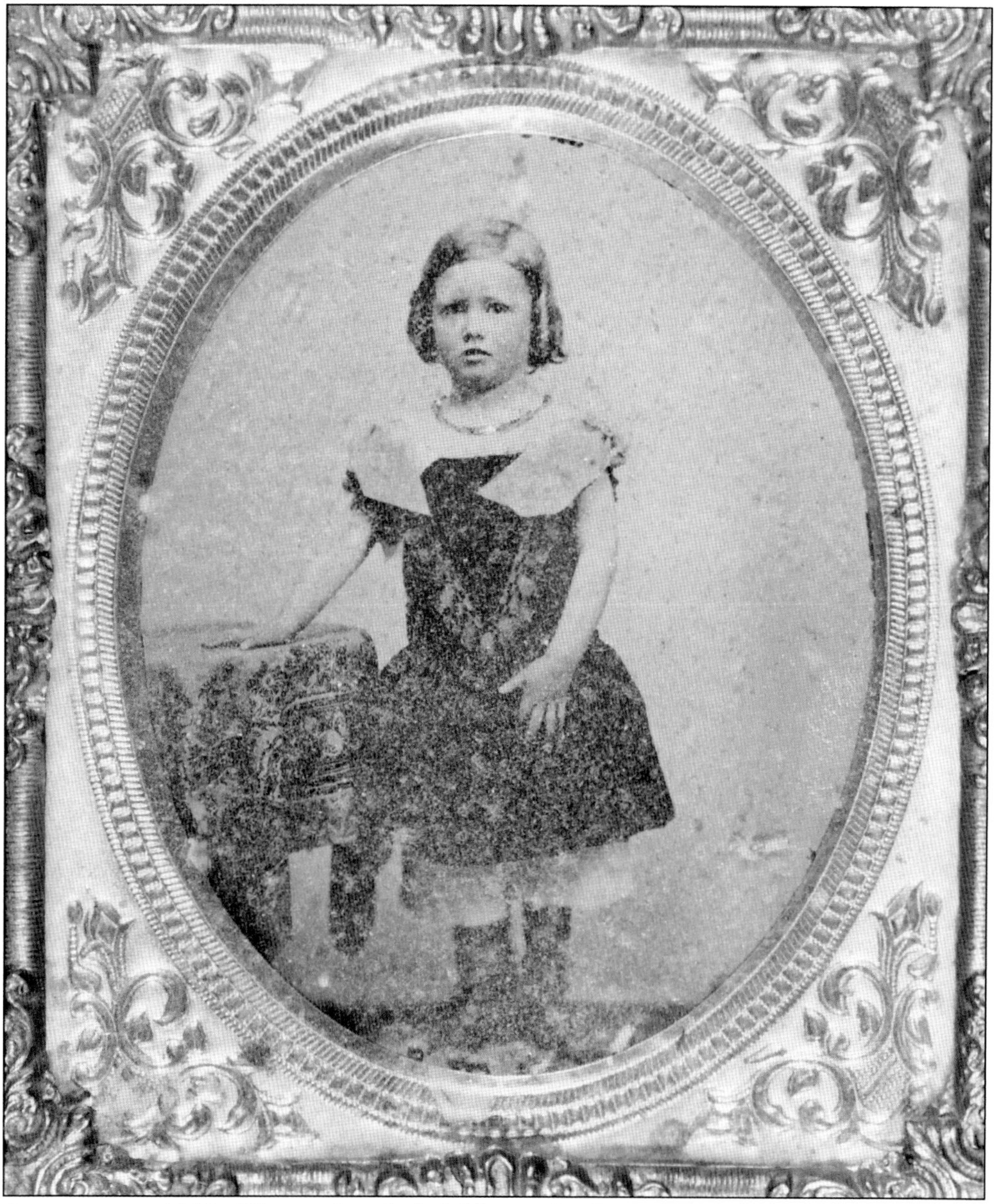

AMBROTYPE C. 1850S. This unidentified child poses for the camera with the typical expression of those who are asked to stand still for a photographer. Possibly a member of the Hay family of Boiling Springs, this young child is oblivious to the political and social upheavals that are to come. The area of Barnwell County known as Boiling Springs, located some 10 miles southwest of Barnwell, was one of the first communities to be formed in the district because of the healthy climate afforded by the lay of the land. Located far enough from the Savannah River to avoid the miseries of swamp land, the community offered a resort-like atmosphere for the early settlers of the district. It was here that the patriarch Tarleton Brown made his home, and his final resting place can be found in a cemetery near the center of the community.

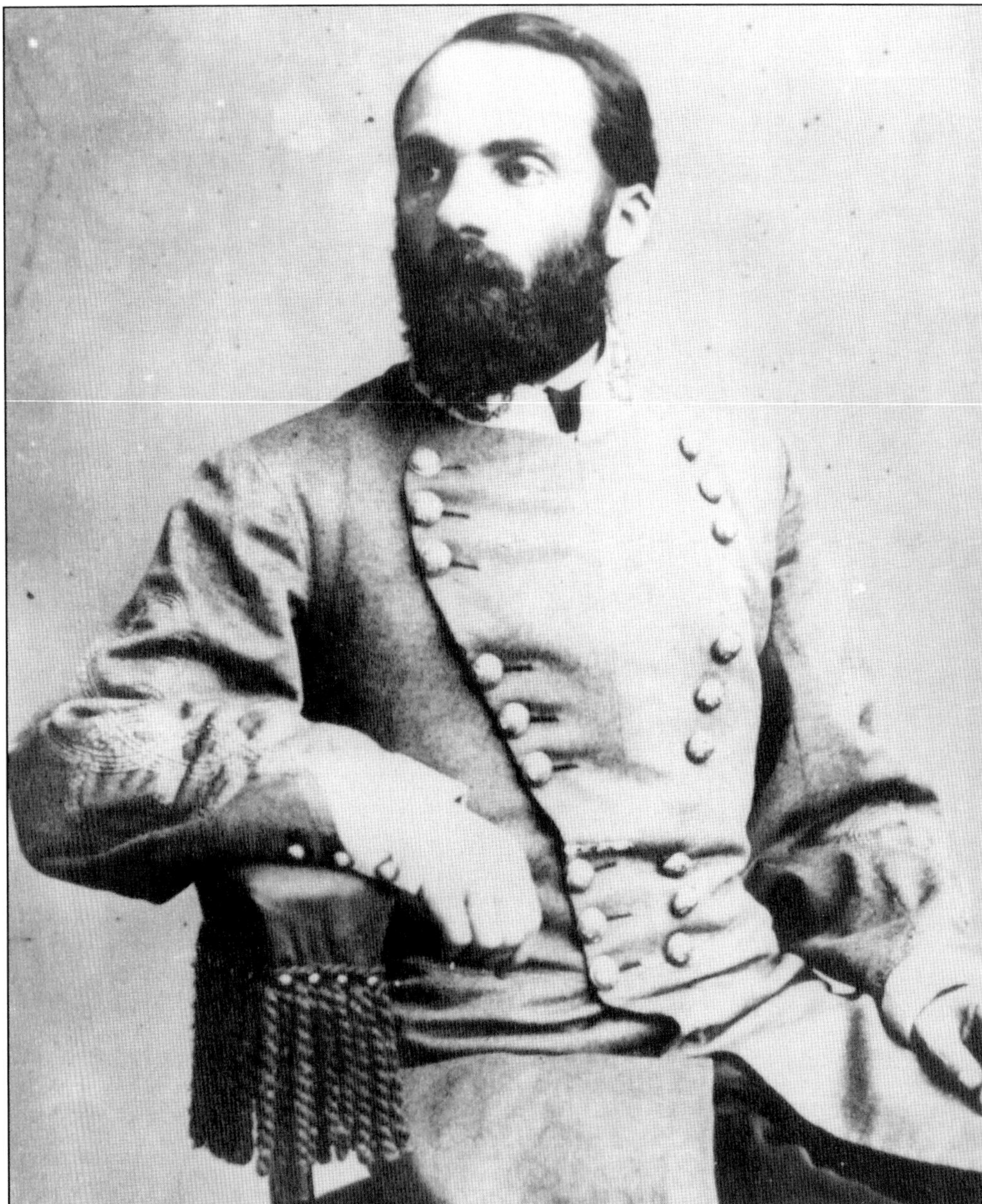

Confederate Major-General Joseph Wheeler. At midnight on February 4, 1865, Major-General Joseph Wheeler dispatched the following message to General G.T. Beauregard: "The enemy have passed Buford's Bridge, moving toward Morris Ford . . . the enemy are also moving northwesterly toward Fiddle Pond." After sending this message from Barnwell Courthouse, he stopped by the earthwork defenses at Morris Ford, just south of Barnwell on the Salkehatchie River, and left a regiment of cavalry to support the artillery battery already in place there. Two days later, the Federal forces, under the command of General Judson Kilpatrick, forced a crossing of the Salkehatchie by outflanking the Confederate defenders, leaving the village of Barnwell at the mercy of the marauding Union army. Local residents struggled to maintain their composure in the face of the enemy, as Kilpatrick's men laid waste to the village, burning the courthouse and many businesses around the town square.

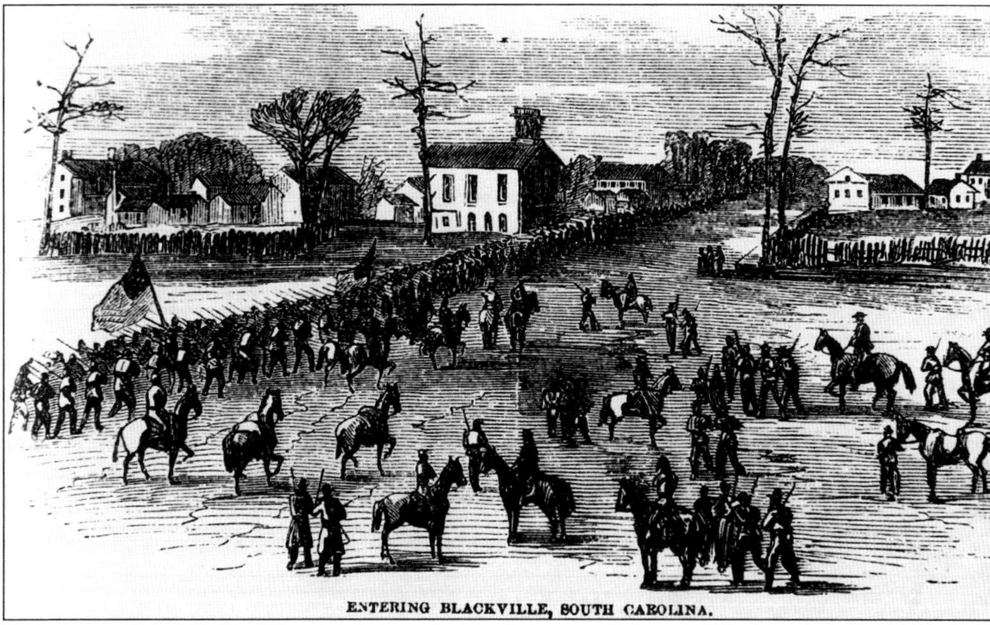

THE 14TH AND 20TH CORPS ENTERING BLACKVILLE. After crossing the Salkehatchie and terrorizing the citizens residing in the village of Barnwell, General Judson Kilpatrick then set his sights on the railroad that ran through Blackville. The Federal infantry followed the cavalry and entered the village of Blackville virtually unopposed.

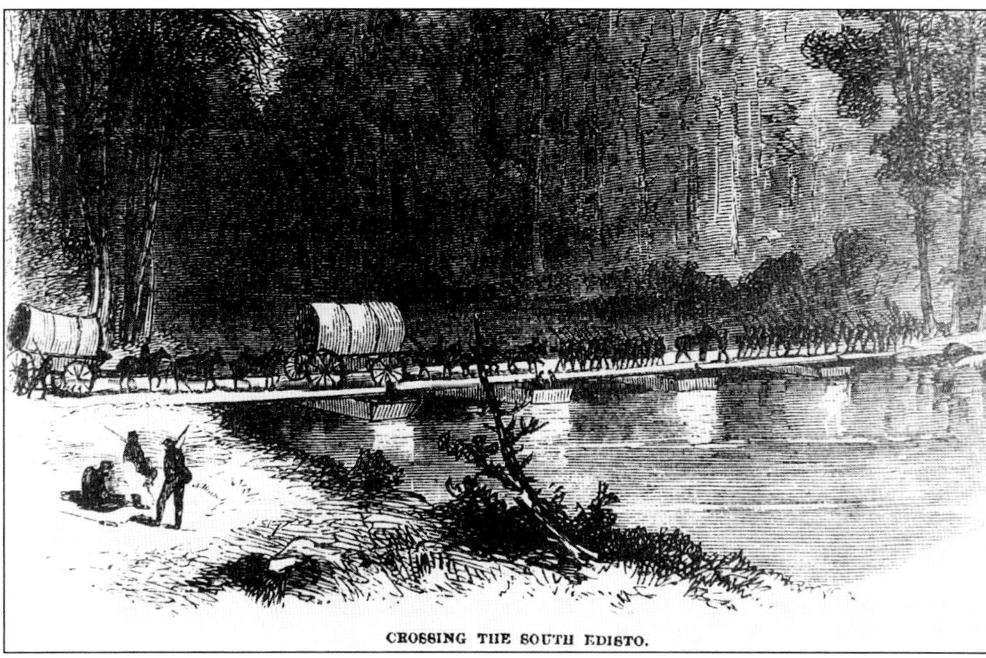

CROSSING THE EDISTO. After General Sherman's 14th and 20th Corps had swept through Barnwell County and destroyed many homes and businesses in the villages of Barnwell and Blackville, they set their sights on the capital and turned toward Columbia. The terrified residents were glad to see the thousands of blue-coated cavalrymen and infantrymen cross the South Edisto and move on.

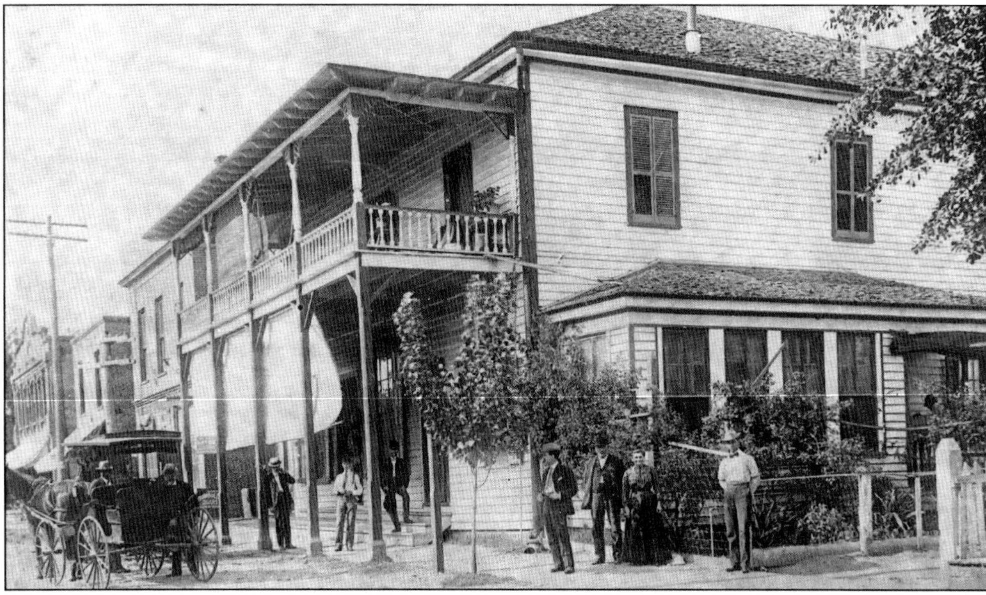

The Molair Store. For many years, one of the circle's most visible landmarks was the building owned by the Molairs. It was first operated as a hostelry, but by the turn of the century, the building housed a general store offering a full line of merchandise for the citizens of Barnwell. In 1936, G. Frank Lindy operated a movie theater in the Molair building until the Ritz Theater was built.

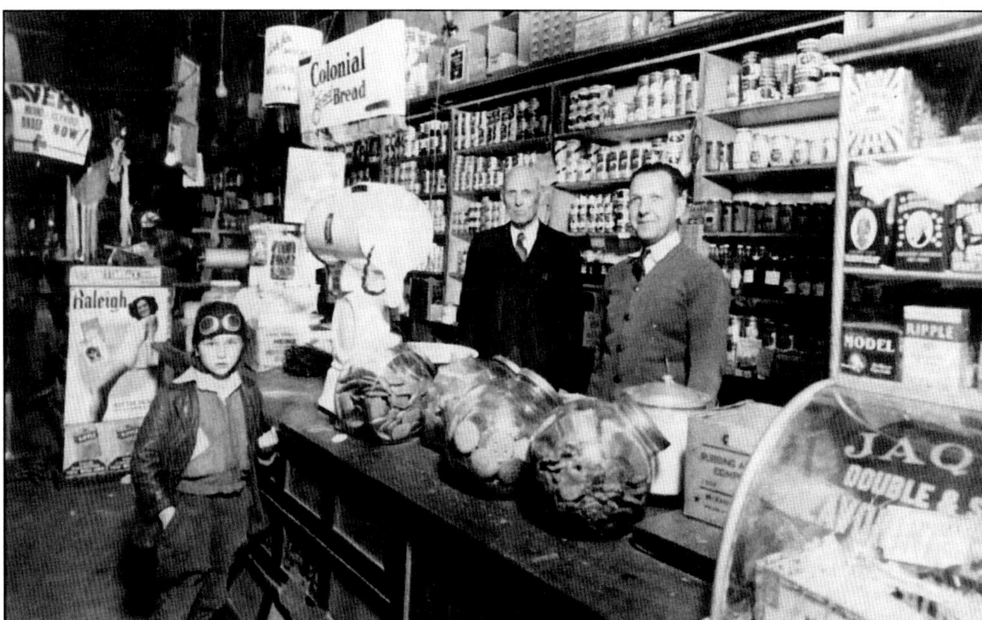

Interior of Molair's. Mr. C.F. Molair first began working in his father's store in 1890, and spent over a half-century serving the citizens of Barnwell County. He took over the operation of the store in 1902 and became a prominent personality as a businessman on the circle in the town of Barnwell.

Two

Barnwell South Carolina

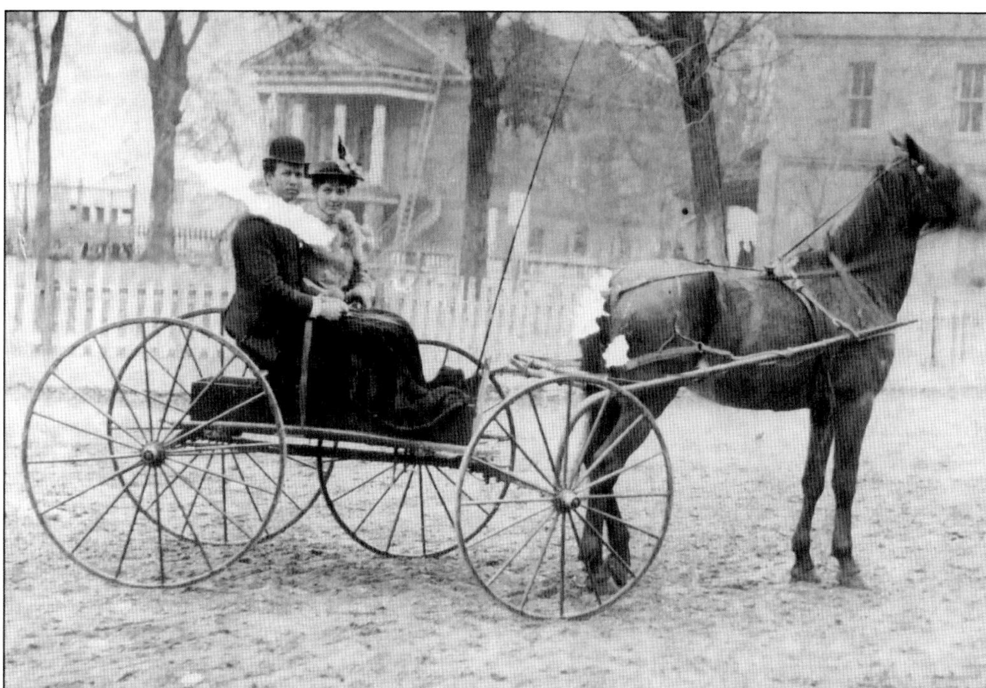

Barnwell's Town Square. Known as "the Circle," Barnwell's town square provided a place for recreation as well as business at the turn of the century. The courthouse and sundial can be seen in the background.

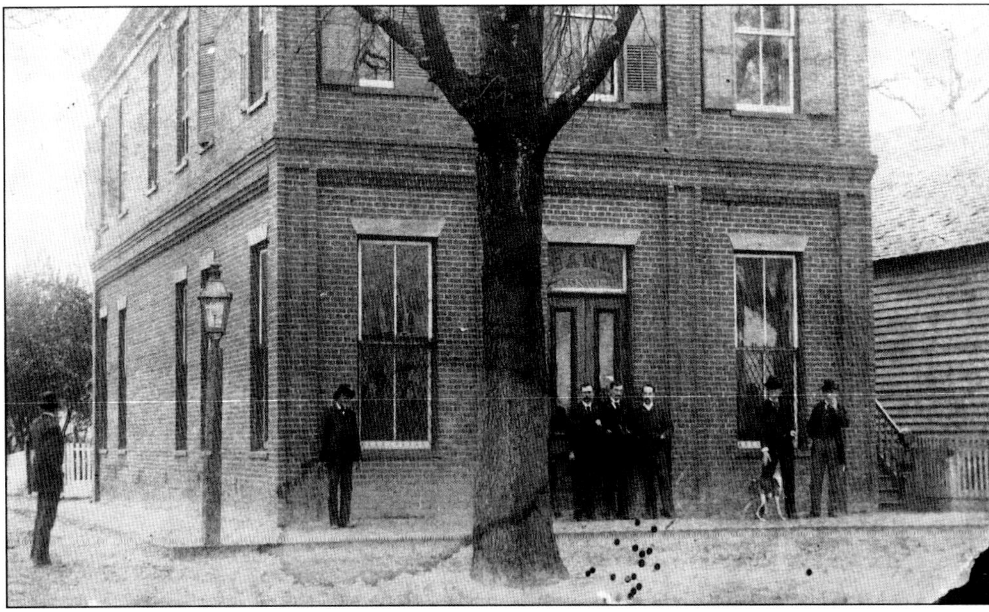

WESTERN CAROLINA BANK. The Bank of Western Carolina stands on the corner of Main and Jefferson Streets just across from the courthouse. Its sturdy construction and elegant architecture make it a landmark which has endured. As can be seen in subsequent photographs, the structure has been remodeled a number of times and gone through some name changes, but continues to function as a banking establishment to this day.

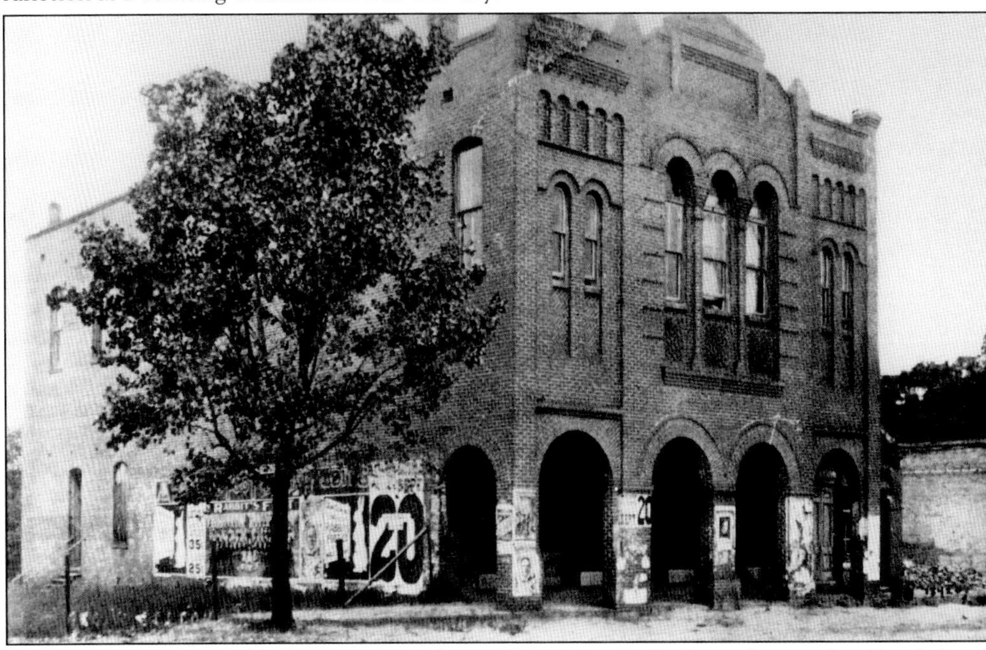

OPERA HOUSE. The old Opera House, located just across Jackson facing the Confederate Monument, was a familiar landmark until around 1915, when it burned in a spectacular fire. The dispensary was located on the ground floor of the building, and for many years after the fire the spot was littered with molten glass from the whiskey bottles that were destroyed during the blaze.

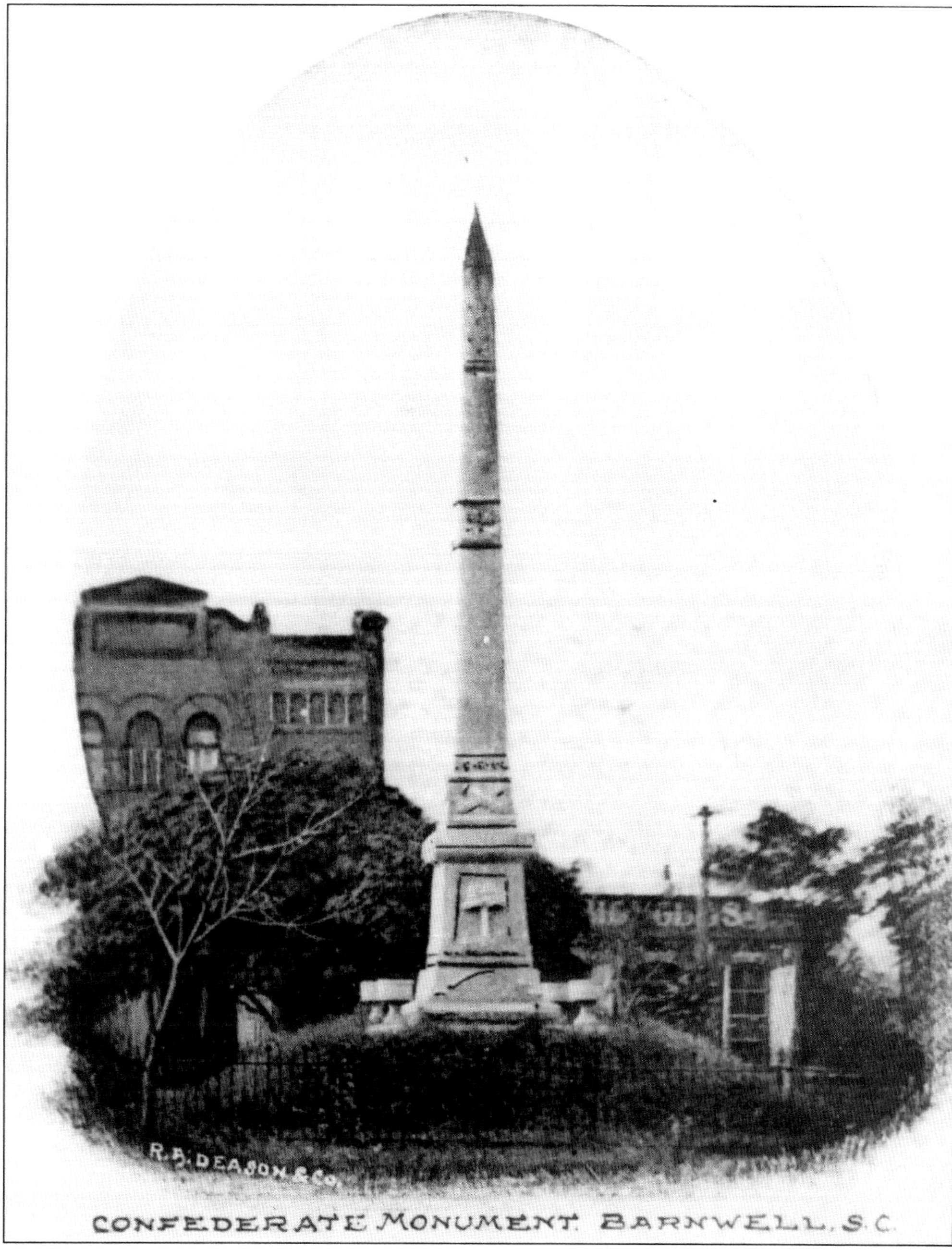

CONFEDERATE MONUMENT. This elegant tribute to the men who fought in the War Between the States stands in Calhoun Park just across from the courthouse. The gray marble and granite obelisk was designed by the Artope and Whitt Marble Yard of Macon, and was erected by the Barnwell Ladies Memorial Society at a cost of $800. On August 22, 1900, the cornerstone was laid with Masonic rites.

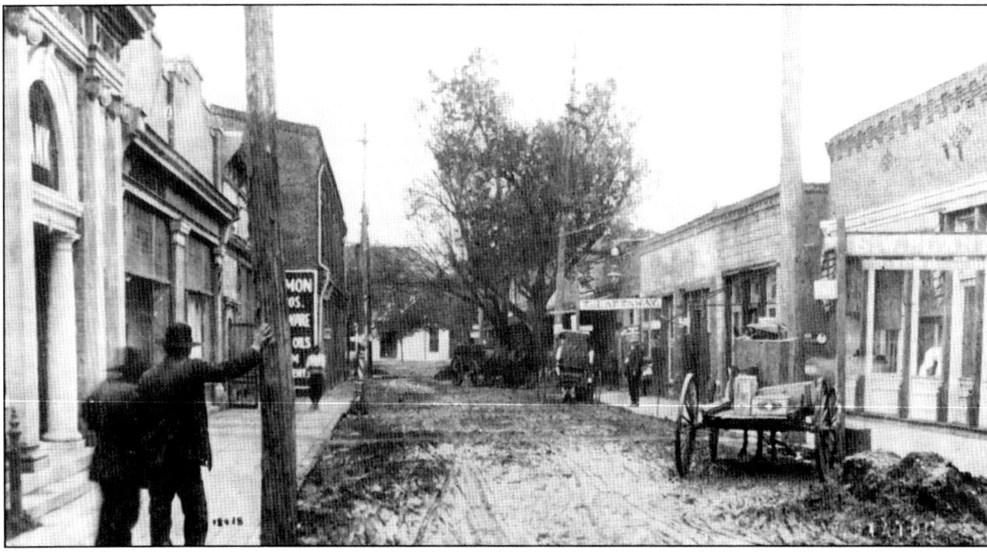

Turn-of-the-Century Main Street. This view of Main Street, taken around 1914, looking west toward the circle, shows the narrow street that was once a part of the Cherokee Trail. Historians speculate that the trail, as well as the road that subsequently was placed upon the same route, crossed Turkey Creek just west of the circle a few hundred yards downstream of the present bridge.

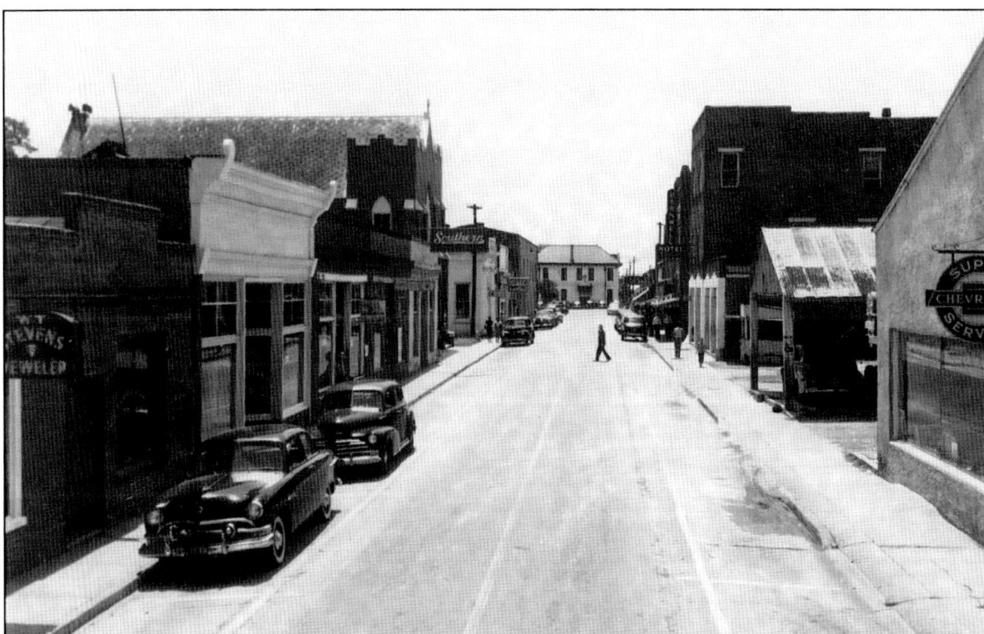

Main Street in the Early 1950s. Looking toward the west from approximately the same vantage point as in the above photograph, this view shows the changes that mid-century brought to Barnwell. The remodeled bank building on the corner of the circle continues to stand as a landmark, and other stores are still recognizable today.

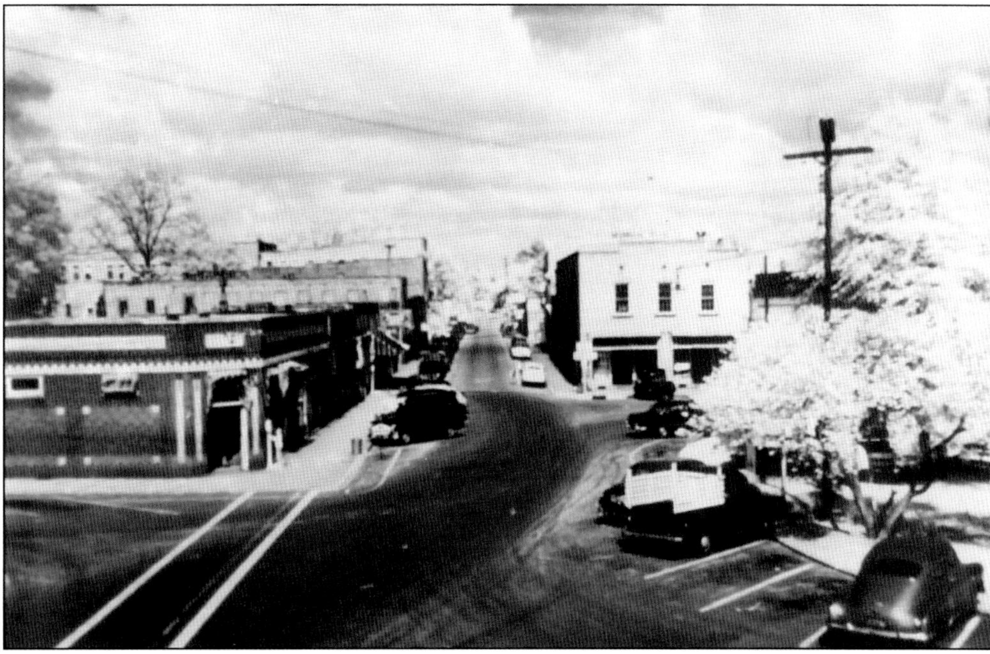

Main Street Looking East. This view of the circle and Main Street taken around 1950 shows the opposite angle from that of the preceding photographs.

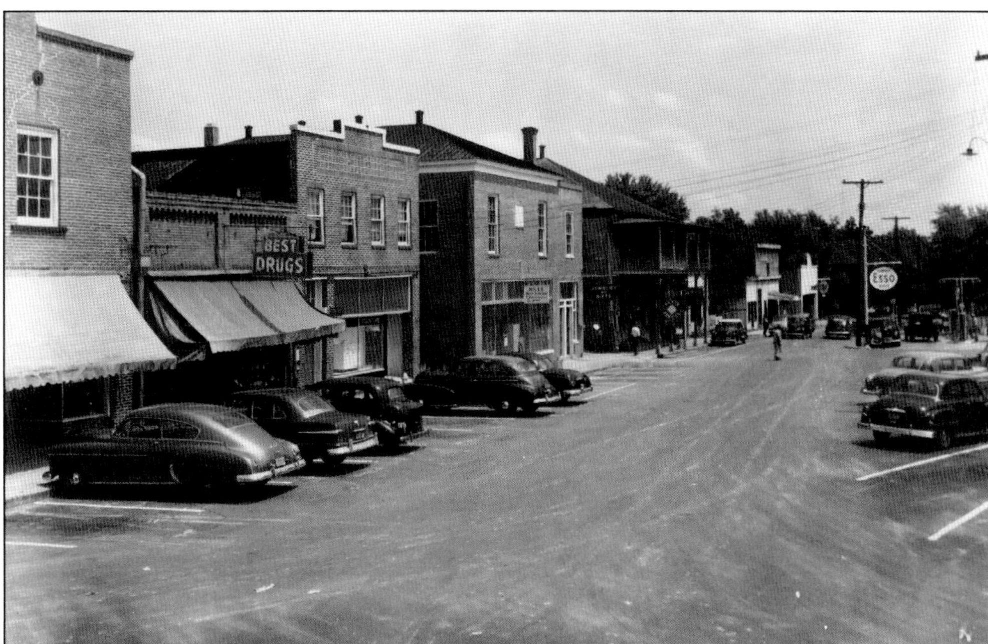

Looking Down Burr Street. The skyline just east of the circle is dominated by several buildings housing businesses. The exception to this is the Masonic Hall, owned by Harmony Lodge #17, Ancient Freemasons of South Carolina.

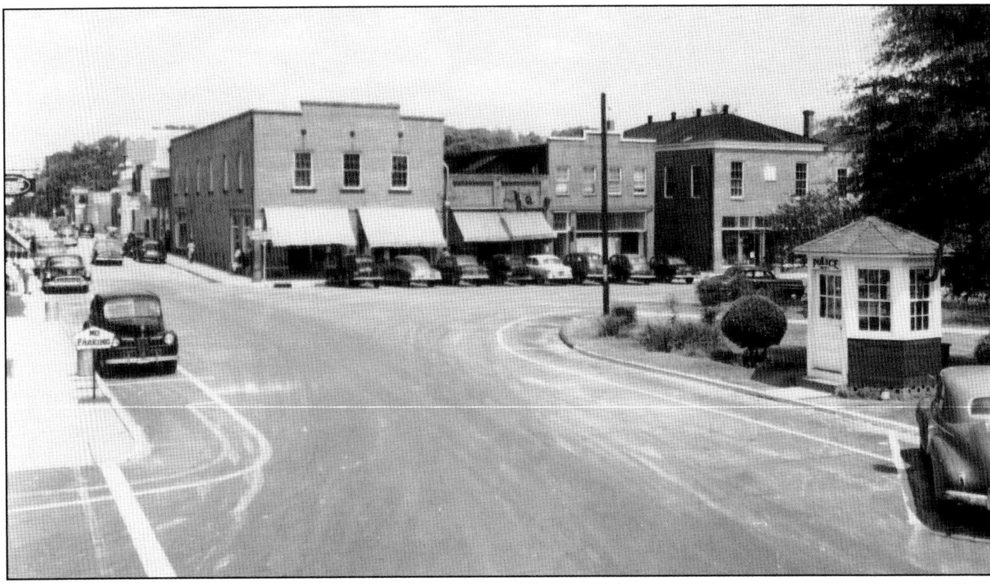

POLICE STATION. The Barnwell policemen could boast having a unique structure for their headquarters. The small, but functional "Little Round House" served the law enforcement personnel well for many years. Situated right in the center of town where the most activity was, the headquarters gave Barnwell policemen a close-up view of the town. Night or day, anyone who needed the lawmen knew just where to find them.

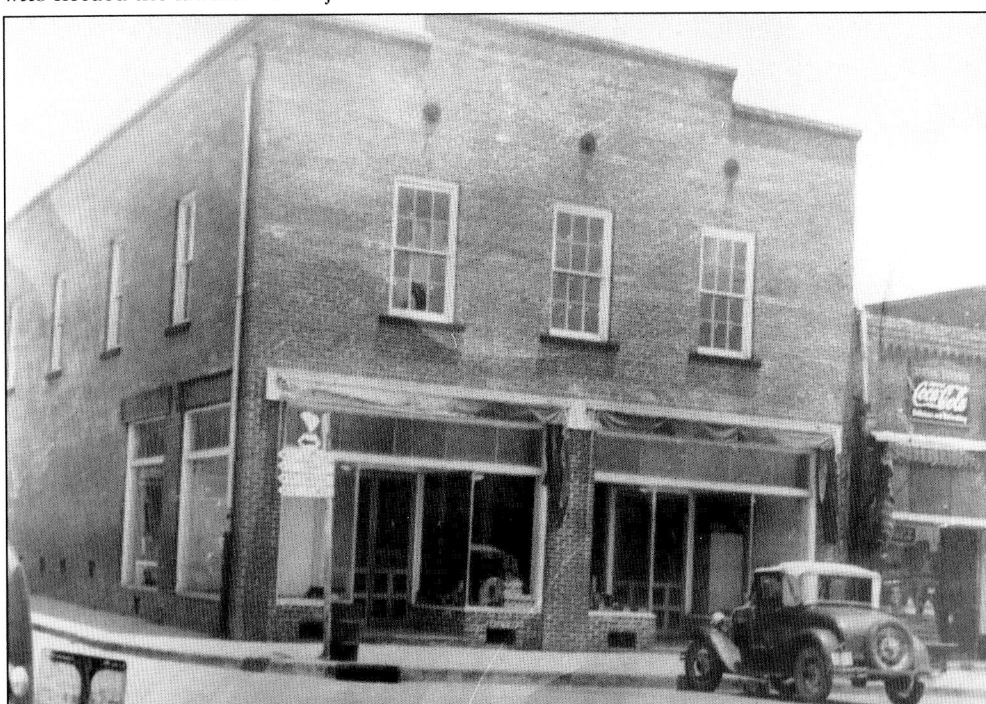

LEMON BROTHERS. Anchoring the northeastern corner of the circle, the Lemon Brothers store was a fixture for many years. Later becoming Stafford's Department Store, the site has always been a profitable location for store owners.

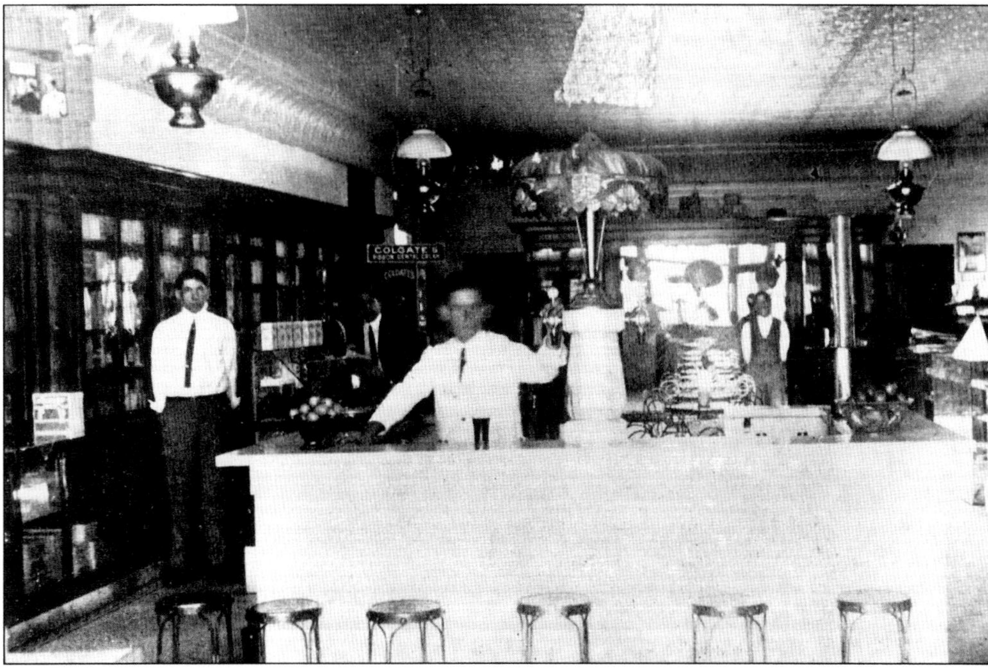

BURCKHALTER'S DRUGSTORE. The interior of Burckhalter's Drugstore shows a typical pharmacy of the early 1900s. Drugstores were a meeting place for the citizens of the community as well as a source of medical necessities. View-cards such as the one shown here were among the items carried in the store.

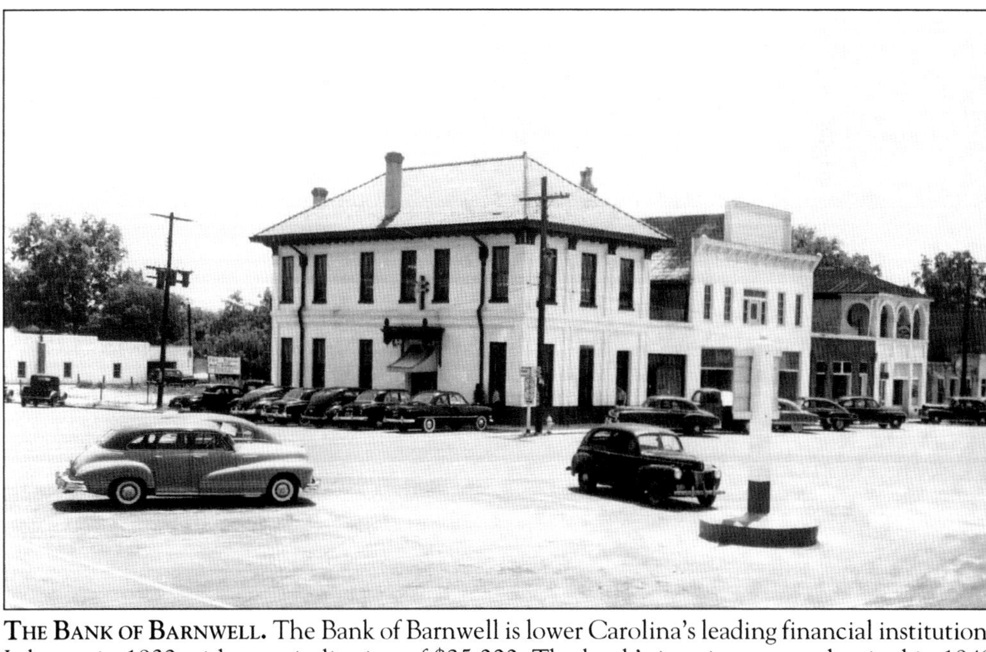

THE BANK OF BARNWELL. The Bank of Barnwell is lower Carolina's leading financial institution. It began in 1932 with a capitalization of $25,000. The bank's interior was modernized in 1949 and then enlarged a few years later, with the relocation of C.G. Fuller's offices. Senator Edgar Brown's law offices occupy the upper floor of this mainstay of Barnwell's economy. The founders of the bank were C.G Fuller, Senator Edgar Brown, and Perry A. Price.

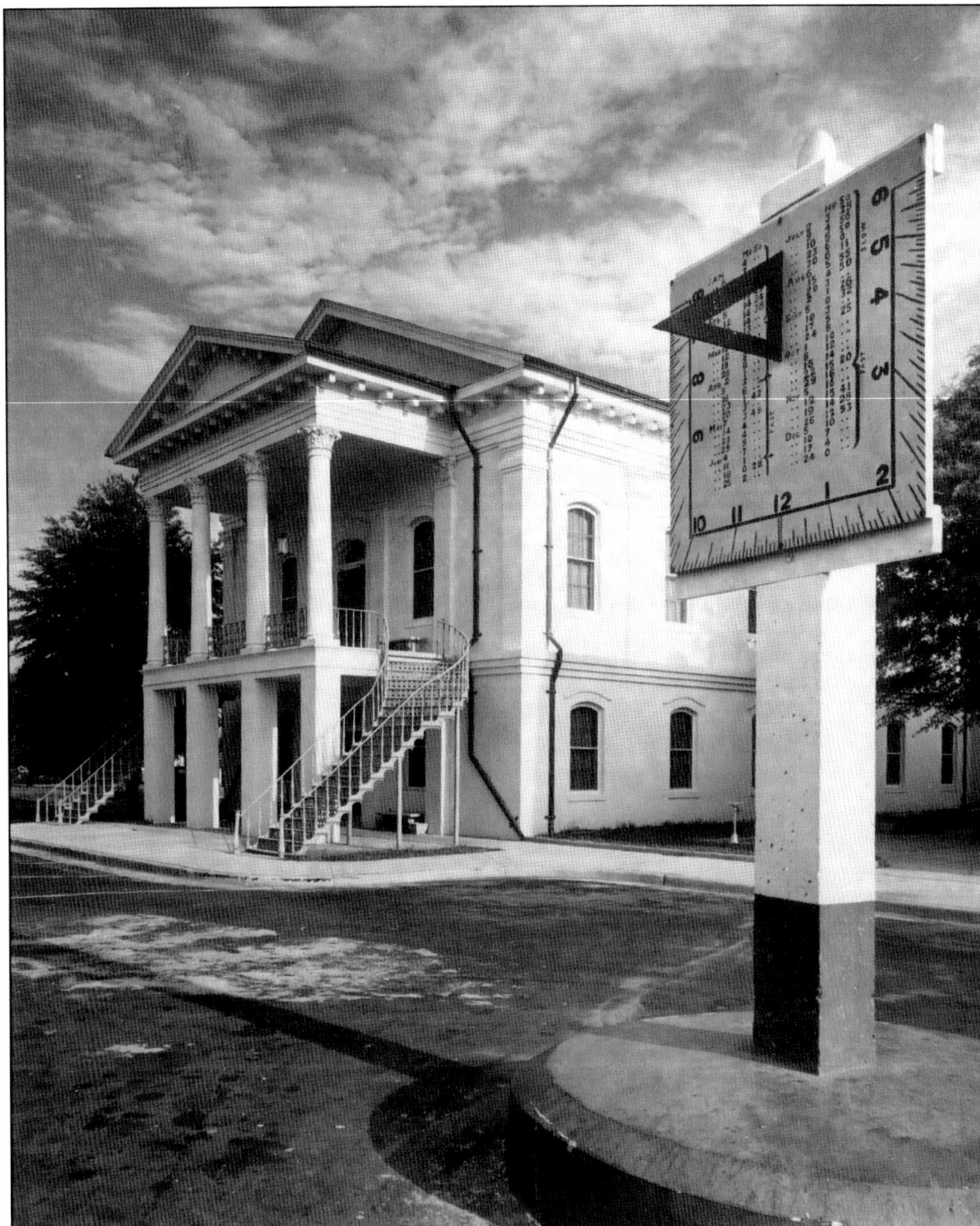

The Vertical Sundial. In 1858, Captain Joseph Allen, one of the wealthiest citizens of South Carolina, gave the village of Barnwell this vertical sundial. The unusual timepiece keeps almost perfect Eastern Standard time and is thought to be the only surviving vertical sundial in the United States. Allen, who owned extensive properties including a very profitable plantation in Louisiana, fell in love with Miss Nancy Louise Myers at first sight and married her in 1838. He built a handsome home, The Cedars, on a 40-acre site located a short distance from the center of town. The old landmark was torn down years ago and replaced by the modern home of Mr. and Mrs. Calhoun Lemon. The remainder of the Allen property was sold to other individuals. Captain Joe was described as being kind and affectionate, but extraordinarily pompous.

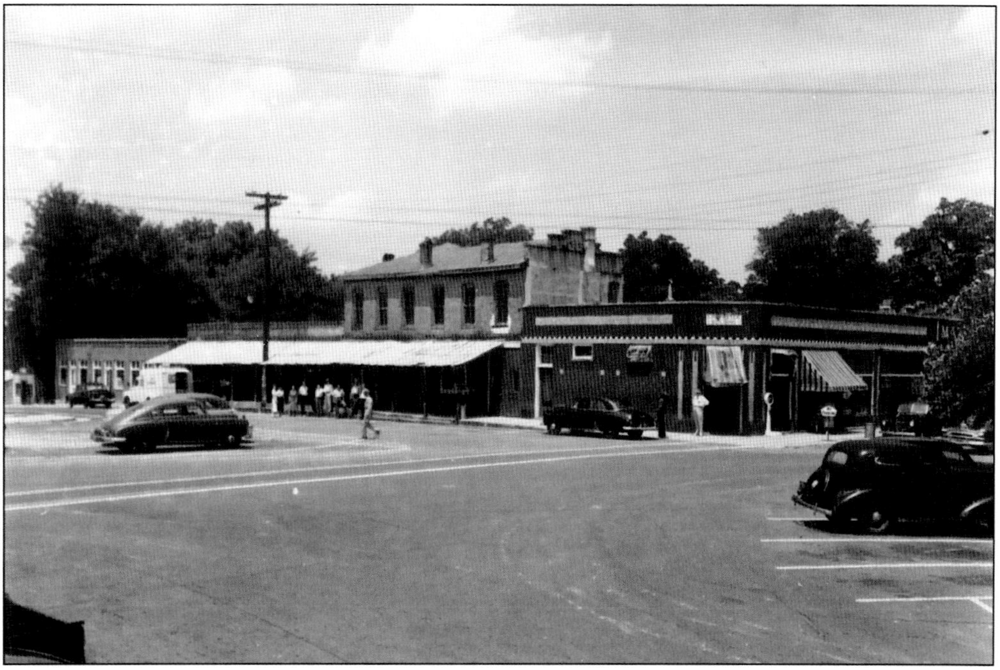

Wall Street. Being situated just across the street from the courthouse and around the corner from the businesses on the circle gave the small grocery store and cafe an advantage that other establishments lacked—proximity. Merchants and shoppers alike could have a leisurely breakfast or make a quick stop for staples before leaving from work.

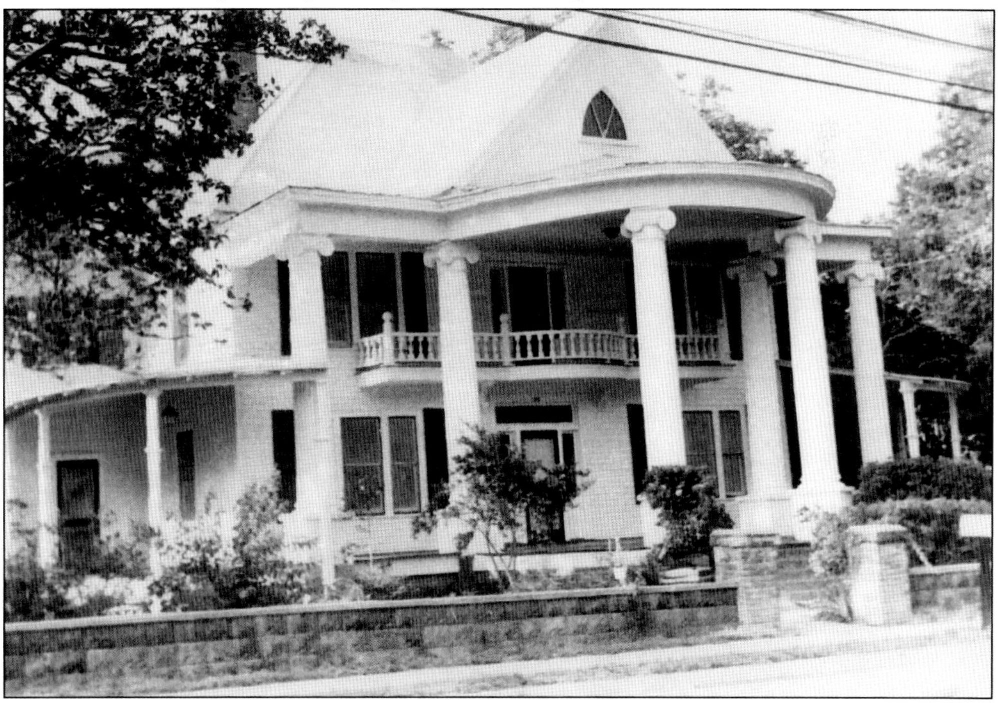

Colonel Mosby's House. This residence, owned by Col. M.S. Mosby, was typical of the grand homes that graced the streets of Barnwell in the late 1800s and early 1900s.

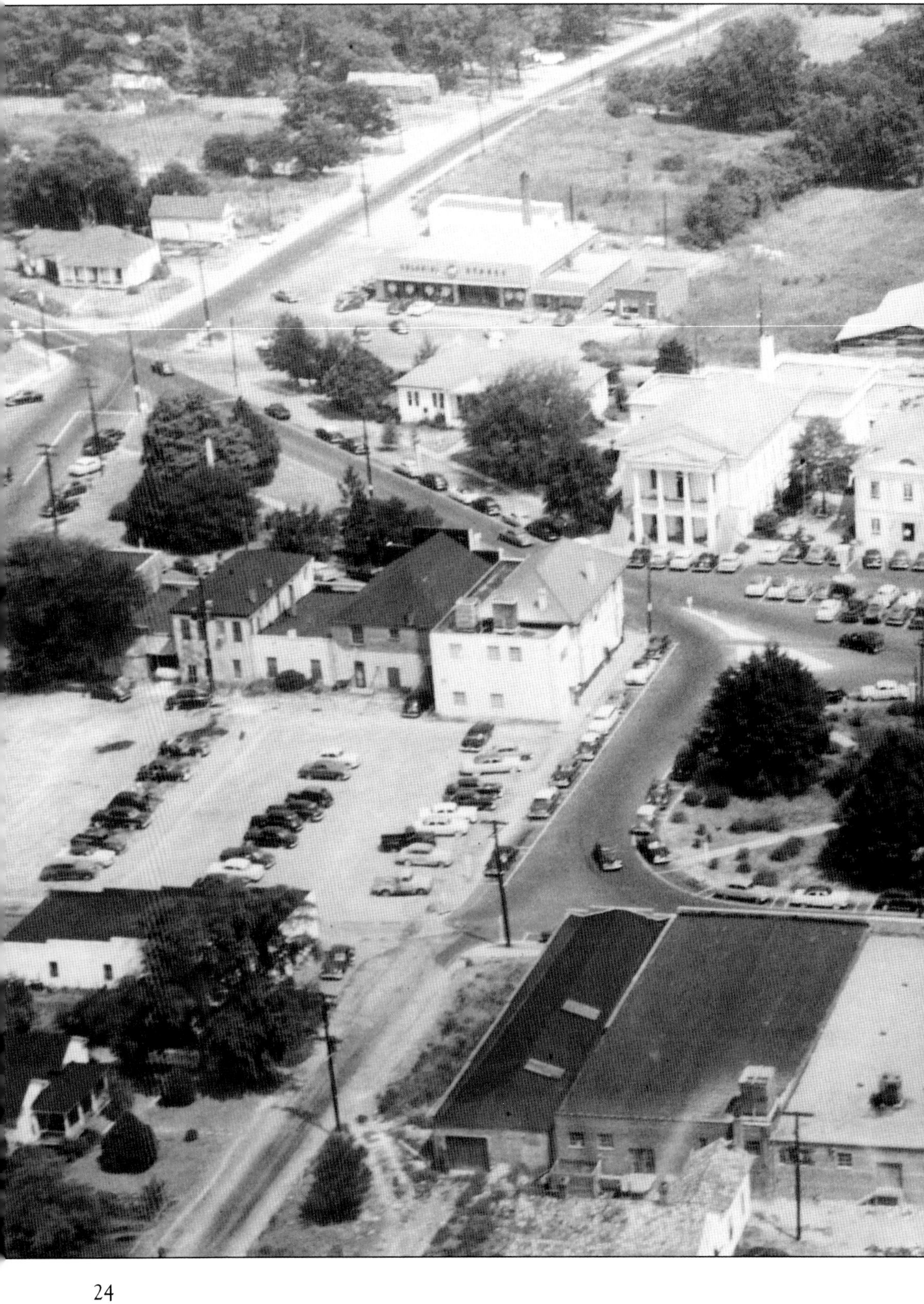

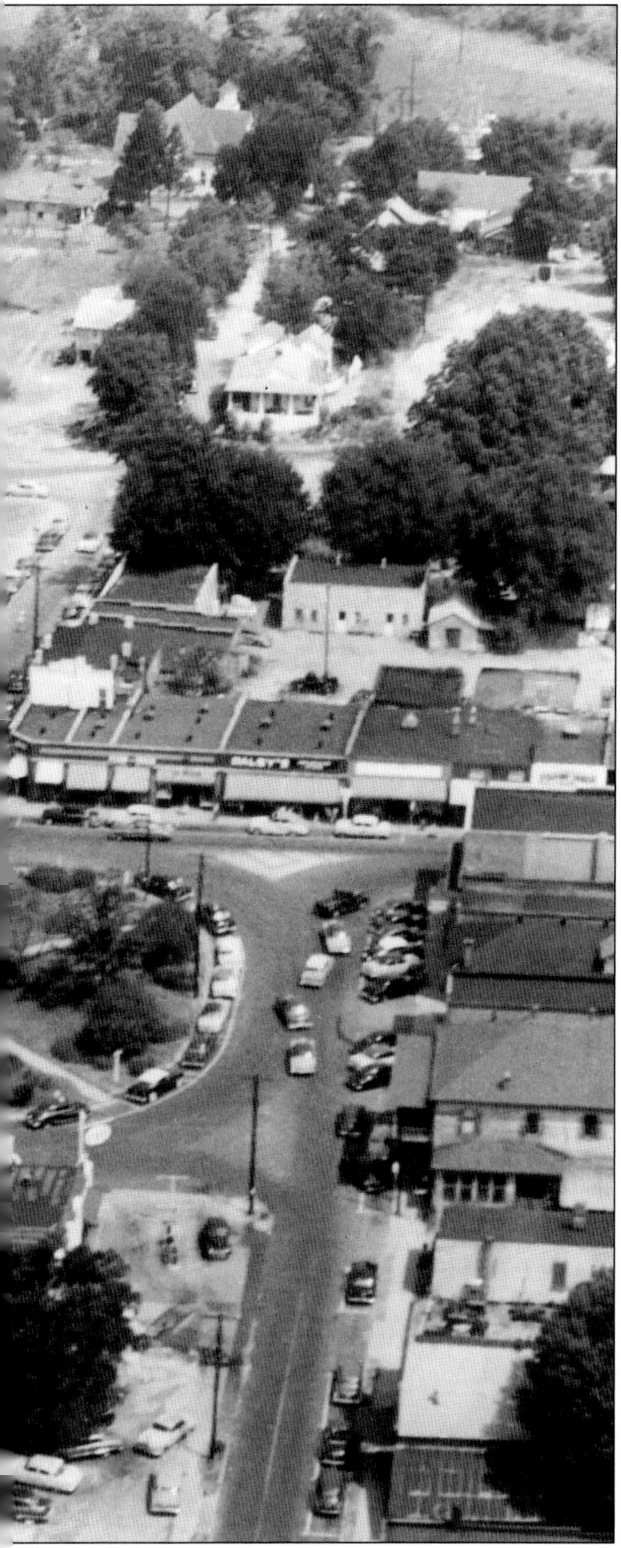

DOWNTOWN BARNWELL. This aerial photograph of downtown Barnwell provides a perfect view of the circle and the surrounding area. The Bank of Barnwell stands in front of the courthouse, and the adjacent empty lot is the site of the old Circle Inn. Buildings now fill most of the frontage of the old lot, and the section in the lower right portion of the photograph now contains parking for new businesses that have been constructed just off of the circle area.

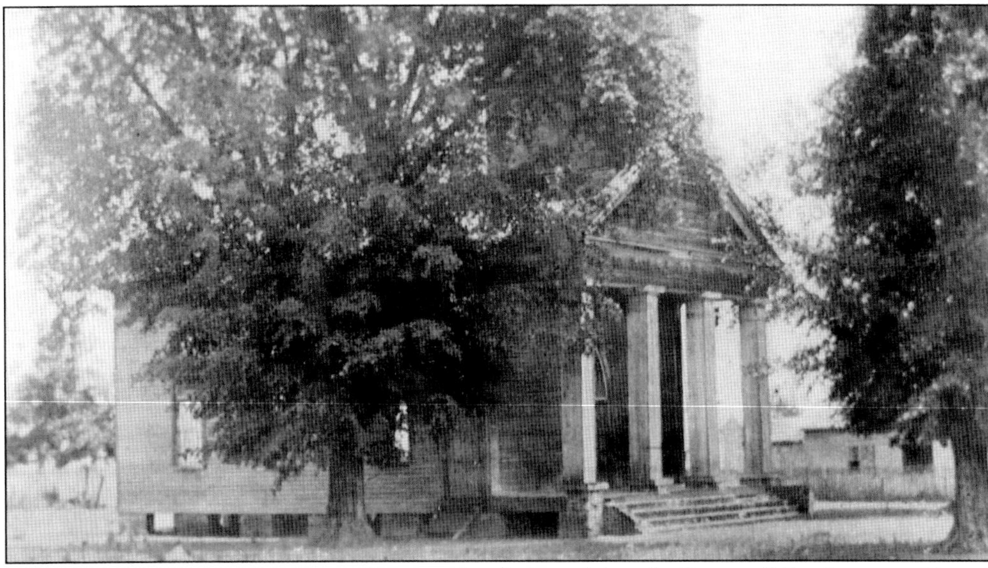

OLD PRESBYTERIAN CHURCH WITH STEEPLE. It is believed that the Barnwell Presbyterian Church was built in 1852. Edwin A. Hagood gave the grounds for the church with the stipulation that no burial of members would take place on the property. The timber for the construction of the church was cut from Hagood land and sawed into lumber at the Hagood's Mill sawmill located a few miles west of town. One of the old Sessions Books lists Dr. James O'Hear Hagood as ruling elder and many families, including the Carrs, Hutsons, and Clarks, as members. From 1865 until 1868, the church was used as a courthouse with Judge A.P. Aldrich presiding. The original courthouse on the circle was destroyed by Sherman's cavalry commander, General Judson Kilpatrick.

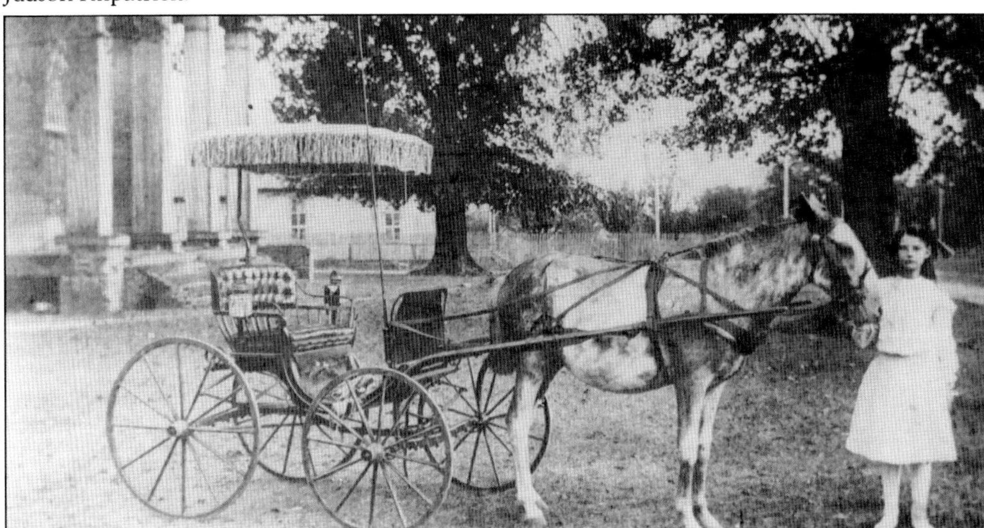

TURN-OF-THE-CENTURY PRESBYTERIAN CHURCH. In 1891, the building was struck by lightning, completely destroying the tall steeple and damaging the interior of the church. For a short time, the church building was abandoned, but by 1894, Dr. H.R. Murchinso began holding services once a month and the congregation began to grow. The church received a boost when Judge Willie Townsend moved from Aiken with his family and organized a Sunday school.

Three

Local Churches

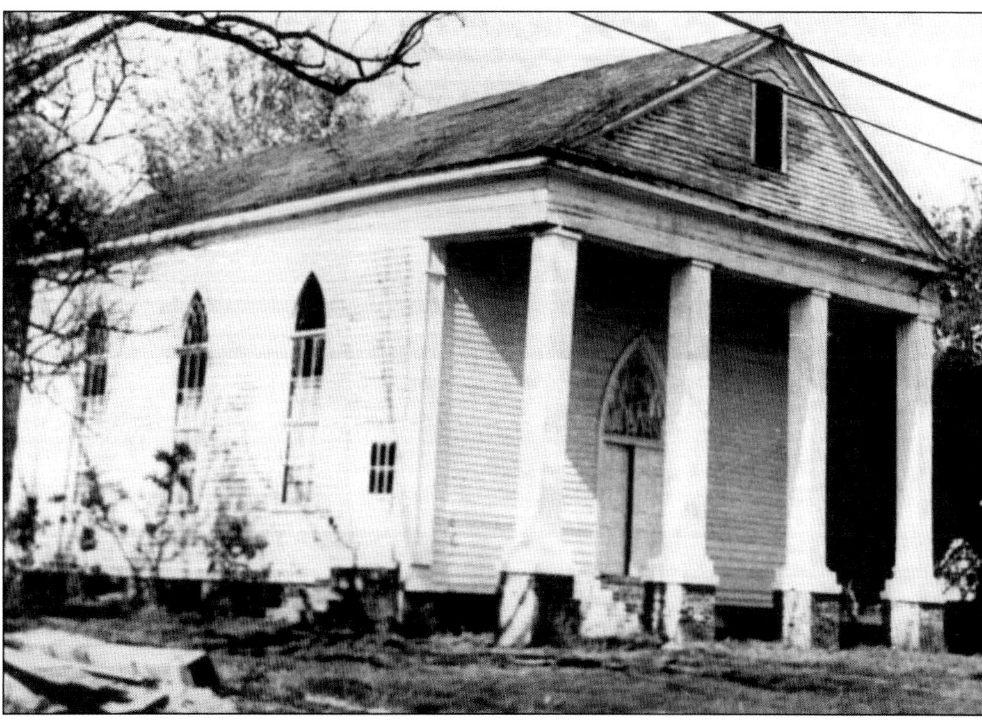

Presbyterian Church. In 1910, after a week of evangelical services, a number of prominent citizens moved their letter to the church. In that same year, a Ladies Aid Society was formed, and the church began to prosper once again. Today, the ministry of the church reaches throughout the community and continues to serve the Barnwell community.

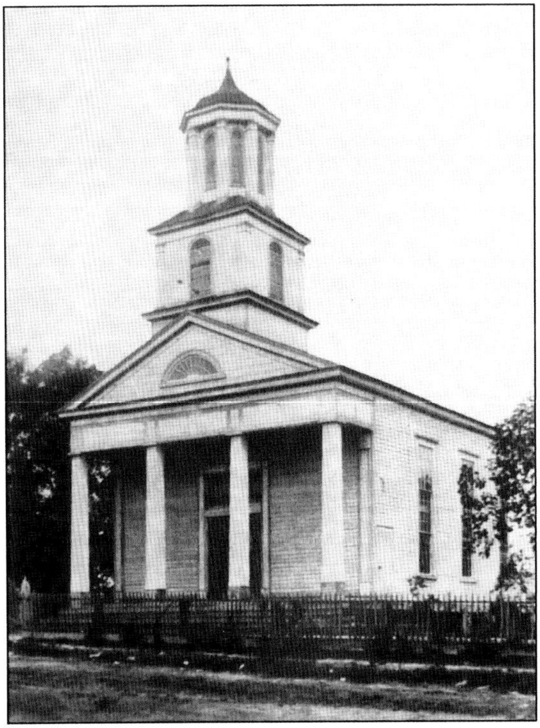

Old Baptist Church. The structure pictured here was the third Baptist church building that the congregation used, the previous sanctuary having been sold to the Bethlehem congregation. The first minister to serve in this church was Rev. T.W. Mellichamp. The dedication services were conducted in 1854 by Rev. W.B. Johnson, president of the South Carolina Baptist Convention and chancellor of Johnson Female University (later Anderson College).

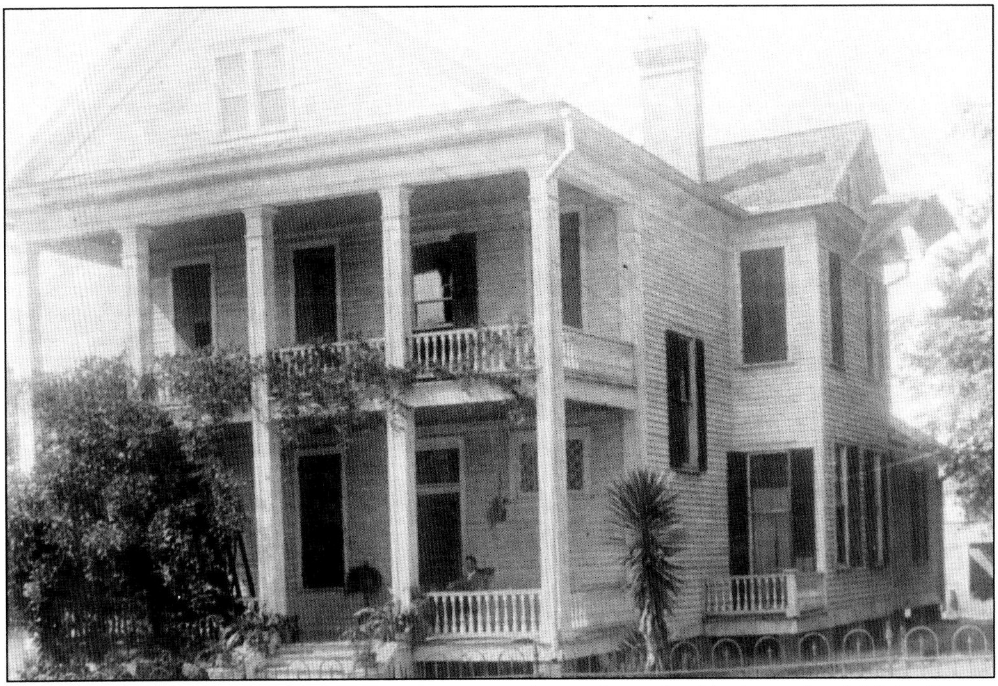

Baptist Parsonage. The Baptist parsonage was located on the block south of Main Street, facing Franklin Street. When the new parsonage was constructed in the 1950s, the old parsonage was sold and moved farther south, although still facing Franklin.

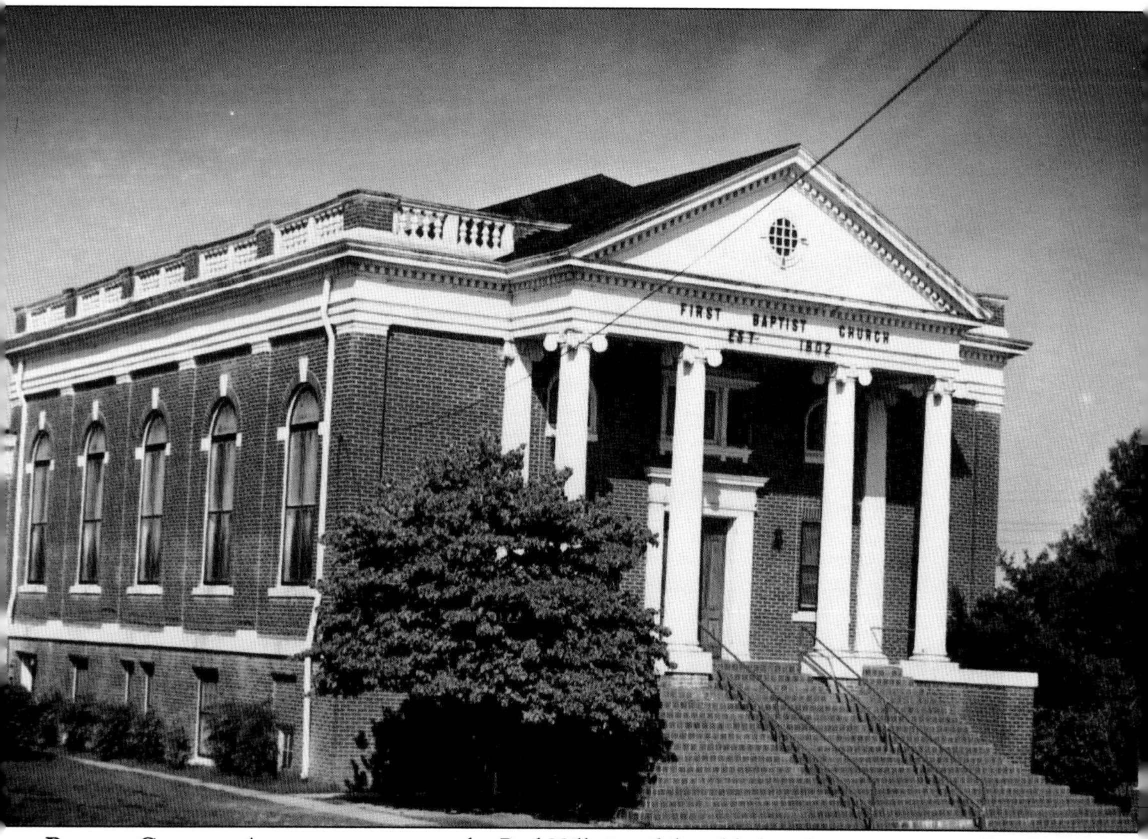

BAPTIST CHURCH. A new sanctuary on the Red Hill site of the old church was constructed and occupied by 1926. The first pastor of this new church was Reverend W.M. Jones. This church building served the needs of the First Baptist congregation until 1962, when a larger church was erected on Allen Street. A few years after the new church was occupied, the old building was lost to a fire.

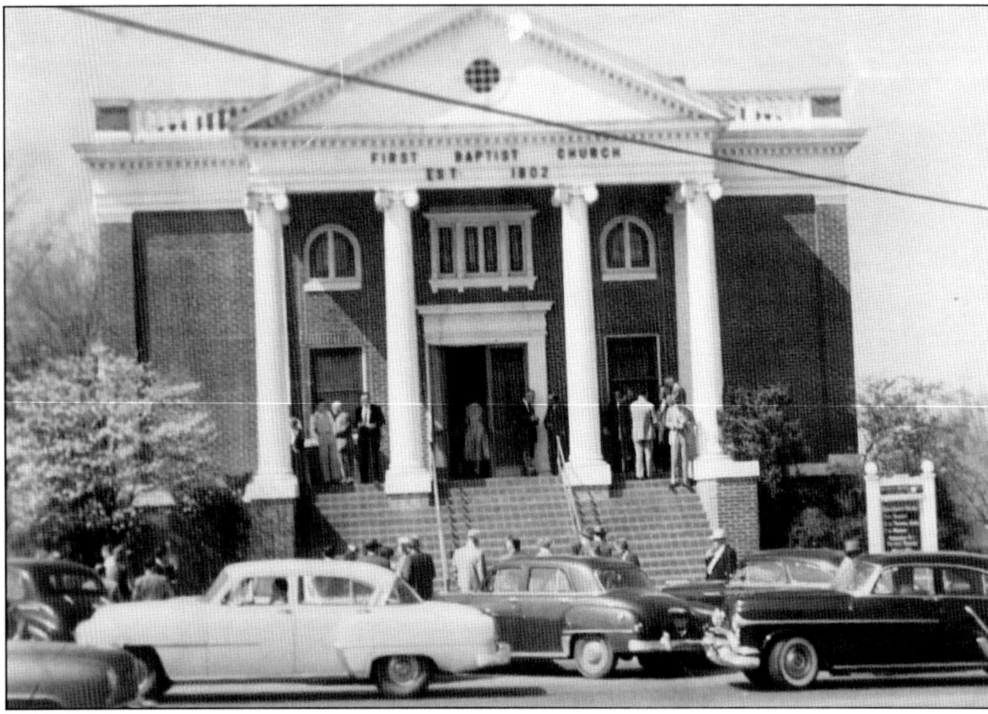

FIRST BAPTIST CHURCH SERVICE. The growth of the Baptist denomination during the Savannah River Plant construction days forced the church to conduct double Sunday services until satellite churches such as Meyers Mill and Hagood Avenue could be formed.

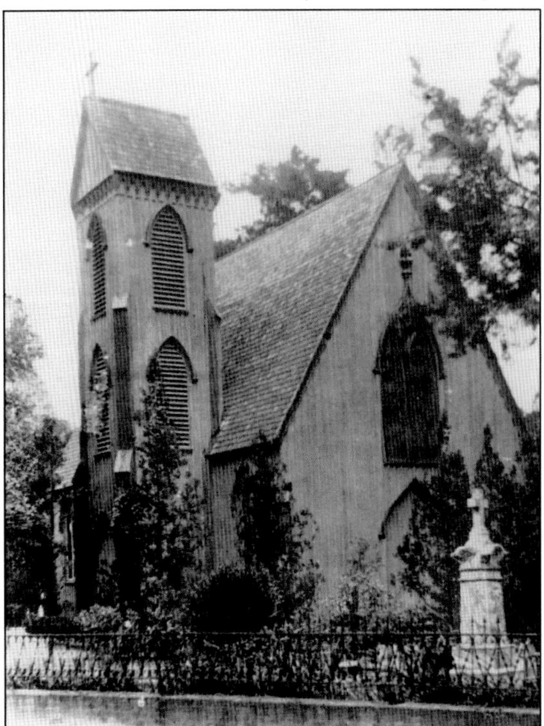

CHURCH OF THE HOLY APOSTLES. The building was consecrated on March 11, 1857, by the Right Reverend Davis, bishop of South Carolina. In February of 1865, the church was desecrated by Union General Judson Kilpatrick's cavalry. They broke the windows out and used the Baptistry to water the cavalry's horses stabled there. The large stained-glass altar window given to the church by Governor James Hammond survived because the members had previously removed and buried it beyond the reach of the vandals. The first rector of the church was the Reverend Edwin A. Wagner, who suggested its English Gothic design. The original altar came from St. Michael's in Charleston and was retained as a side altar in the church.

OLD METHODIST CHURCH. Organized in 1885 with 13 charter members, the church was constructed on a lot donated by Charlie Pechman, a public-minded citizen. The plan of the church was in the shape of a "T," ostensibly to honor an evangelist named Charlie Tillman, who encouraged the people to organize their church. The bell tower and tall graceful spire were in keeping with the customs of church architecture of the day. The windows were fitted with folding shutters, and the panes were painted white to simulate frosted glass. The east wing had a door entering upon the church yard and was used by the choir and any late-comers who wished to slip in unobtrusively. At first there were no musical instruments installed, but in later days, a reed organ was purchased, and Miss Virgie Patterson became the organist. A near disaster was averted when a fire was extinguished by John Eve, an African-American brickmason who pulled shingles from the roof for a foothold. The grateful congregation presented the brave man with an engraved silver water set. The original church was remodeled extensively in 1928.

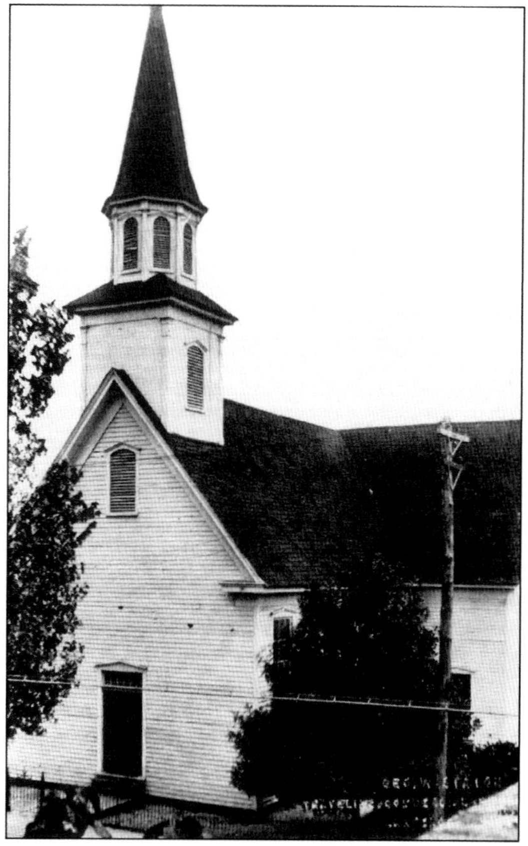

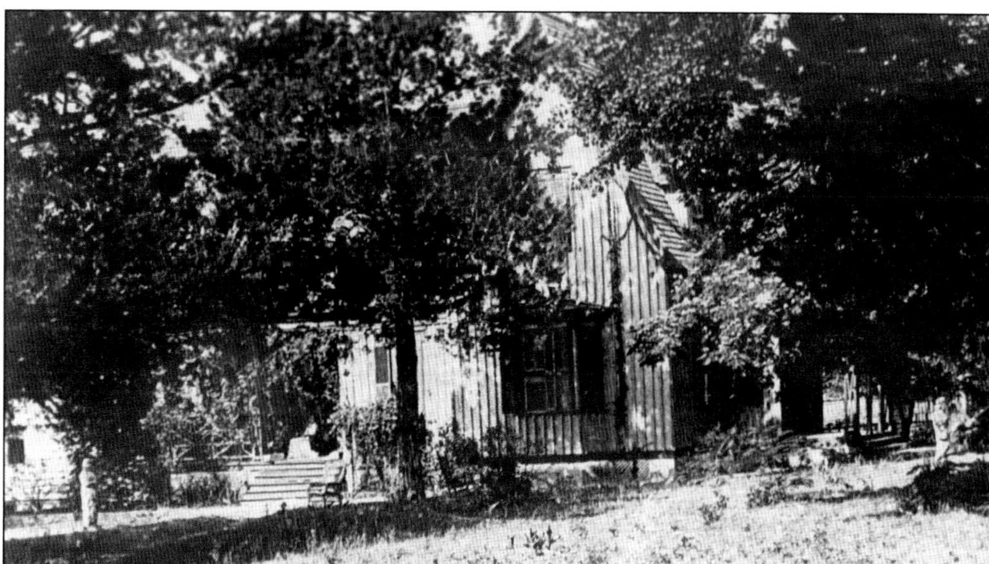

THE "RECTORY." This structure, located adjacent to the Church of the Holy Apostles, was constructed around the middle of the 19th century. It was nicknamed "The Rectory," although it was a private residence and was never owned by the Episcopal church.

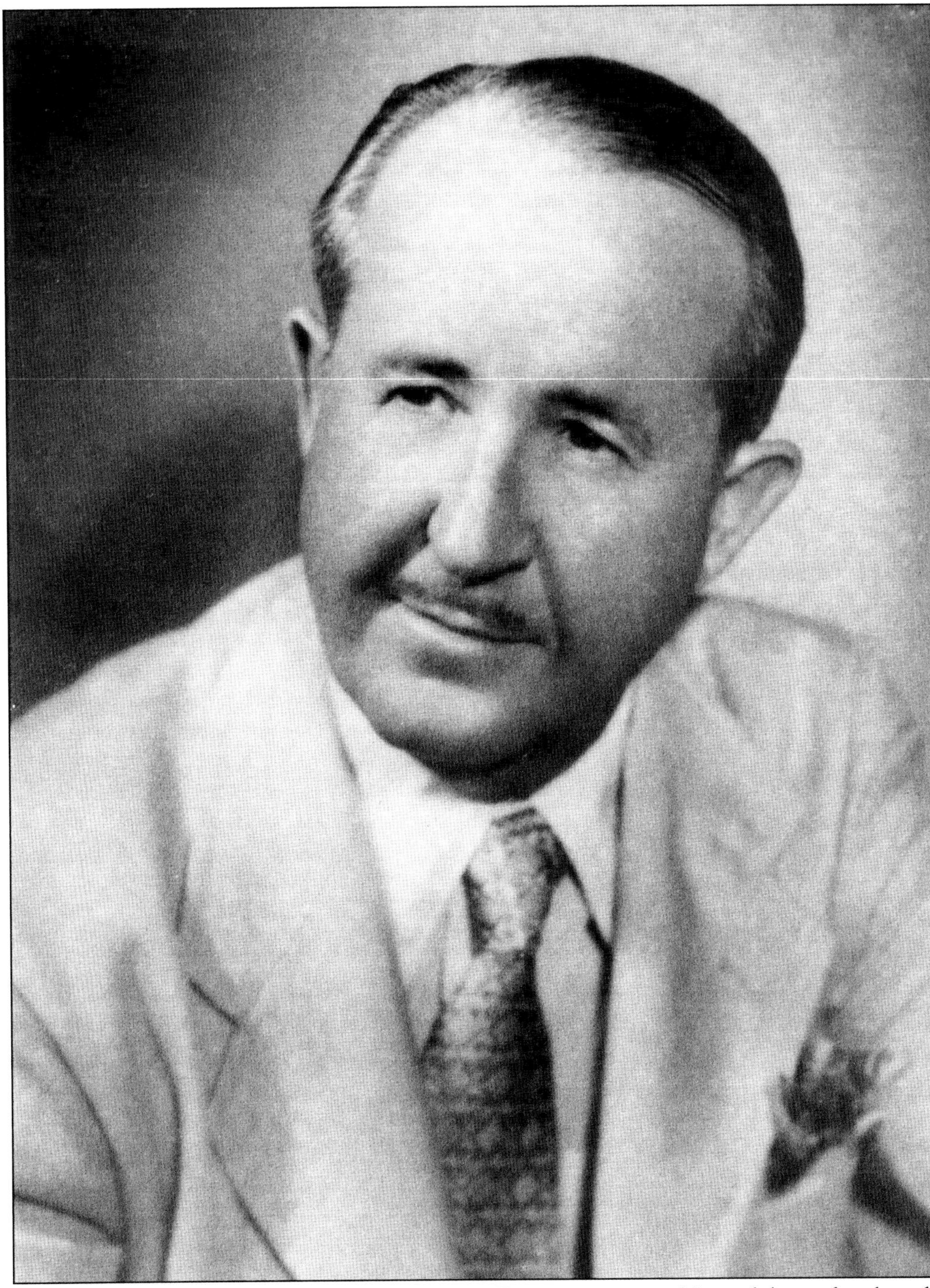

Cornell Goldsmith Fuller, Businessman and Philanthropist. Most of the surfaced roads in Barnwell County were built by C.G. Fuller. His operation encompassed all of South Carolina and many neighboring states. While visiting one of his sites nearby, he became interested in Barnwell and established his home here. He was extremely active in civic affairs, serving as mayor of the town in 1932 and supporting many projects throughout the community, including the local bank and other business ventures.

Four

THE LEGACY OF C.G. FULLER

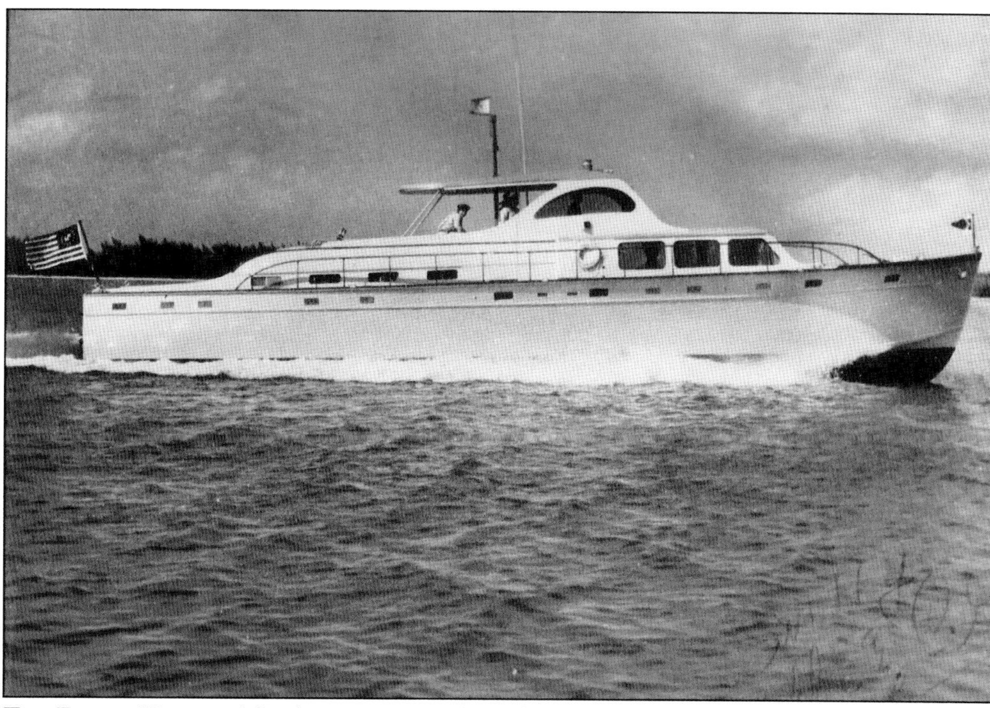

THE FULLER YACHT. After his retirement from the contracting business in 1941, C.G. Fuller spent much of his time at his residence in Bal Harbour, North Miami Beach, Florida. Mr. Fuller loved yachting, and the area was perfect for berthing a succession of boats, including *Snuffy*, pictured here. However, he still visited his residence in Barnwell often and kept in close touch with his friends and business acquaintances in the county.

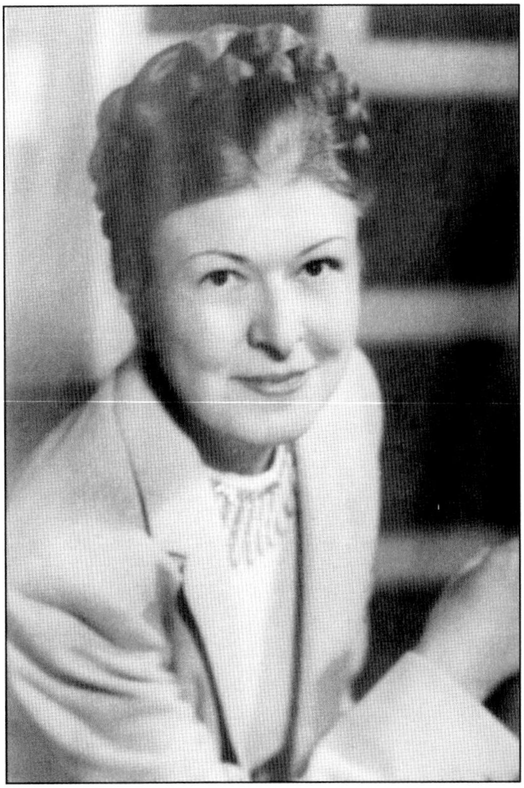

MRS. EFFIE FULLER. Being the wife of business tycoon and philanthropist C.G. Fuller was no easy task. His interests kept him traveling all over the United States, and she often accompanied him to baseball games and other events that interested him. She was quite an individual in her own right, with outstanding talent as a "needlewoman." The Barnwell County Museum is housed in a building that bears her name and a fine piece of her crewelwork is displayed there.

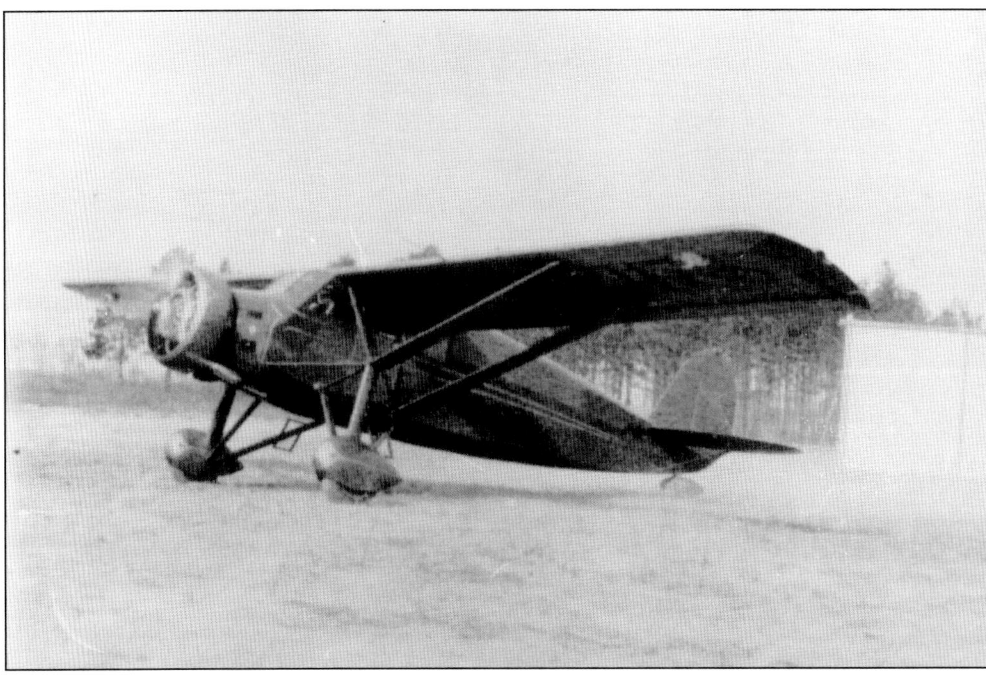

FULLER AIRPLANE. Among C.G. Fuller's many other business accomplishments is a commercial airline, which he organized and operated. Mr. Fuller's airplane was the first in Barnwell County and a curiosity to behold.

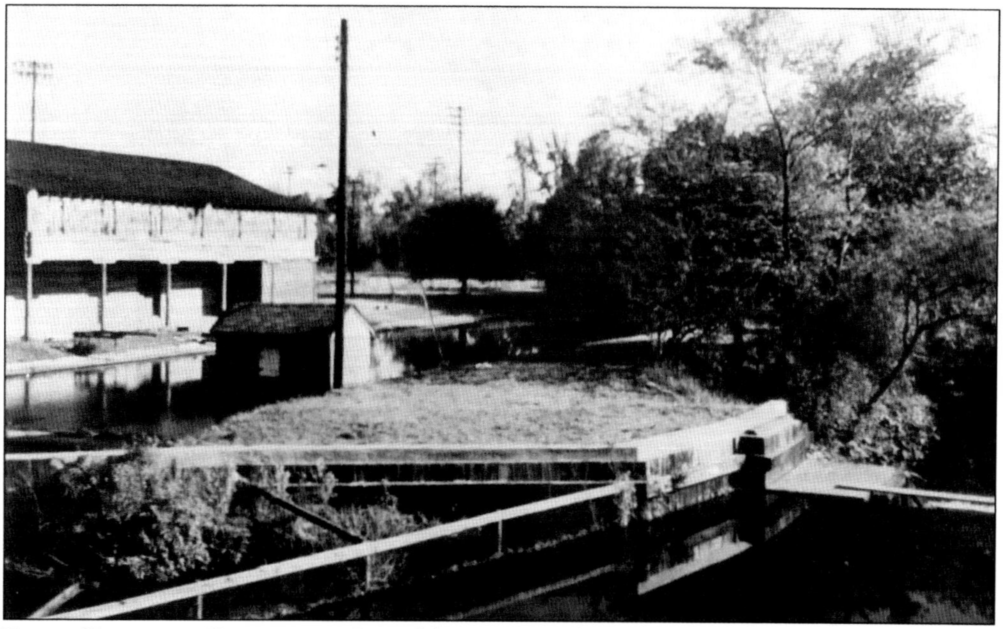

Fuller Park with Bathhouse. One of the most popular recreation areas around Barnwell was the Fuller Park swimming pool, located at the base of Red Hill. The bathhouse and pavilion near the pool were used by the swimmers and other visitors to Fuller Park. Beyond the pool area was a baseball stadium with a large covered grandstand that once attracted minor league teams to train. The Fuller Park pool was used until the 1960s.

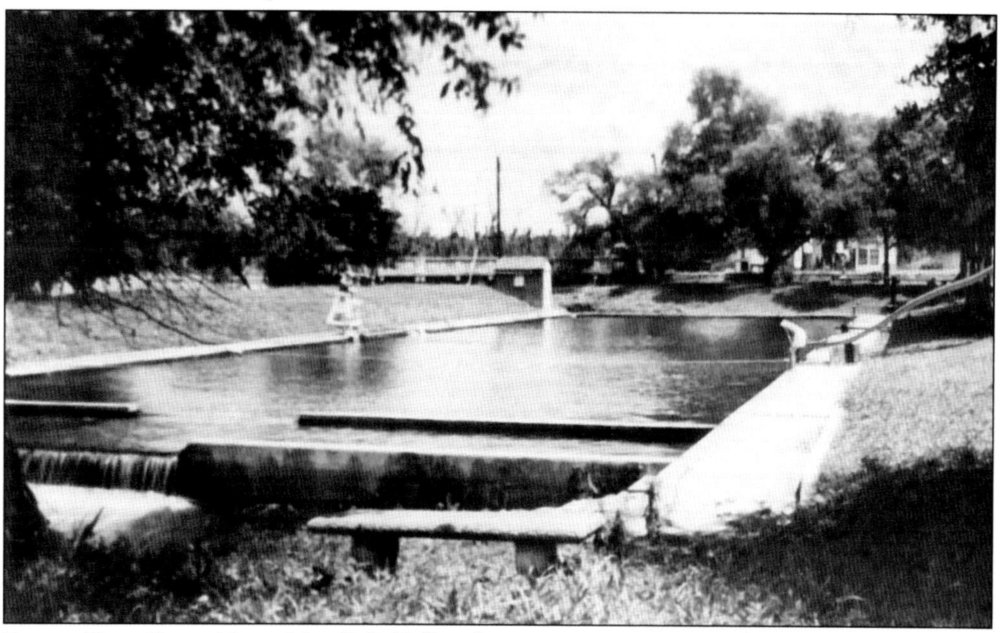

Fuller Park Pool. Named for C.G. Fuller, the area was, in a sense, a beautification project as well, for the location was used as a trash dump for many years prior to the construction of the park. The concrete construction was fed by the waters of Turkey Creek, which was allowed to flow through it. The western end of the pool was extremely shallow so that small children could safely splash in the cool water.

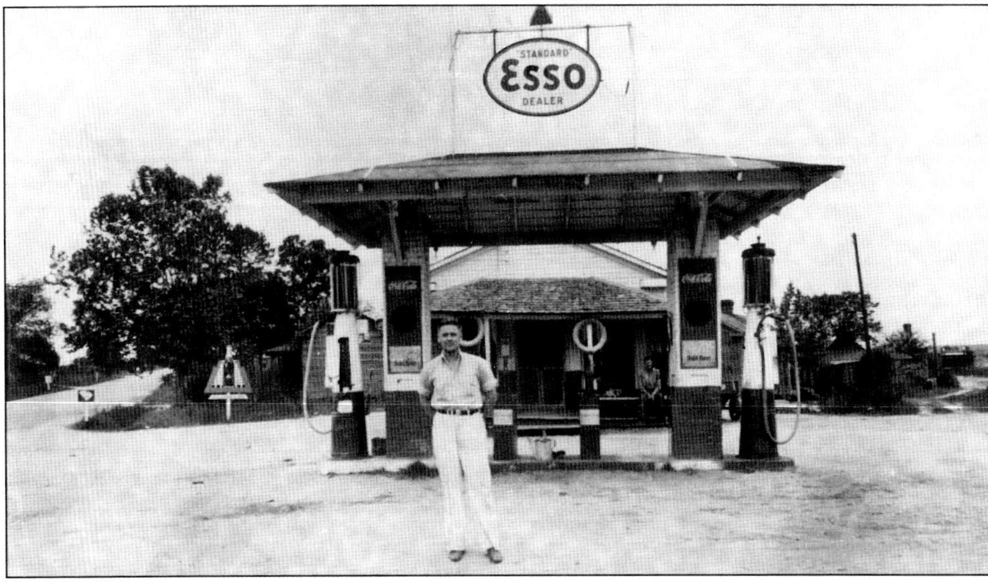

Holland's Grocery in the 1930s. Carrying on the family tradition, owner Lawson Holland stands proudly in front of his store. Its ideal location at the foot of "Red Hill" just across Turkey Creek promoted business, and the store became a well-known landmark in the area.

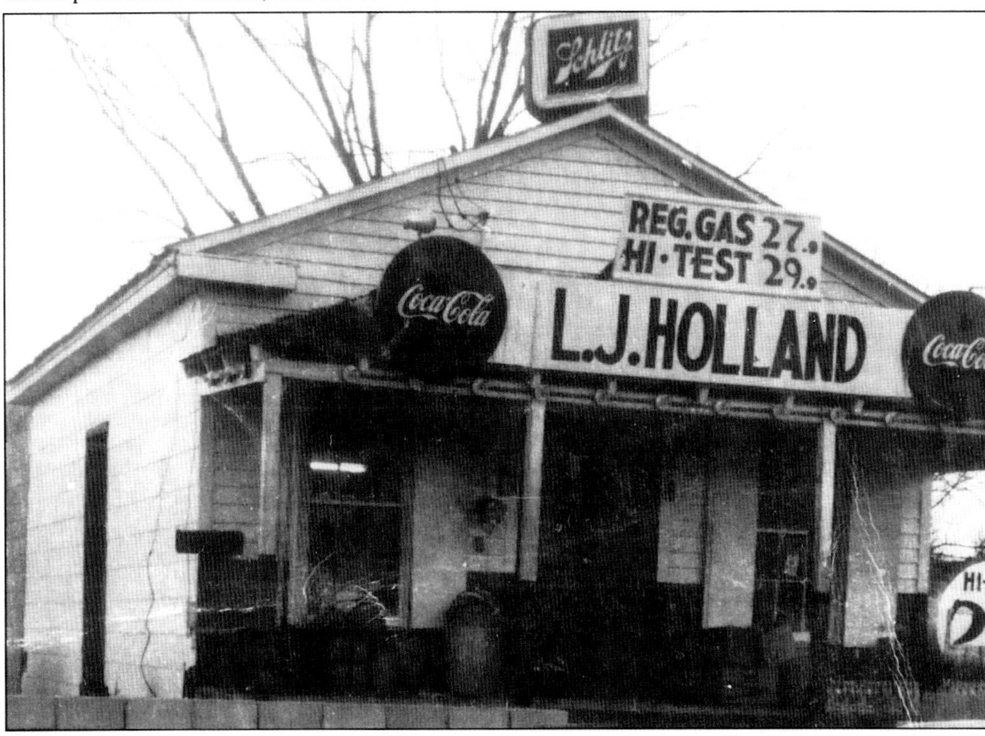

Holland's Grocery in the 1950s. The original structure was moved back farther on the lot to make room for expansion of the highway coming into town. With the arrival of the Savannah River Plant, Holland's became a popular stop after work. Being located at the junction of two roads leading from the "Bomb Plant" area guaranteed a booming business, thus necessitating enlargement of the facilities to accommodate the rush of business.

Five

Away from the Circle

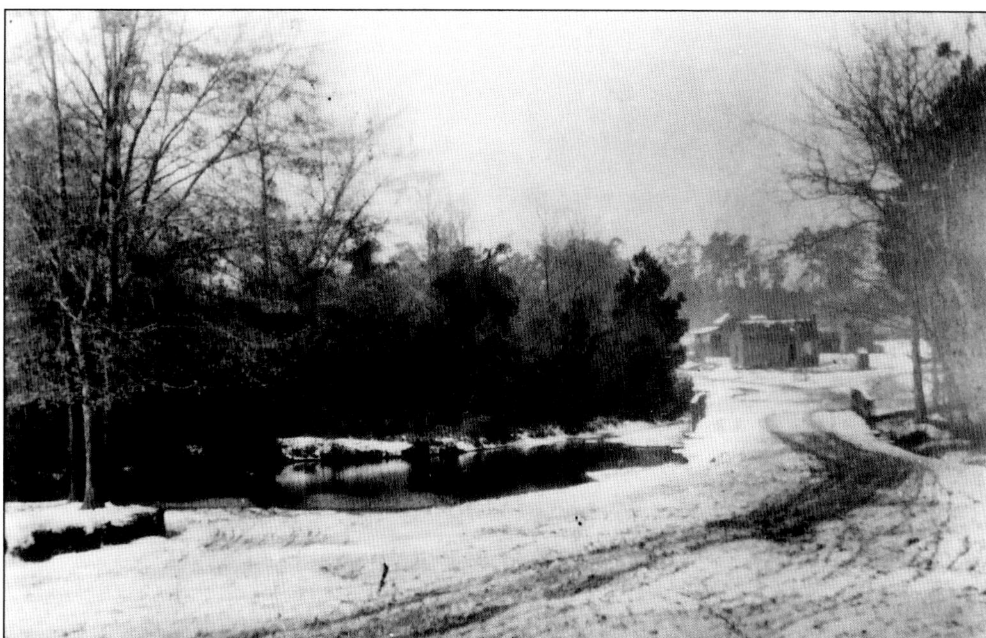

Turkey Creek Bridge. Located upstream from the old crossing, the Turkey Creek bridge became one of the factors that made the town of Barnwell thrive. After crossing the bridge, travelers climbed Red Hill to enter the main business section of town.

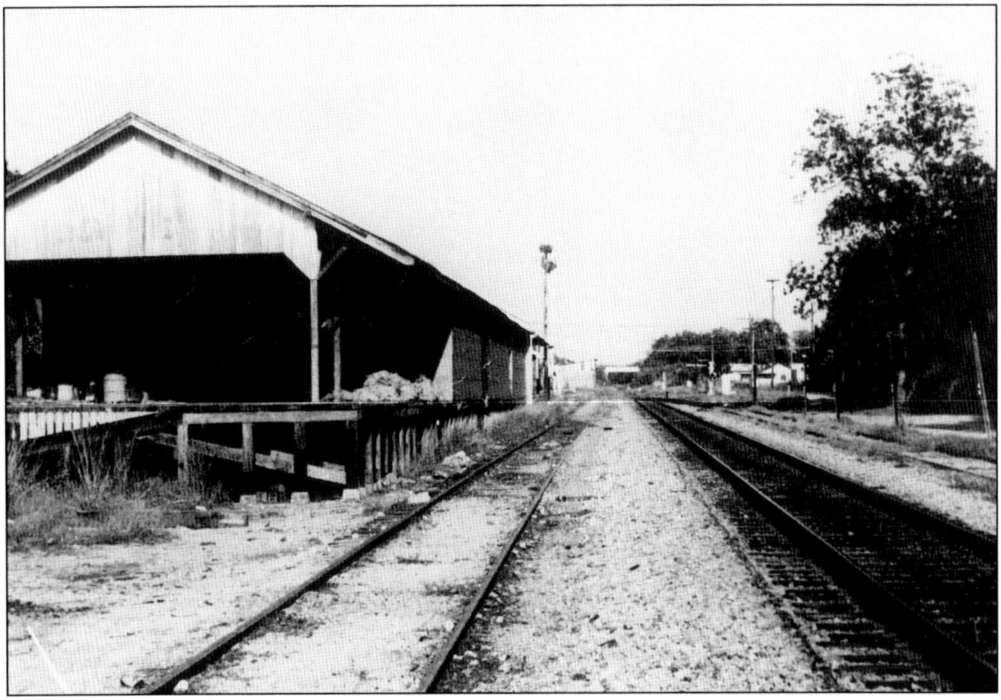

Atlantic Coastline Warehouse. Slightly to the west and adjacent to the Atlantic Coastline Railroad Depot was the warehouse and loading dock. This structure outlasted the depot itself and survived for a few years before it was torn down in the 1980s.

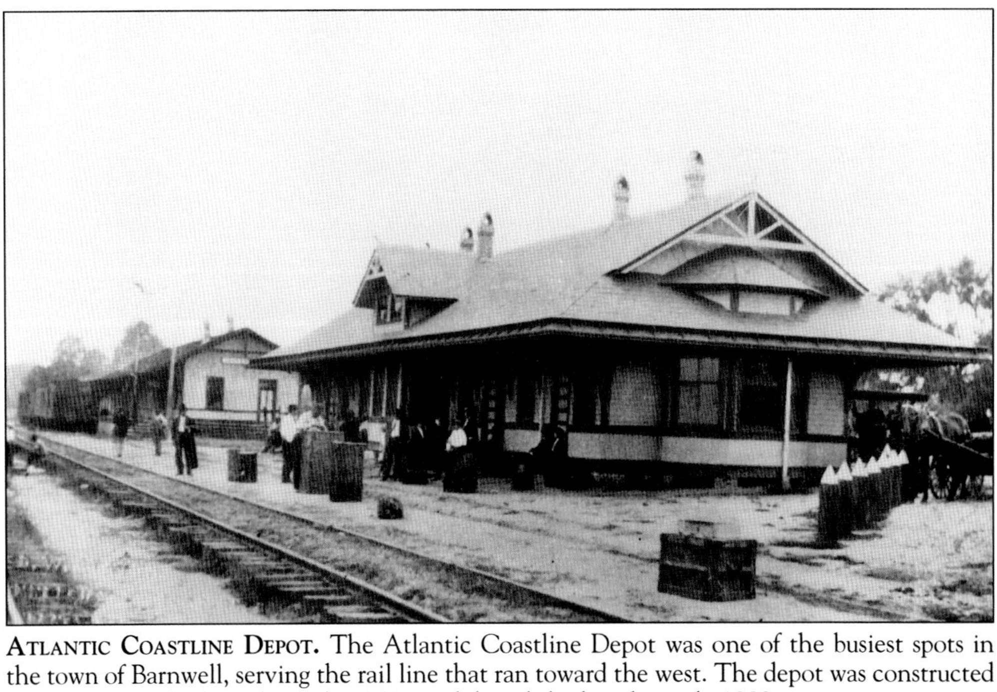

Atlantic Coastline Depot. The Atlantic Coastline Depot was one of the busiest spots in the town of Barnwell, serving the rail line that ran toward the west. The depot was constructed around 1900, rebuilt in the early 1950s, and demolished in the early 1980s.

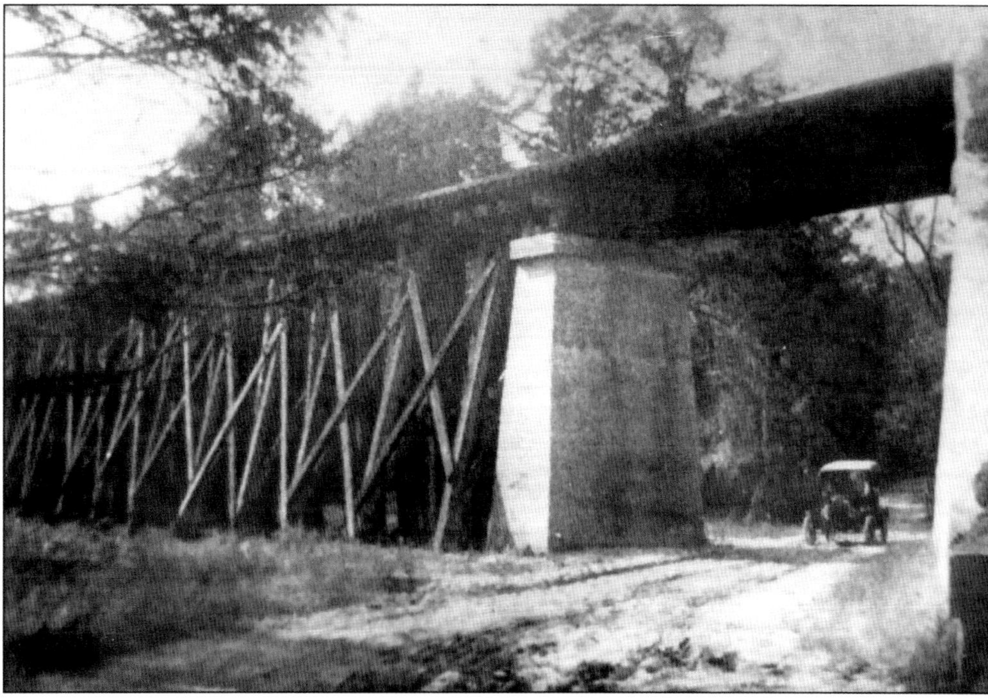

Salkehatchie Trestle in the 1930s. For those accustomed to traveling on the causeway, which was constructed to build the highway across the Salkehatchie River, the swamp does not look imposing. It is only when one considers the true width of the swamp and the height of each of the riverbanks that the true magnitude of the swamp becomes apparent. Here, the trestle dwarfs an automobile passing underneath.

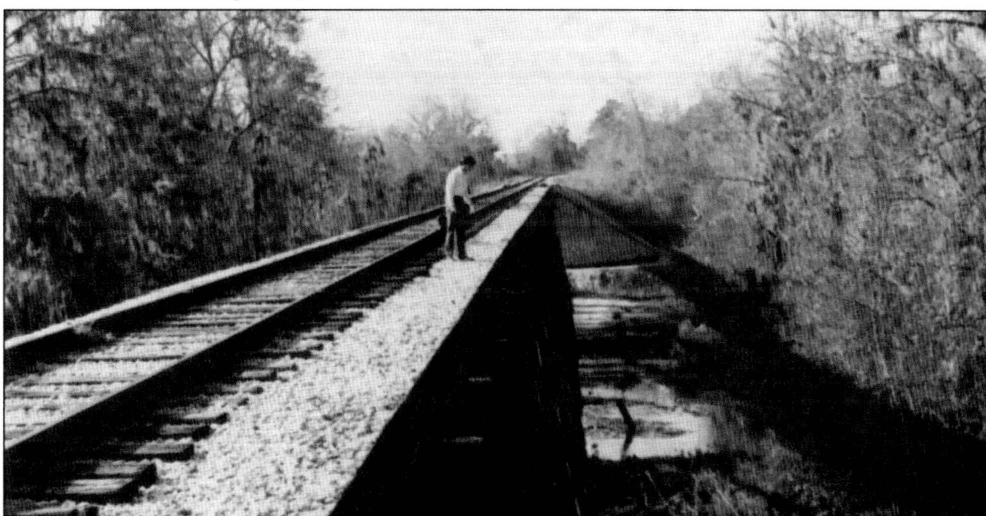

Salkehatchie Trestle in the 1960s. For years, people used the trestle to cross the Salkehatchie River to reach fishing sites on the other side. As long as one remembered train schedules, there was no problem making the trip back and forth. However, when a train came along, a person on the trestle had two choices: jump in the river and take his chances, or lay down on the cross ties and pray the train would clear.

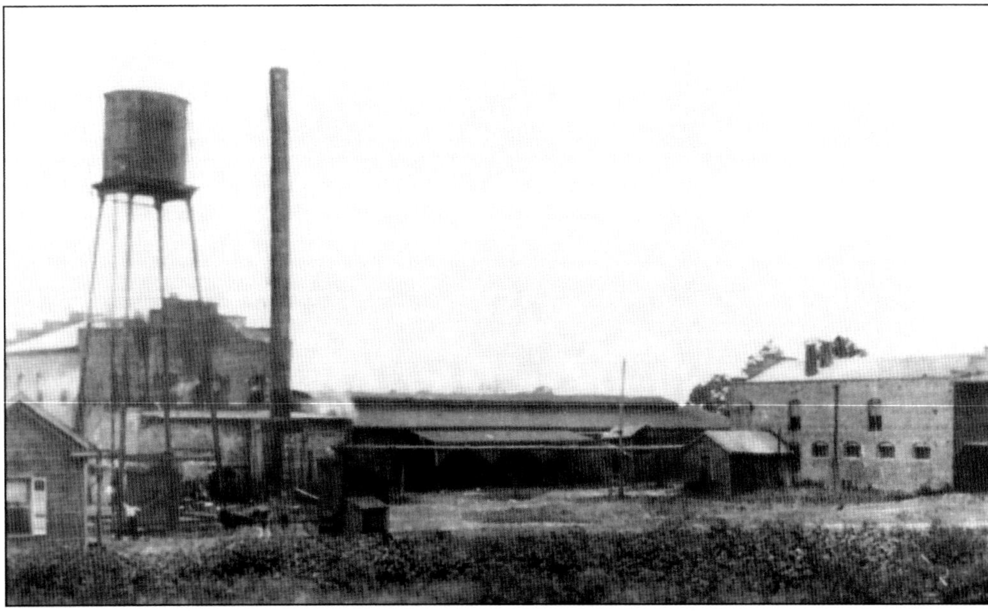

Oil Mill, c. 1914. The Southern Cotton Oil Company was located on the eastern side of the railroad tracks about a half mile northeast of the Barnwell County Courthouse. The 60-foot water tank shown in this view had a capacity of 12,000 gallons of water. Behind the water tower is the press room and linters, the long, low cotton seed house, and at the far right, the engine room attached to a cotton house.

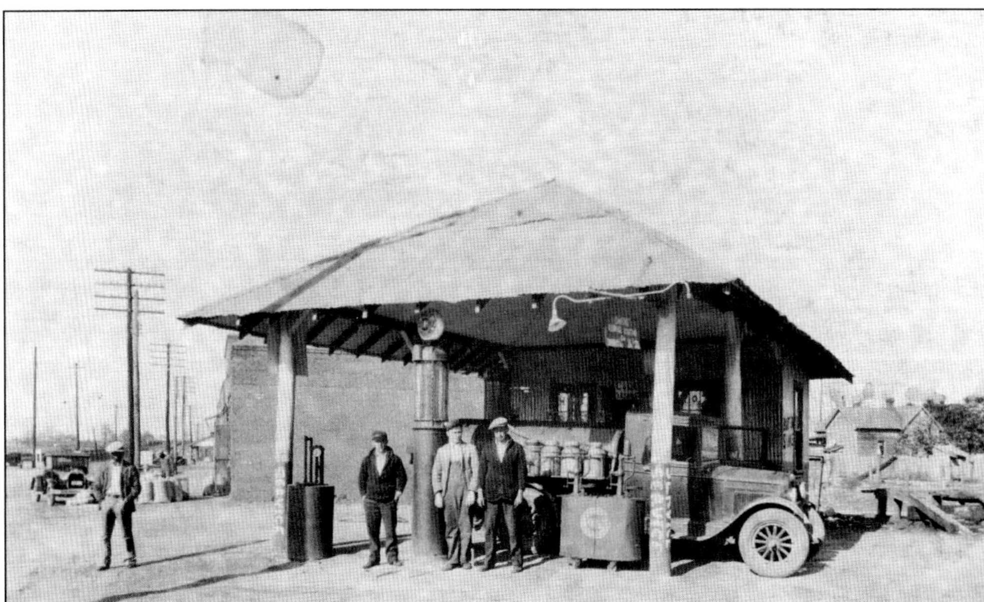

Delivery by Vickery Oil. Vickery Oil Company served the surrounding communities as well as that of Barnwell. Here, the delivery man carries oil to a service station in Olar.

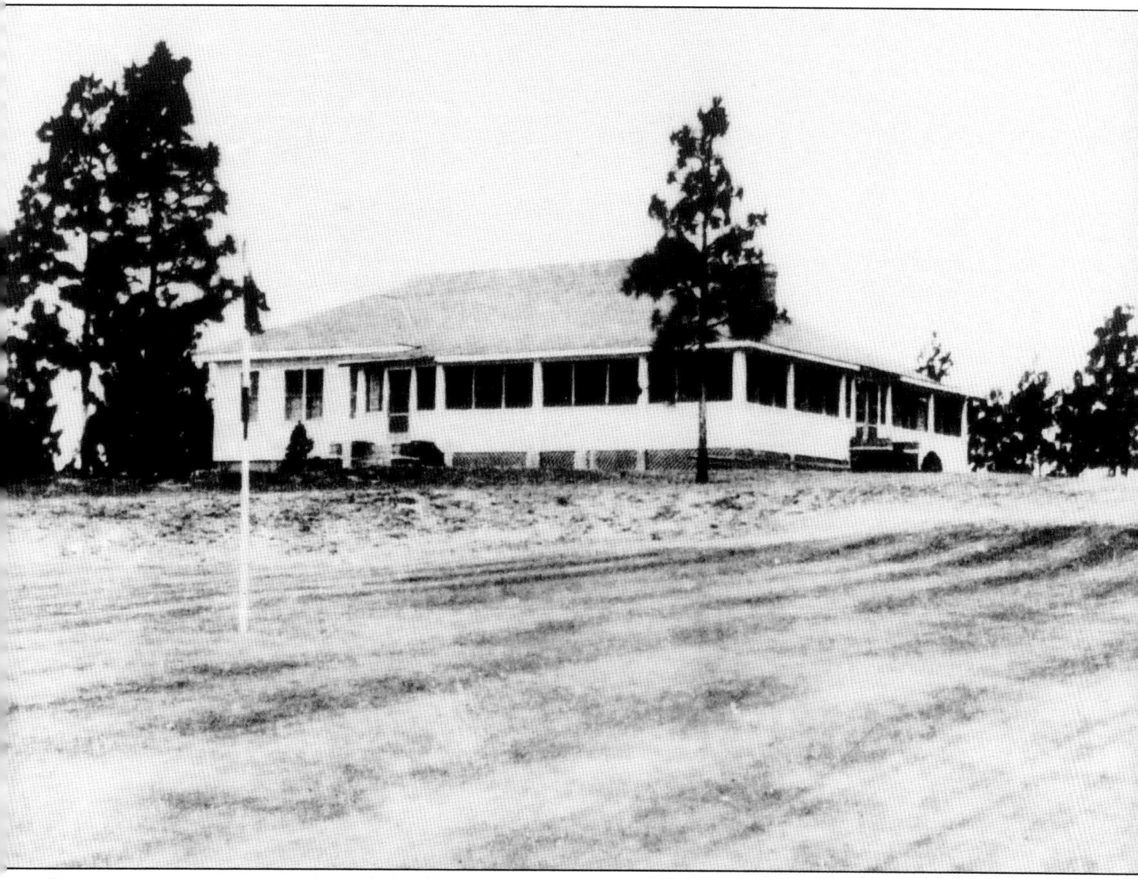

SWEETWATER COUNTRY CLUB. The Sweetwater Country Club was constructed as a part of the New Deal legislative initiatives during the Great Depression. The Civilian Conservation Corps designed and built recreation areas for public use. This nine-hole golf club was one of the finest recreation facilities of its time. Much of the work on this and other public service projects in the Barnwell area was encouraged and supervised by C.G. Fuller, who was instrumental in seeing that Barnwell received its fair share of the opportunities afforded by the national legislation. Mr. Fuller infused much of his own money in these projects, such as donating $15,000 for a modern watering system for the golf course and giving the land upon which the course and clubhouse were built. Now operated as a private club, it has been expanded to 18 holes and continues to be one of the premier golf courses in the surrounding counties.

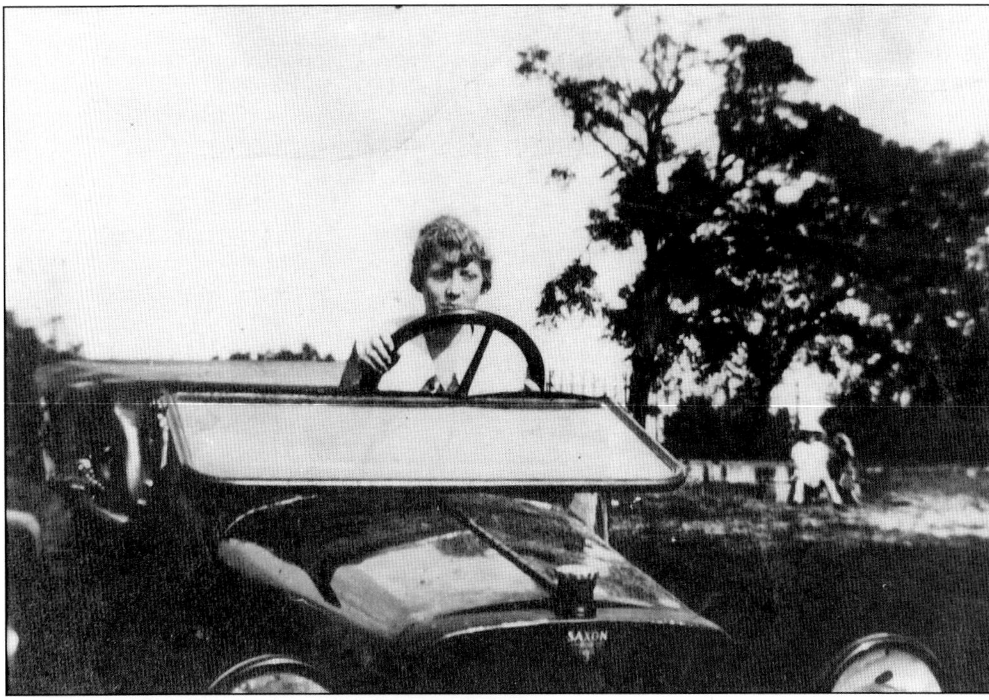

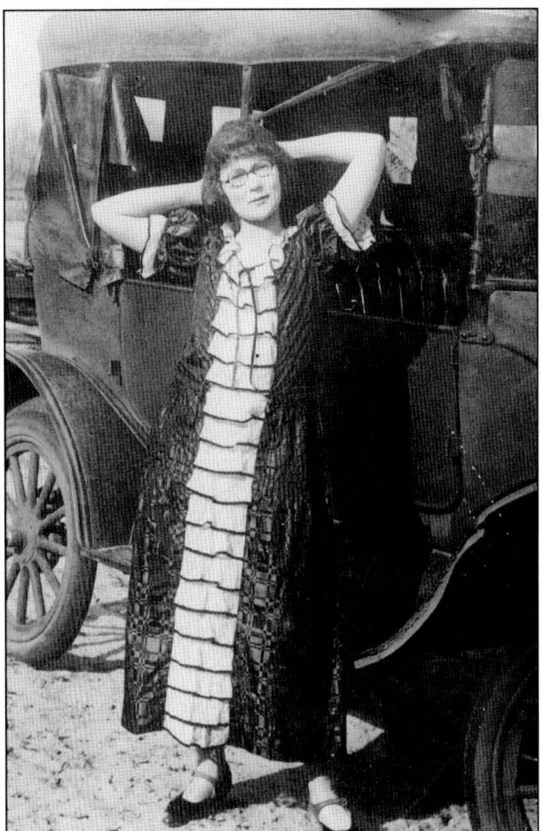

RIDING IN A SAXON. America's love affair with the automobile is well documented. At the turn of the century, there were 8,000 motor vehicles registered in the United States. By the time of the Great Depression, a total of 27 million automobiles were registered. In 1908, there were 250 companies manufacturing automobiles, but by 1929, only 44 of those companies remained. In the mad scramble for profit, many automobiles like the Saxon, pictured here, disappeared from the scene altogether.

FLAIR FOR FASHION. The automobile gave Americans a freedom they had not experienced before. The relatively cheap price of Henry Ford's automobiles allowed everyone to be adventurous. Women in Barnwell County were beginning to take advantage of this newfound sense of self-reliance, as this young lady's pose suggests.

Six

Living in the Country

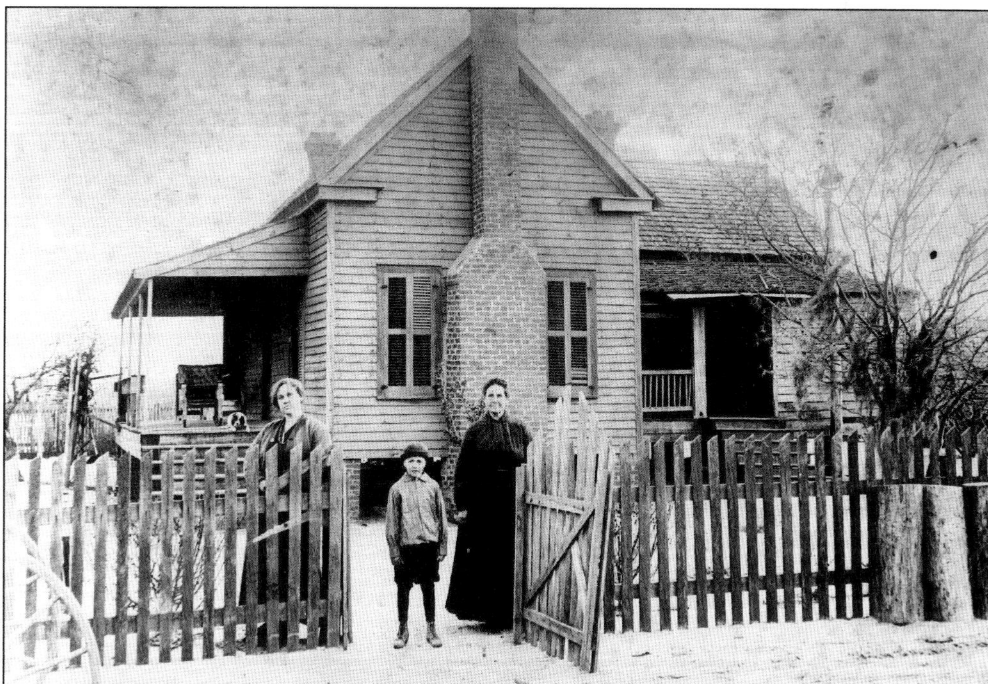

W.P. Morris Residence, 1915. The union of the Harden and Morris families came in the late 1900s when Robert Morris married his neighbor Mary Jane Harden. After her husband died, "Mama Jane" moved in with daughter Mattie and her husband, Preston. This type of arrangement was very common in the early part of the century, and the extended families that were formed became the basis for very stable relationships that helped rural families through the uncertainty of the 1920s and 1930s. In the case of the Morris family, the majority of the land passed down was saved during the trying times of the Great Depression. The house pictured here was remodeled and enlarged just before hard times rolled in, and the family kept the farm going.

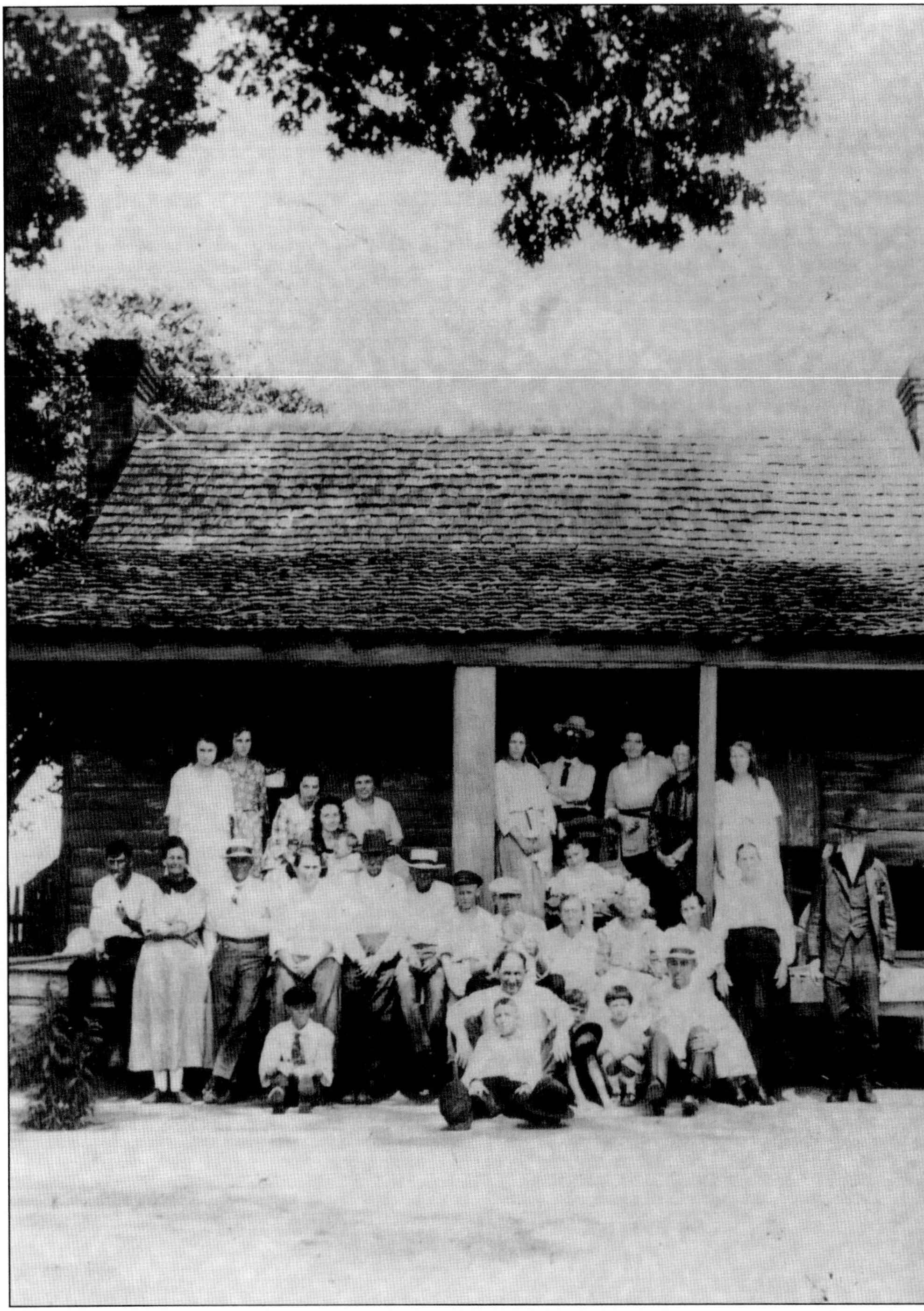

FOURTH OF JULY AT YENOME, 1920. The Morris family gathers at the W.M. Morris homestead for a celebration of our nation's birthday. This structure, which still stands today, was rebuilt in 1865 after being destroyed by Union cavalry on General Sherman's sweep through South Carolina. Located a few hundred yards from the railroad depot at Yenome, South Carolina, the Morris household was a favorite gathering spot for those who lived near the crossing.

YENOME STATION IN THE 1920S. Southern Railway constructed railroad depots approximately every 5 miles along its route through Barnwell County. In addition to the stations in Barnwell and Blackville, Ashleigh Station, Kline Station, and Yenome Station served the farmers in the surrounding countryside. Visible in the background here is the depot at Yenome, formerly known as Morris Station, located 5 miles south of Barnwell.

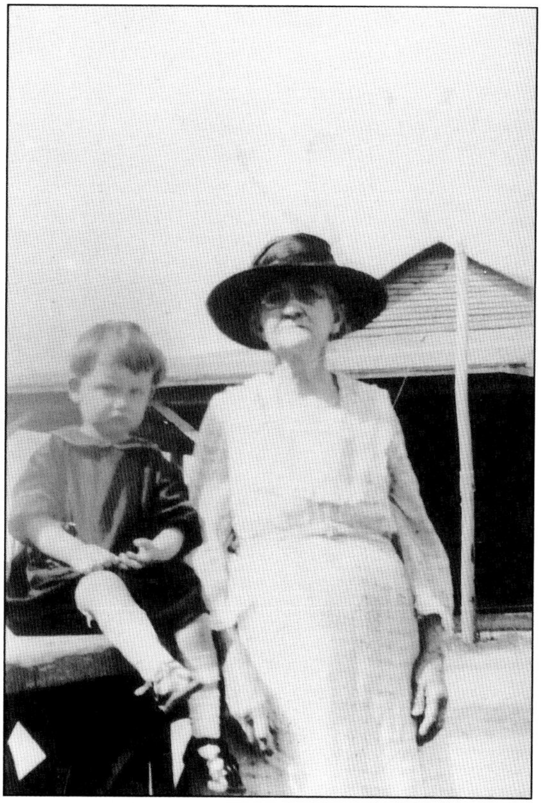

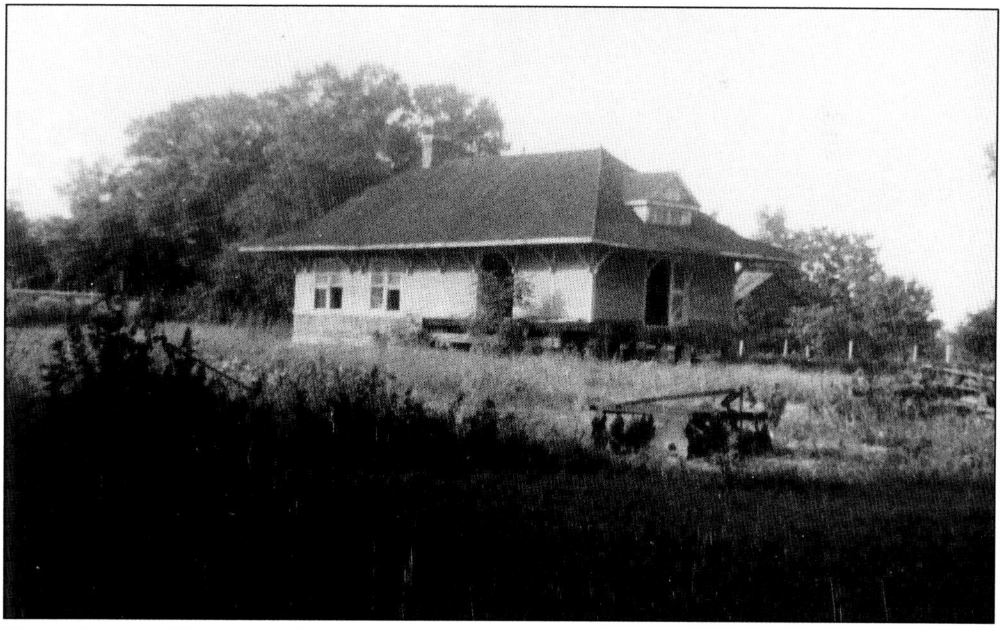

KLINE DEPOT. Kline was the southernmost stop on the Southern Railway's line through the county. Located between Barnwell and Allendale, the depot was in a strategic spot, enabling farmers to ship and obtain goods easily without having to travel all the way to one of the larger towns.

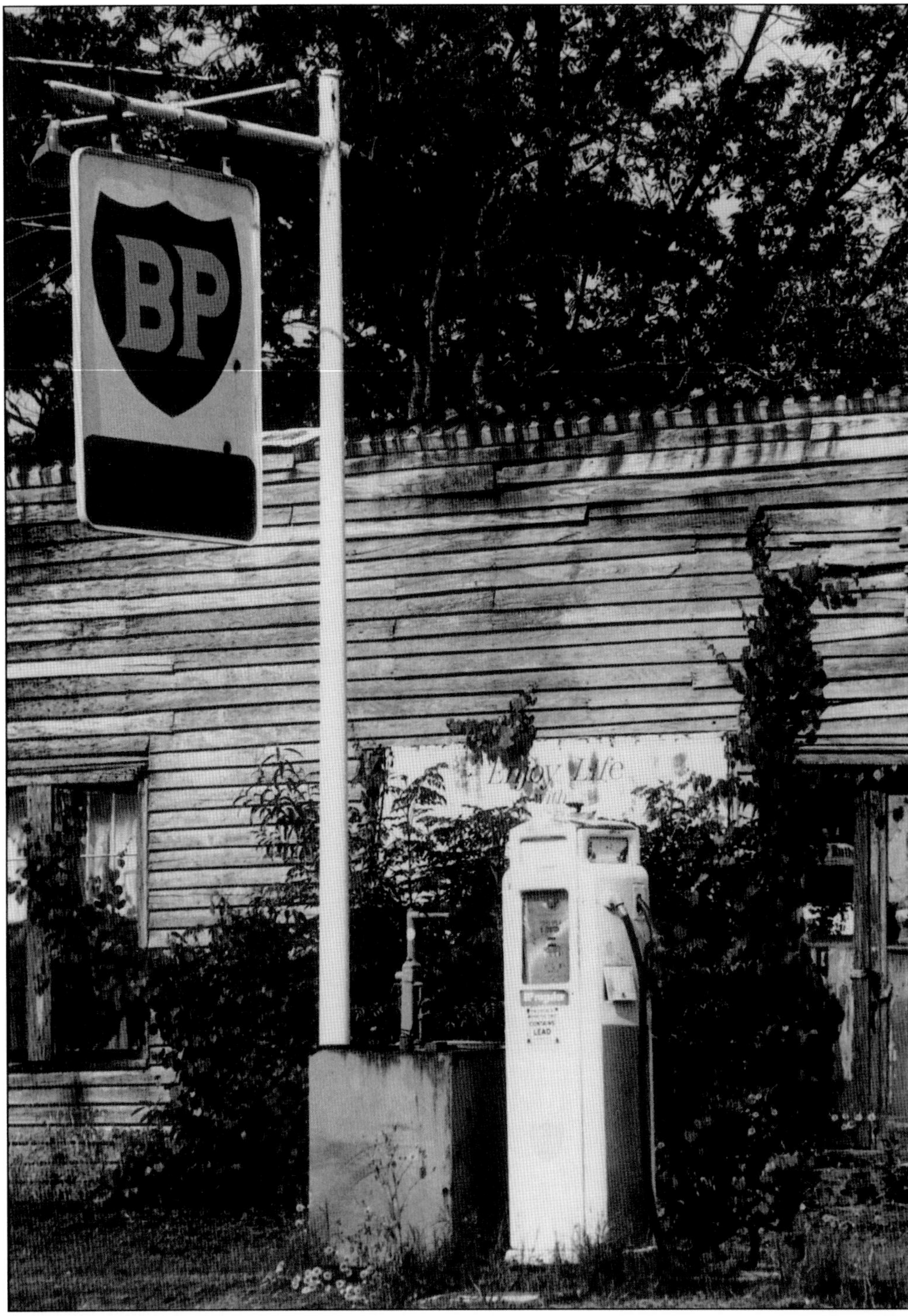

Barker's Store. Every community had its general store, and Yenome was no exception. For many years, Mr. Clyde Barker ran this store, which sat beside the road approximately 4 miles south of Barnwell. Even after the store closed in the late 1960s, it was opened on election days for use as a voting location for the area's residents.

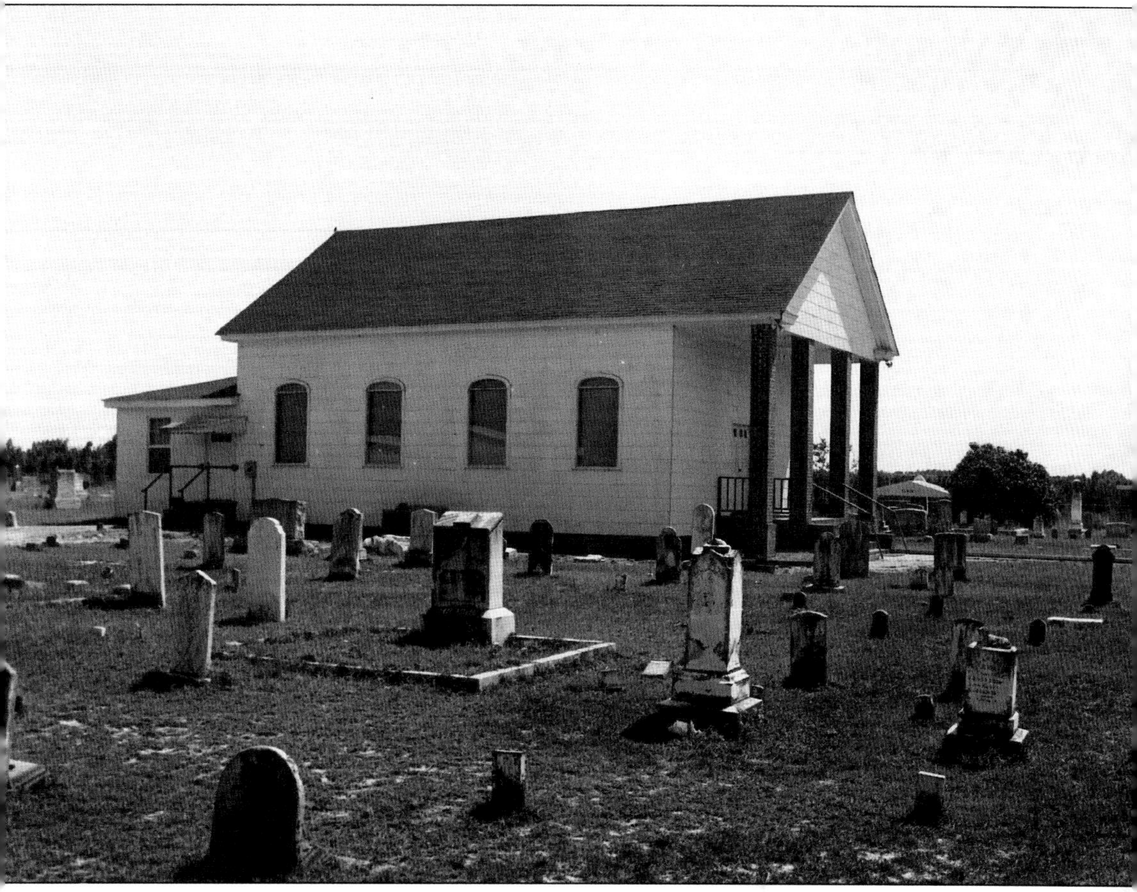

SILOAM METHODIST CHURCH. Siloam Methodist Church, chartered in 1885, is the only rural Methodist church in Barnwell County. The congregation has shared ministers with a number of other churches during its lifetime. Once a part of a charge that included other small country churches such as Speedwell and Gillette, in Allendale County, Siloam now shares a minister with the United Methodist Church in Barnwell.

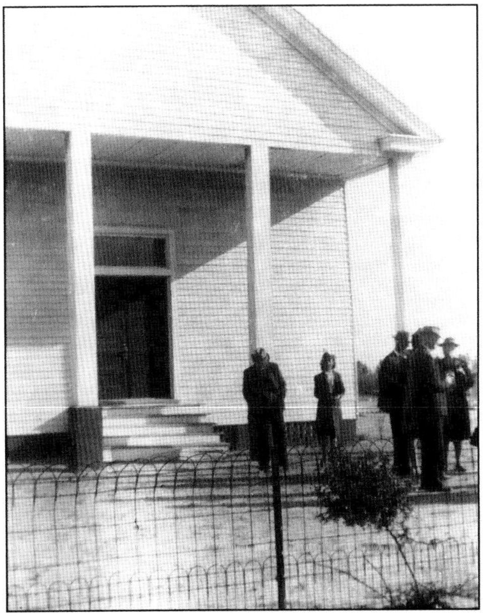 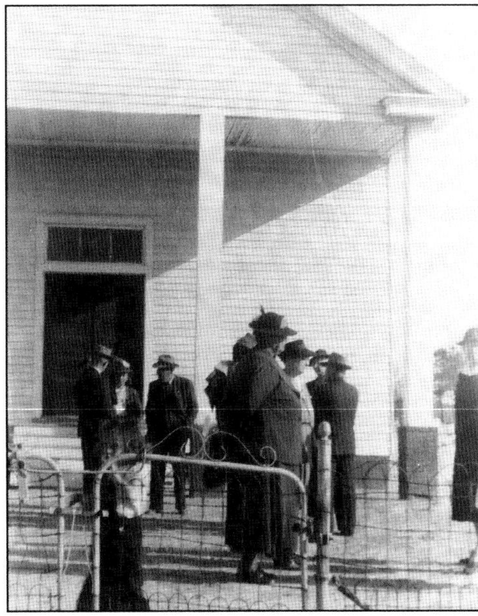

Afternoon Services at Siloam. For many years, Siloam's Sunday services were conducted in the afternoon because the minister had to preach at several other churches in addition to Siloam. This situation is reminiscent of the origins of the Methodist denomination, where circuit riders traveled from church to church delivering sermons at each stop. Services are now held at 9 a.m., which allows the minister to hold services in Barnwell at the traditional eleven o'clock hour.

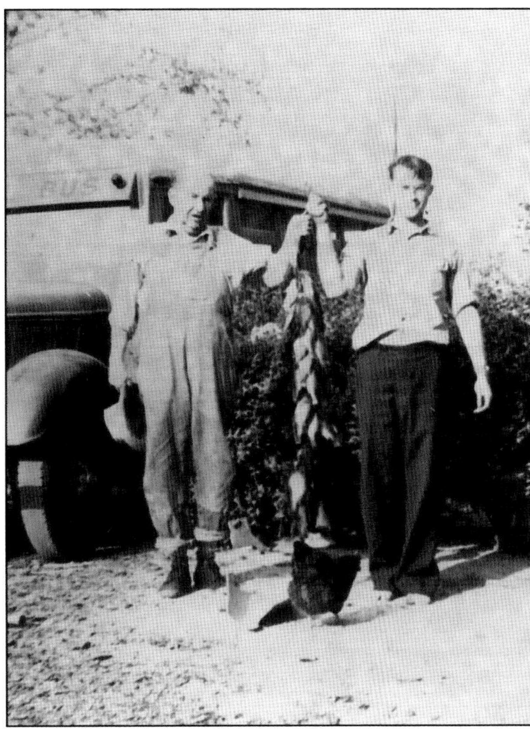

Showing Off a "Mess of Fish." The Depression years were bleak for everyone, but all family members pitched in to help. In 1929, W.P. Morris was depot agent at Yenome, then served at Cave Station, 5 miles below Kline, until 1934, when he was transferred to White Oak Station, north of Columbia. His son, Heyward, helped out by driving a school bus. They both hunted and fished to put food on the table during these hard times. While her husband served at White Oak, Mrs. Morris supervised the family farm and kept the family focused on making it through these stressful years. Their older son, Harris, graduated from Barnwell High School in 1931 and moved to Columbia, where he worked as a radio repairman.

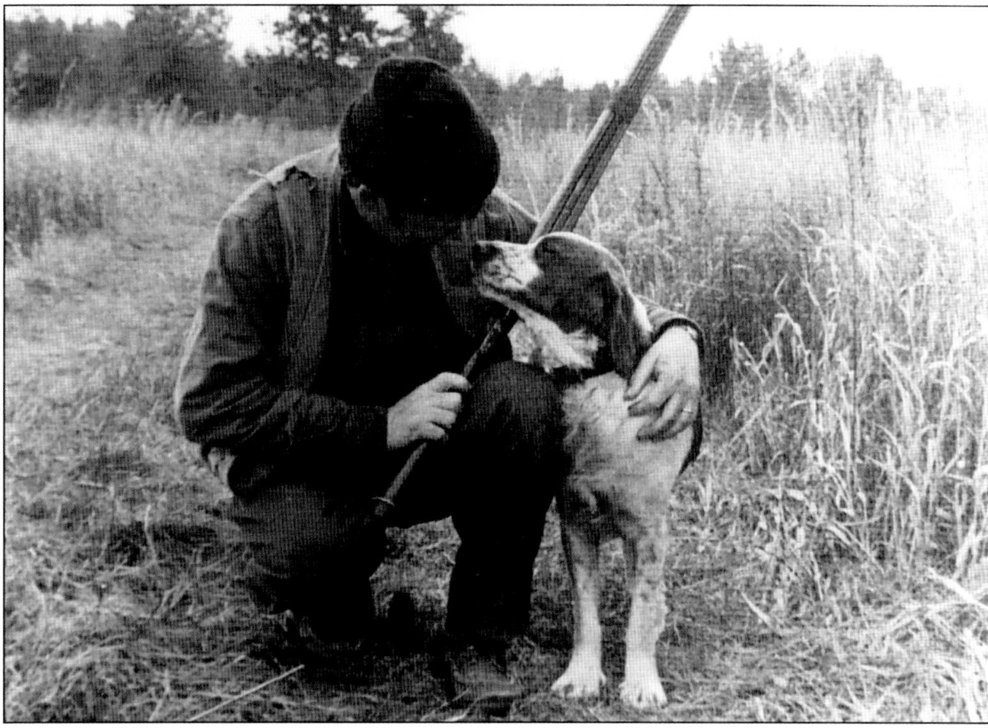

Man's Best Friend. Before the slash pine arrived in great numbers to the South Carolina countryside, habitat for game birds such as quail abounded. Great expanses of fields containing "broom sedge" offered sportsmen a chance to work their dogs and enjoy many hours of superb hunting.

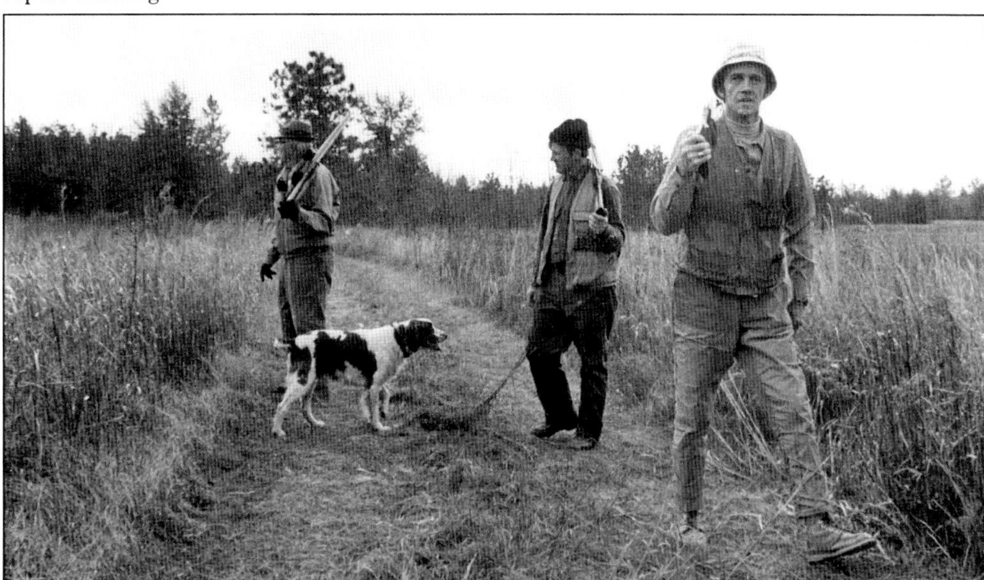

Visiting Sportsmen. The ideal conditions in Canada during the off-season afforded many opportunities for trainers to take their dogs up north and then return for the hunting season in South Carolina. Many out-of-state sportsmen took advantage of the county's excellent hunting.

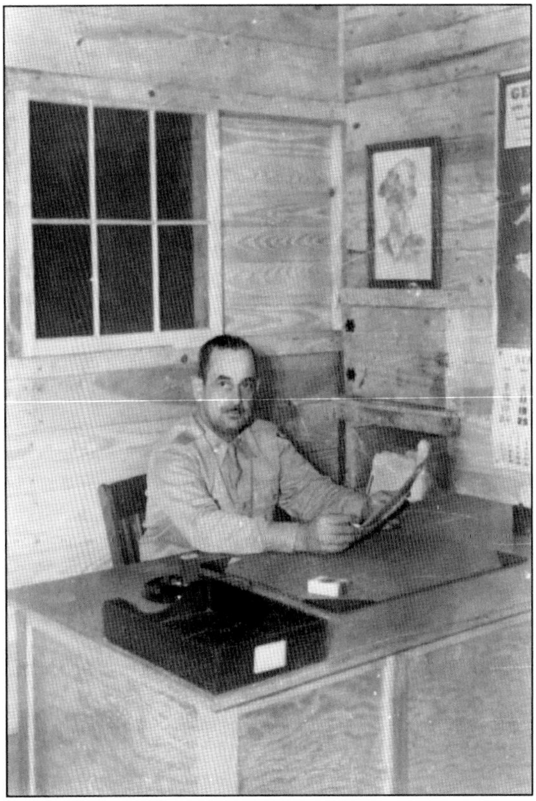

COMMANDANT OF THE POW CAMP. Captain J.R. Jarrell, a native of Indiana, was in charge of the Prisoner of War Camp. Captain Jarrell's responsibilities required him to ensure the safety of his men, the prisoners, and the citizens of Barnwell. His job was made a bit easier by the fact that these prisoners were not likely to attempt an escape. They were treated well at the camp and in any case, language barriers would hinder them if they had attempted to leave.

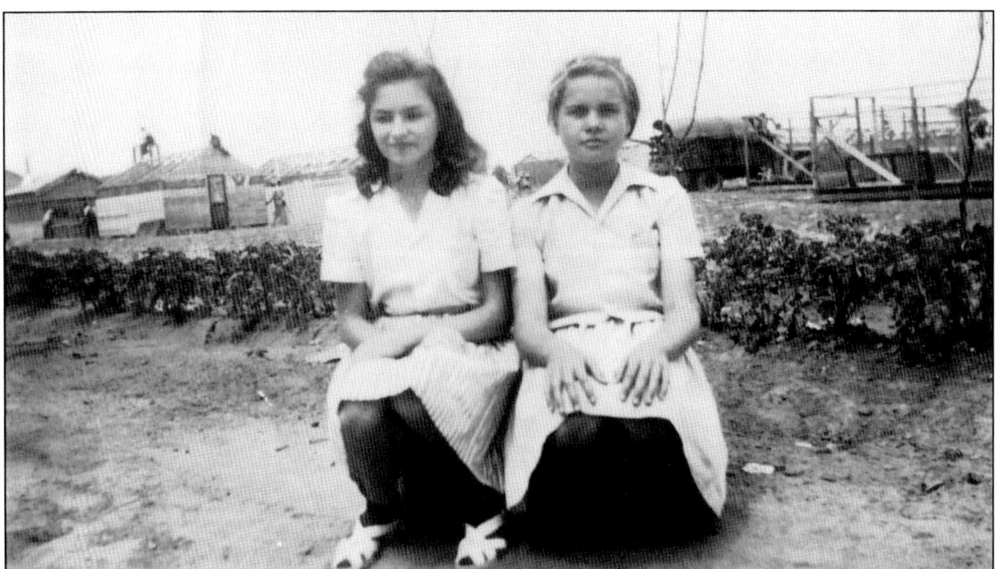

CONSTRUCTION OF POW CAMP. Misses Esther Cheek and Annie Laurie Fort pose in front of the Prisoner of War Camp being constructed in Barnwell. After the war, National Fastener, or "the Zipper Plant" as the facility was more popularly called, was constructed on the same property.

Seven

German Prisoner of War Camp

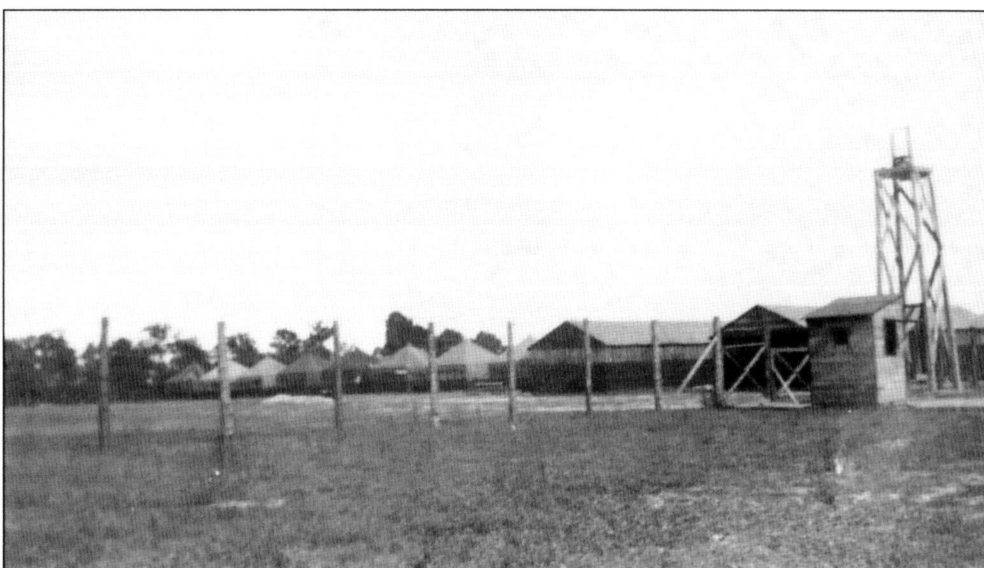

Guard Tower and Enclosure. This overall view of the Prisoner of War Camp shows the layout of the facility. The accommodations for both the prisoners and the guards were essentially the same, except, of course, that the prisoner's quarters were fenced in.

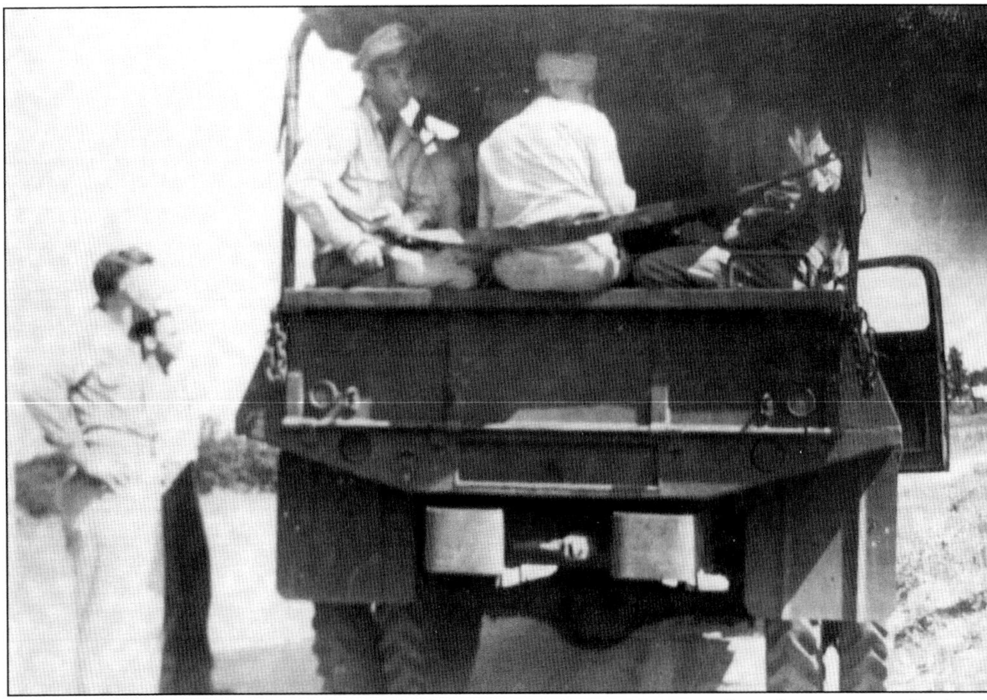

Work Details at the POW Camp. Each morning, the prisoners gathered in groups of a dozen or so for their work assignments. After the guards were given their orders, the prisoners were loaded into trucks to be taken to their respective work sites. The men were treated humanely by the citizens of Barnwell; it was not an uncommon sight to witness prisoners being given water and snacks during their breaks.

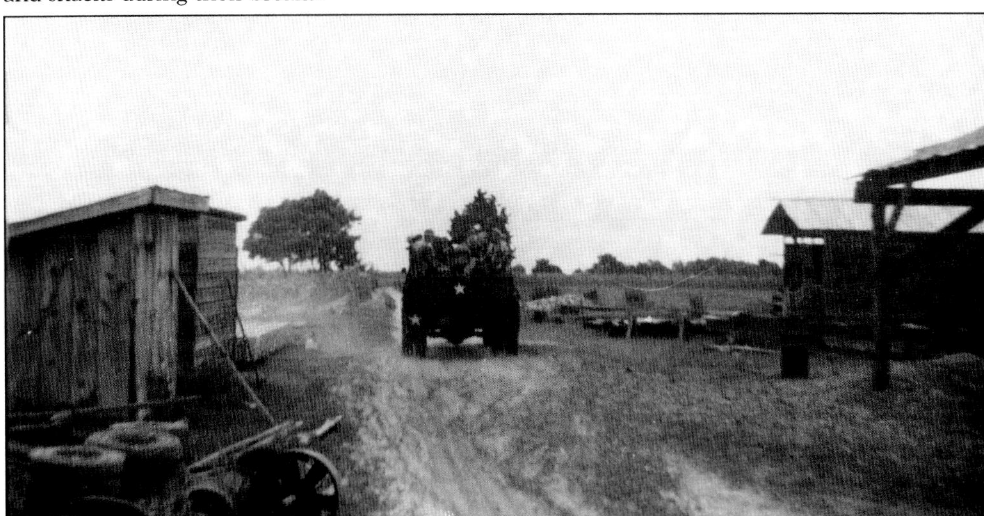

Heading to Work. Once the assignments were made and the prisoners loaded onto the trucks, they were driven to the work sites and expected to put in a good day's work. The prisoners appreciated the kind treatment given to them by the guards and citizens of Barnwell. Years later, many of the prisoners maintained correspondence with local residents, and a few years ago, at least one former prisoner returned to Barnwell for a visit, but had problems finding people who knew about the camp.

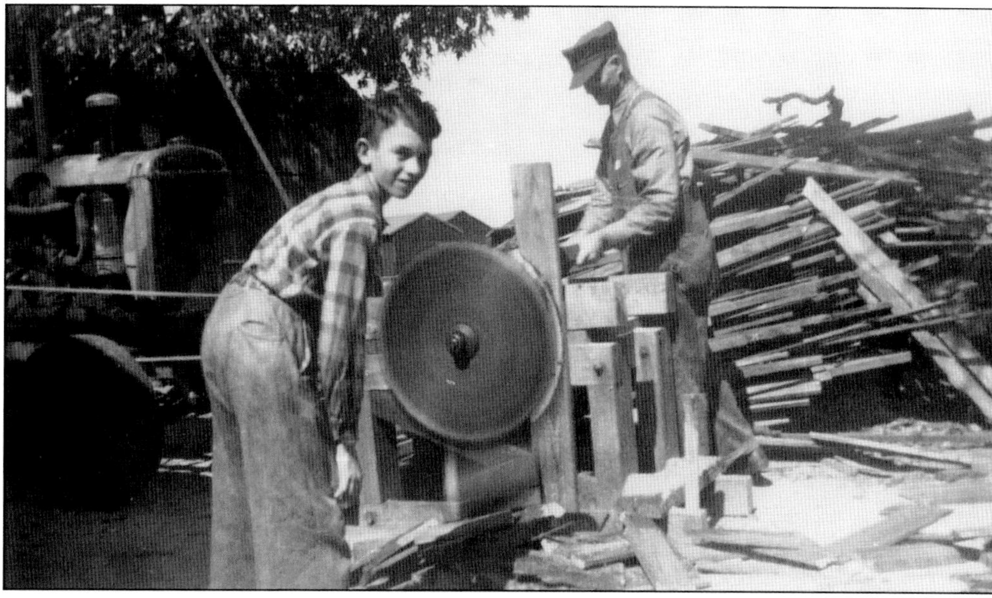

The Cheek Sawmill. One of the reasons that the Prisoner of War Camps were constructed was the critical worker shortage in the United States during World War II. The agricultural areas suffered greatly, and the prisoners were used to great advantage in smaller communities such as Barnwell. Here, Mr. C.C. Cheek can be seen working in the sawmill where prisoner labor was often used.

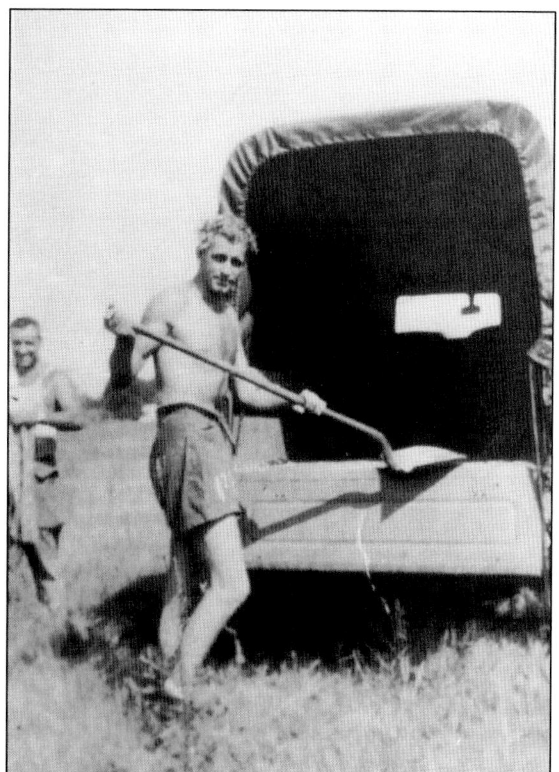

Wielding a Shovel. The work details kept the men busy so they didn't have as much time to dwell on the fact that they were, in fact, prisoners of war. They made connections with a land that they never dreamed of, and lived to be released after the war was over.

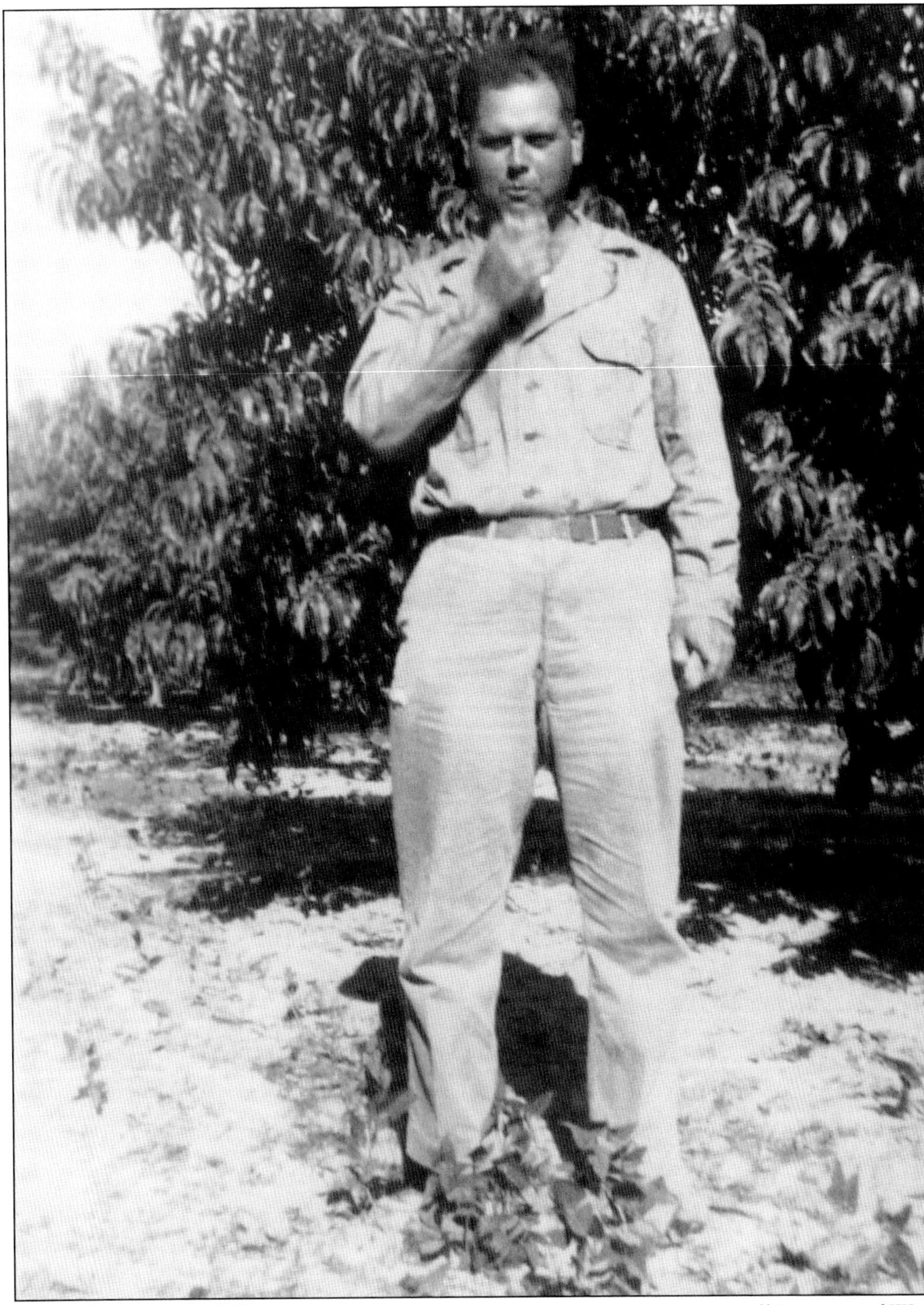

ORCHARD NEAR THE POW CAMP. One of the guards assigned to the Barnwell Prisoner of War Camp enjoys a peach from the orchard located southeast of the camp. During the "boom" associated with the construction of the Atomic Energy Commission's Savannah River Plant, the orchard area was selected as the site of a neighborhood of duplex apartments constructed by Knox Carolina Homes, appropriately named "Peachtree Gardens."

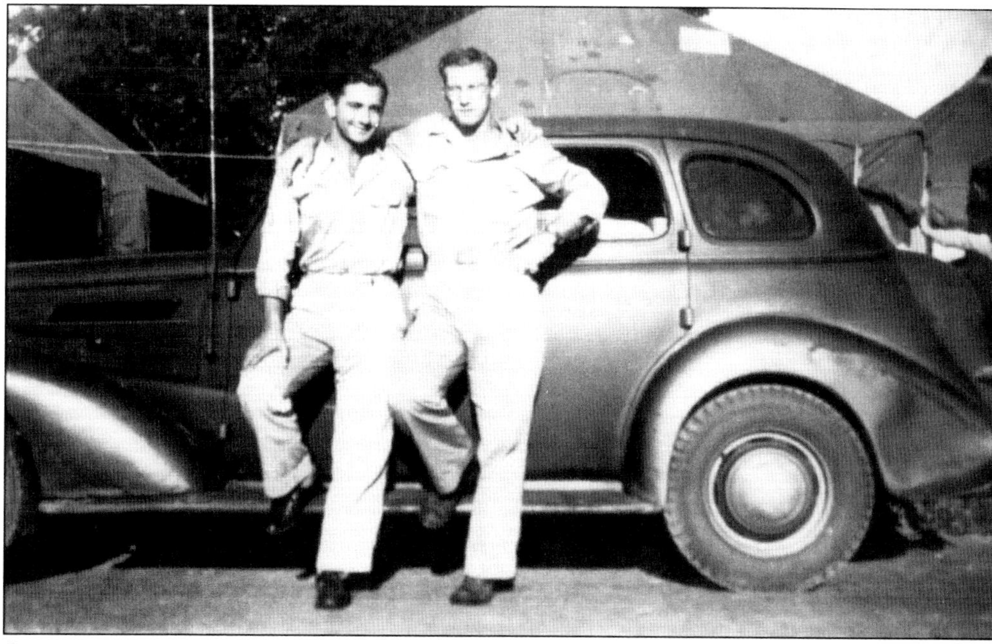

Guards at the POW Camp. The guards who were assigned to the Prisoner of War Camp in Barnwell became very close. They became an integral part of the community and were respected by the local citizens. Here, two of the men strike a characteristic pose in their dress khakis.

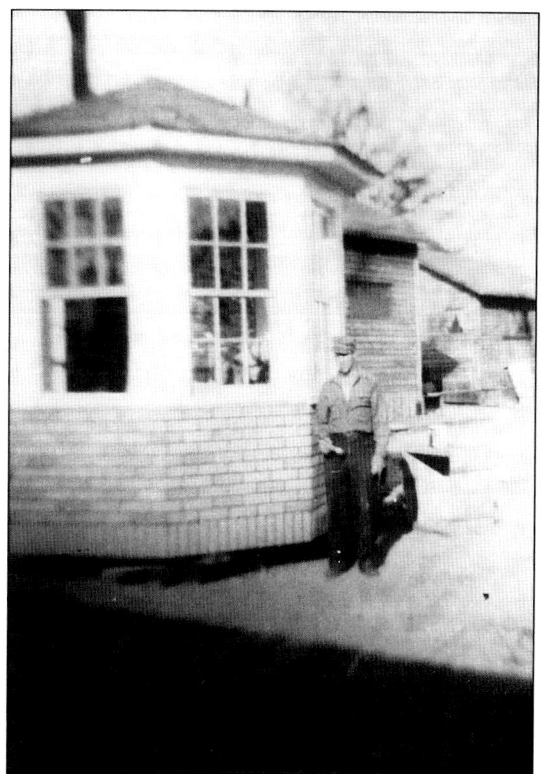

Guard Hut. Mr. C.C. Cheek constructed the guard hut that was located at the entrance to the Prisoner of War Camp. This was a small, but functional place for the guards to stay out of the weather and maintain records on a daily basis.

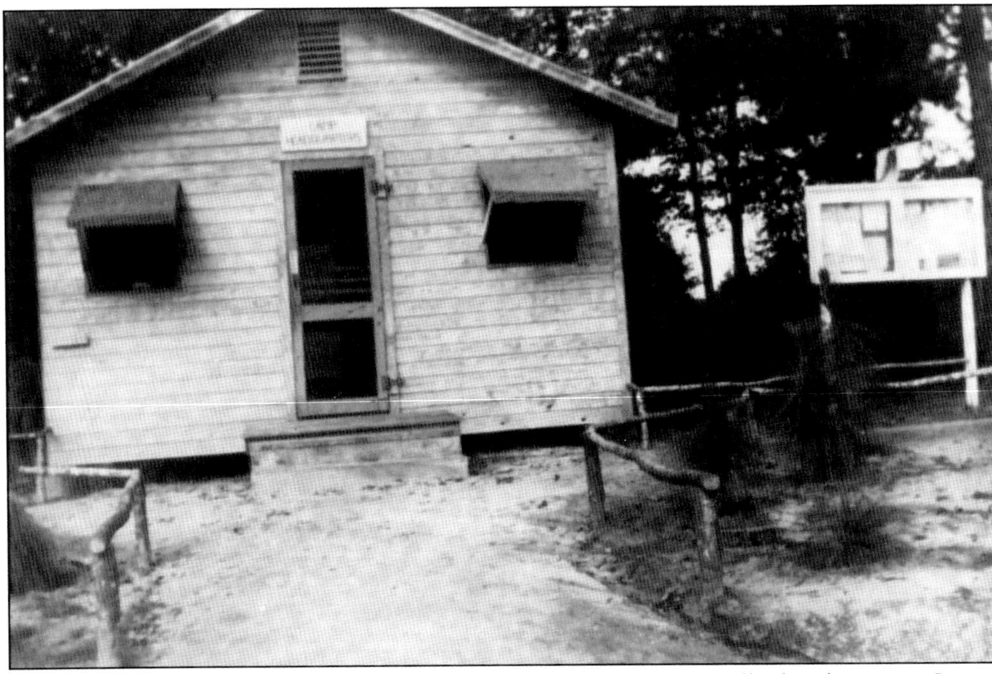

POW Camp Headquarters. This structure housed Captain Jarrell's headquarters. It was here that the citizens of Barnwell County came to place requests for prisoner labor in their communities. Other nearby buildings contained recreation areas for the guards who were assigned to duty at the camp.

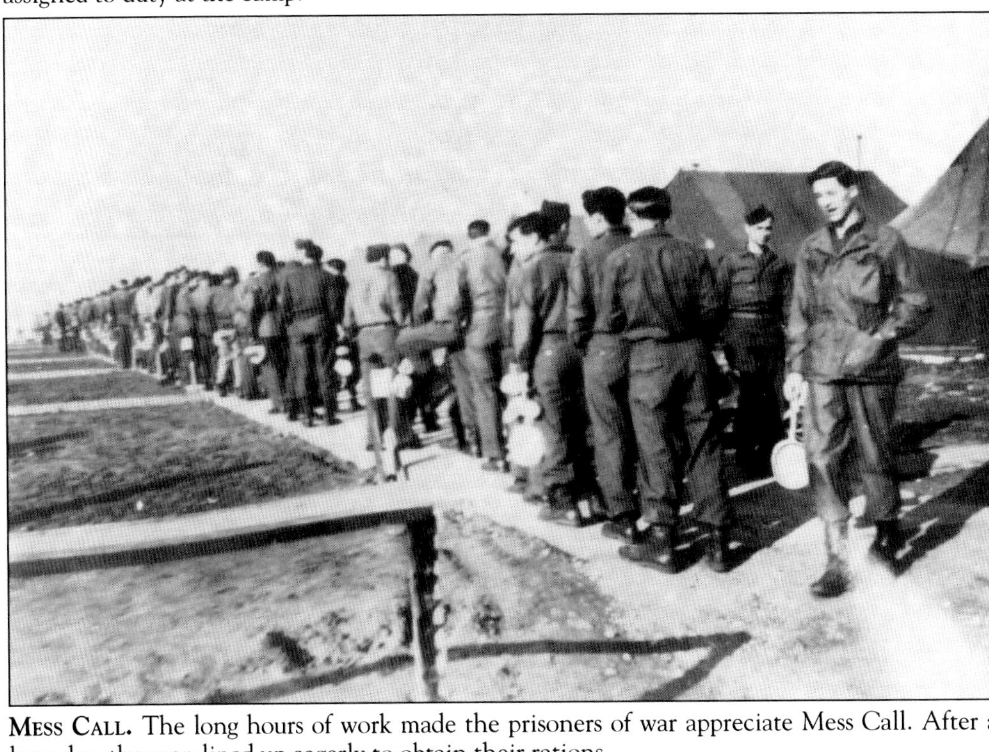

Mess Call. The long hours of work made the prisoners of war appreciate Mess Call. After a long day, the men lined up eagerly to obtain their rations.

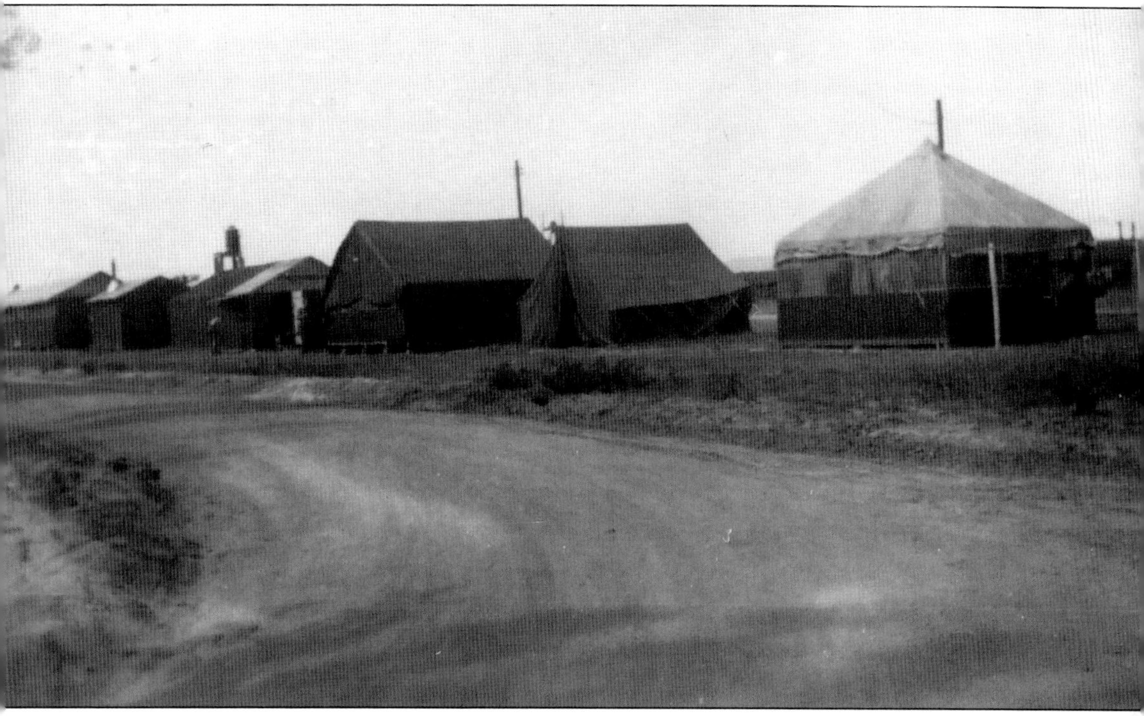

Guard's Quarters. This view of the Prisoner of War Camp shows the quarters used by the guards.

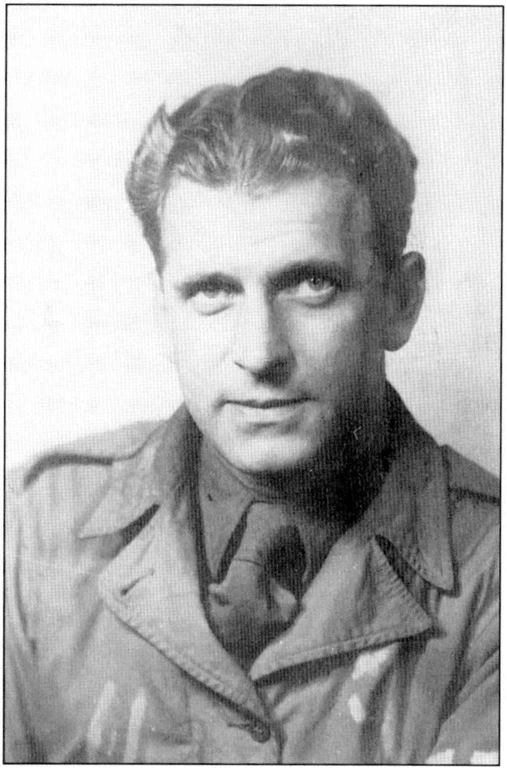

Captain Seigfried Rackl. He was an interpreter of English for the German prisoners of war.

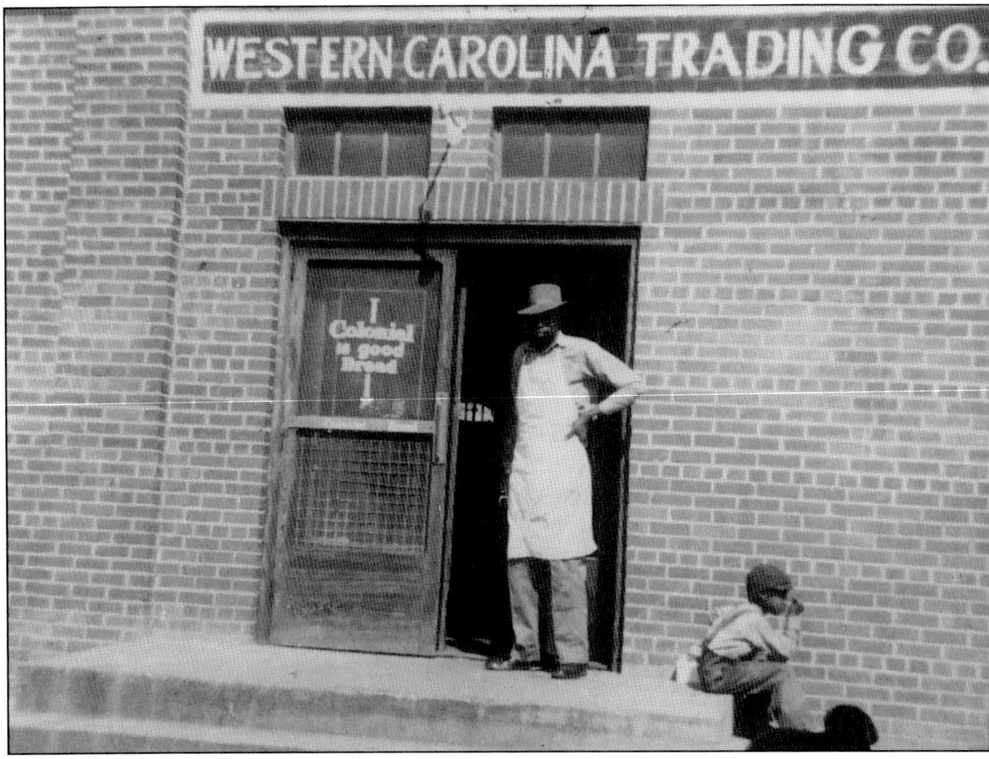

WESTERN CAROLINA TRADING COMPANY. The Western Carolina Trading Company was the first self-service grocery store in Barnwell County, making it the forerunner of the massive shopping department stores to come. Mr. Heyward Geddings and Miss Margaret Anderson were faithful employees, along with "Slick" Mixon, who helped with the operation of the store.

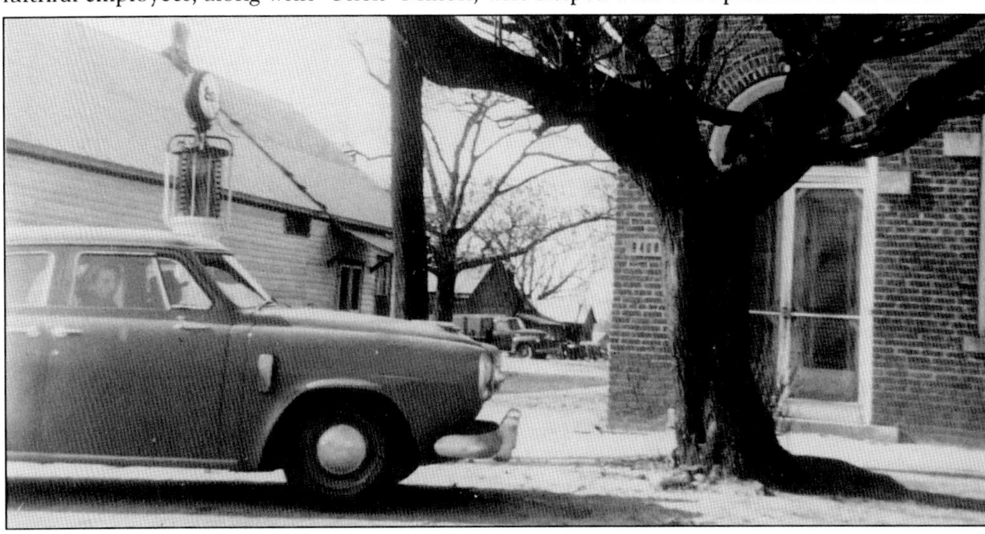

WESTERN CAROLINA DEPOSITORY BANK AT DUNBARTON. The Western Carolina Depository Bank was one of the most successful banking institutions in Barnwell County. Situated in the center of town, the bank was a focal point for the citizens. The owner of this Studebaker would soon be forced to change banking habits, as the bank ceased to operate in this location after the Savannah River Plant moved in.

Eight

The Savannah River Plant Comes to Barnwell County

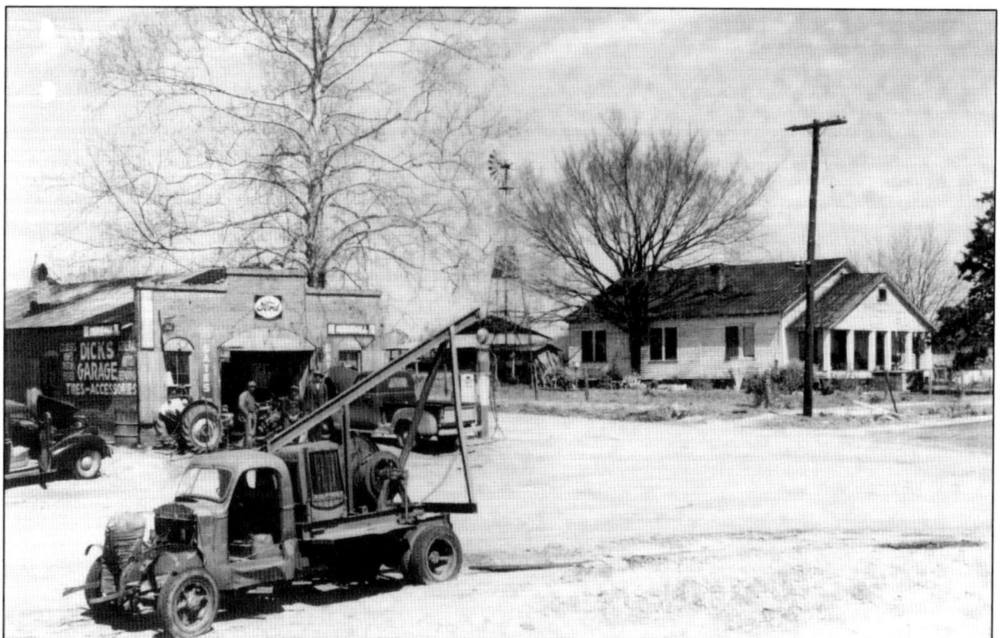

Dicks Garage. Horace Dicks Sr. ran this garage in Dunbarton when the announcement of the Savannah River Plant came. Mr. Dicks would be forced to move his establishment as the modern world of atomic energy closed in around him.

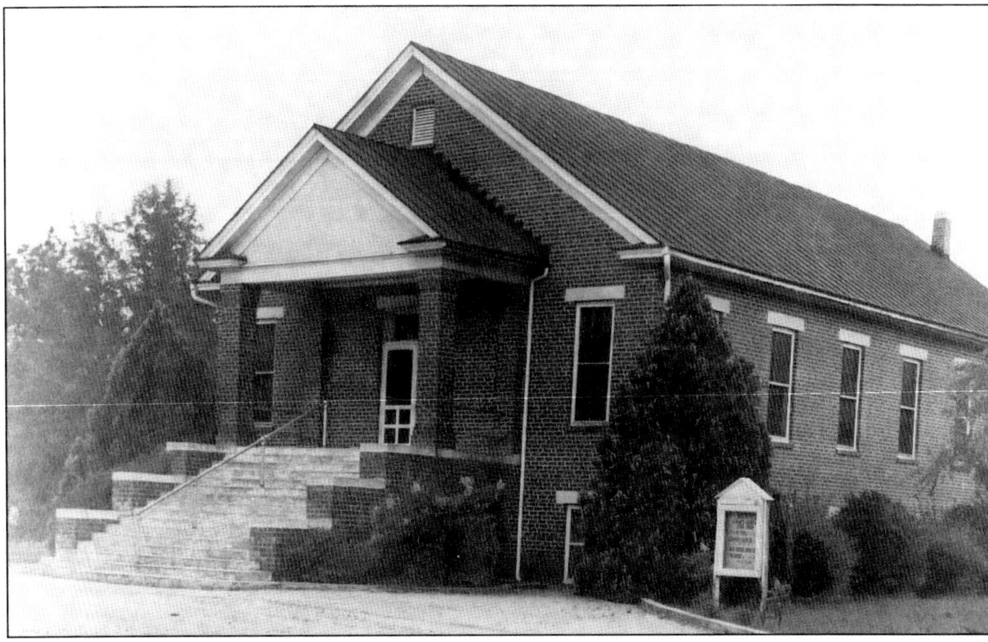

Dunbarton Church. On May 1, 1952, the small town of Dunbarton, South Carolina, ceased to exist. Institutions such as this local church were swept away forever from the landscape.

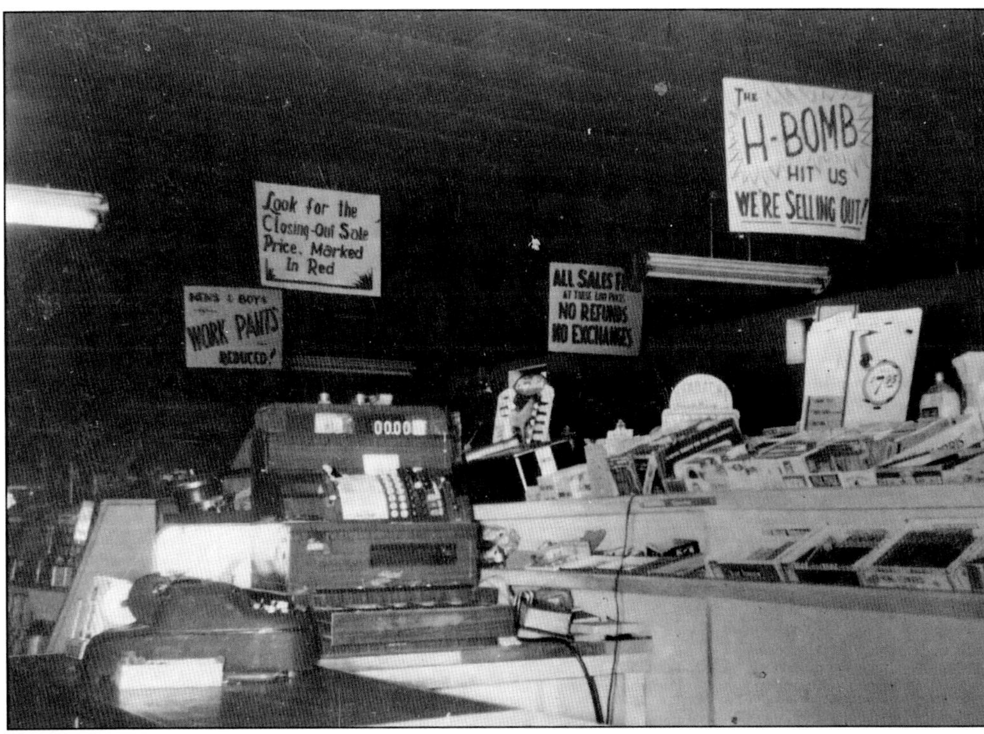

SRP Announced. Throughout the ordeal of making plans to evacuate, many of the citizens of Dunbarton never lost their sense of humor, as the sign prominently displayed indicates. The people resigned themselves to being good citizens and took the displacement in stride.

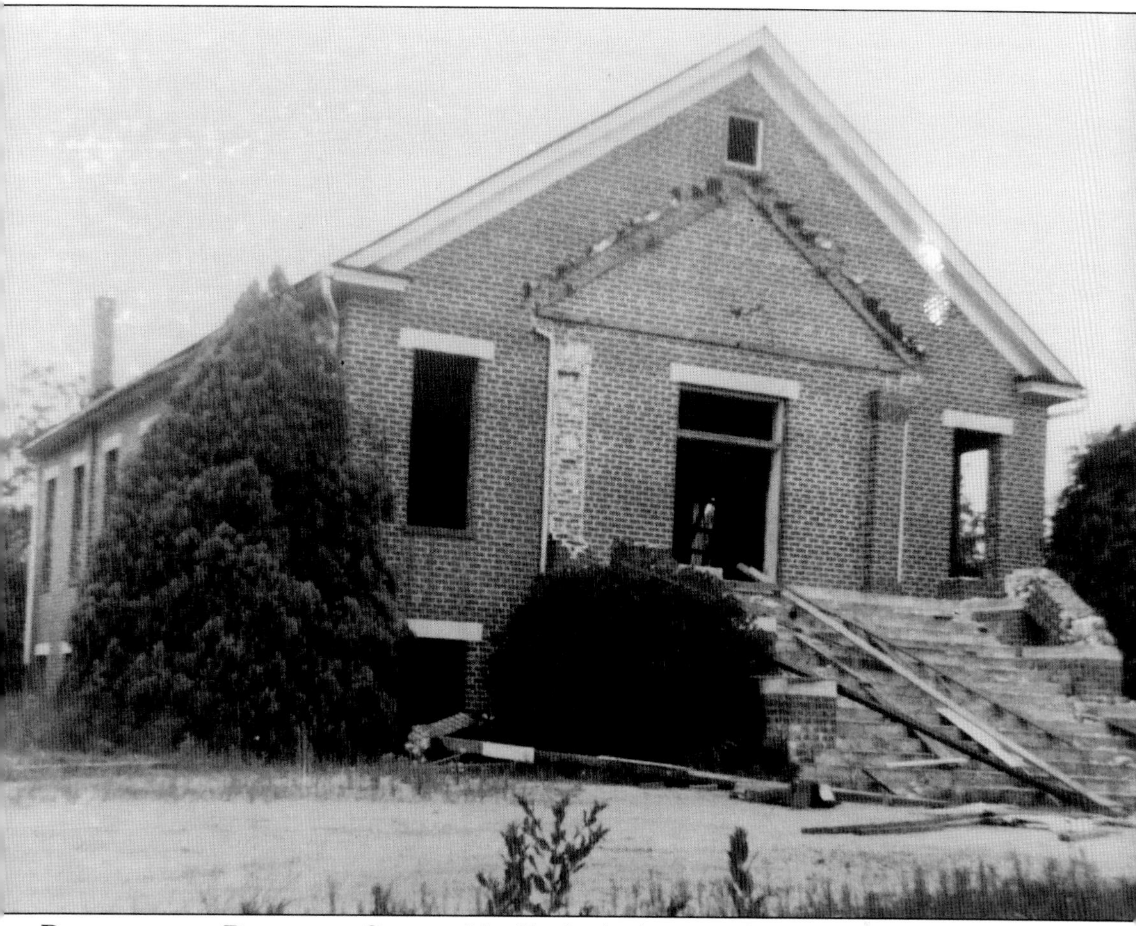

DESTRUCTION OF DUNBARTON CHURCH. Mr. Charlie Anderson wryly commented that the only time this kind of damage was sustained to a community was when General W.T. Sherman's troops laid waste to Barnwell County in 1865. In both cases, the United States Government was behind the destruction; only this time, the community would not recover from the damage.

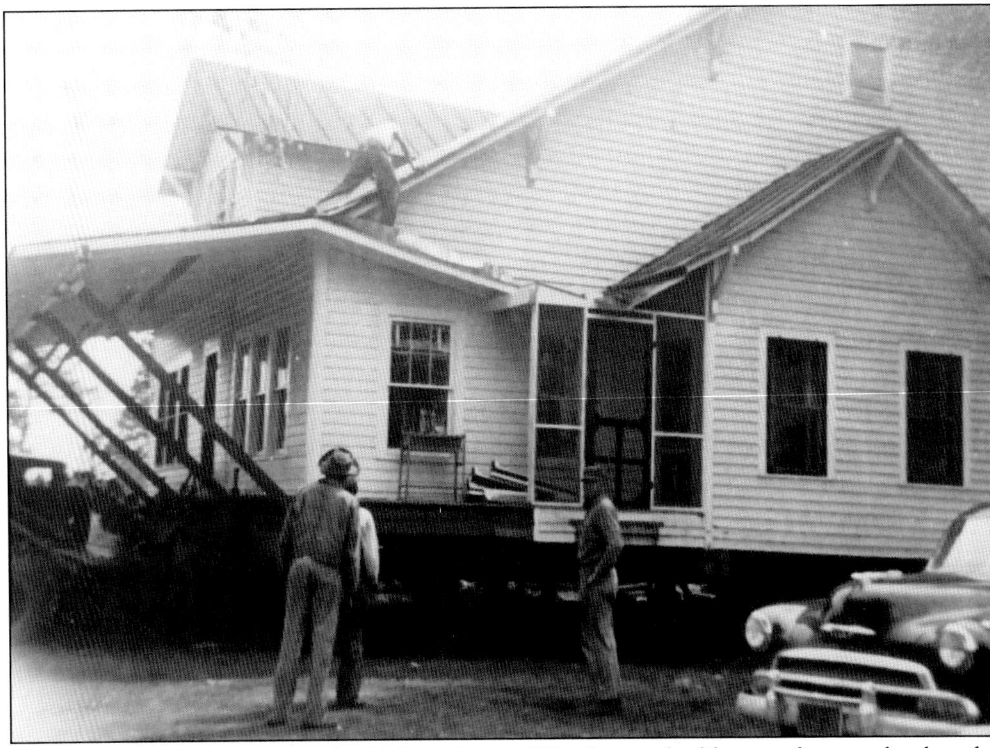

Preparations for Moving. The 300 residents of Dunbarton had known for months that the day would come when they would have to make actual preparations for moving their town. The work crews that prepared Mr. Dicks's house went about their forlorn business with a stoic attitude, holding the community together even in the face of this sad task.

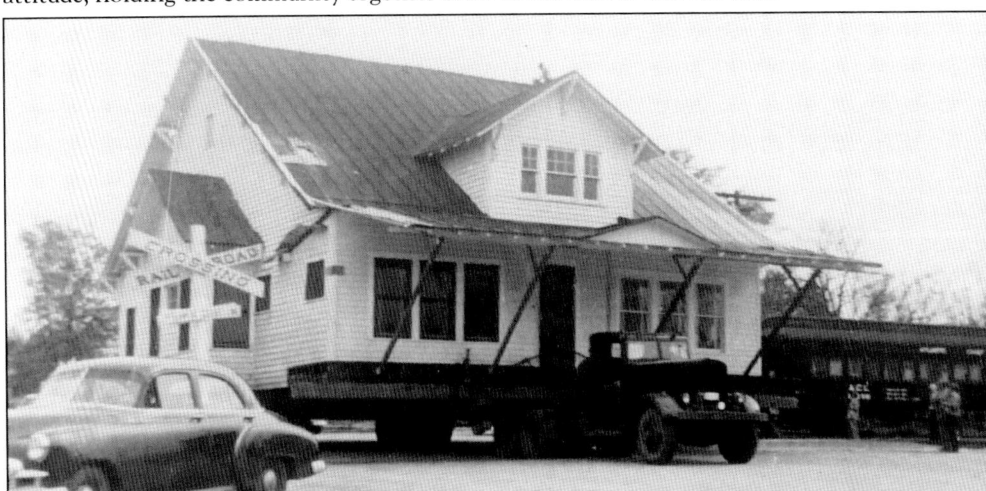

Crossing the Tracks. The day that the citizens of Dunbarton had feared finally arrived, and the job of moving the homes to another location could not be postponed any longer. Crossing the tracks with a house was not something that Mr. Dicks had thought he would ever have to do, but now he faced the reality of the situation. He would move his house to Barnwell and take up residence there along with many of his friends and neighbors.

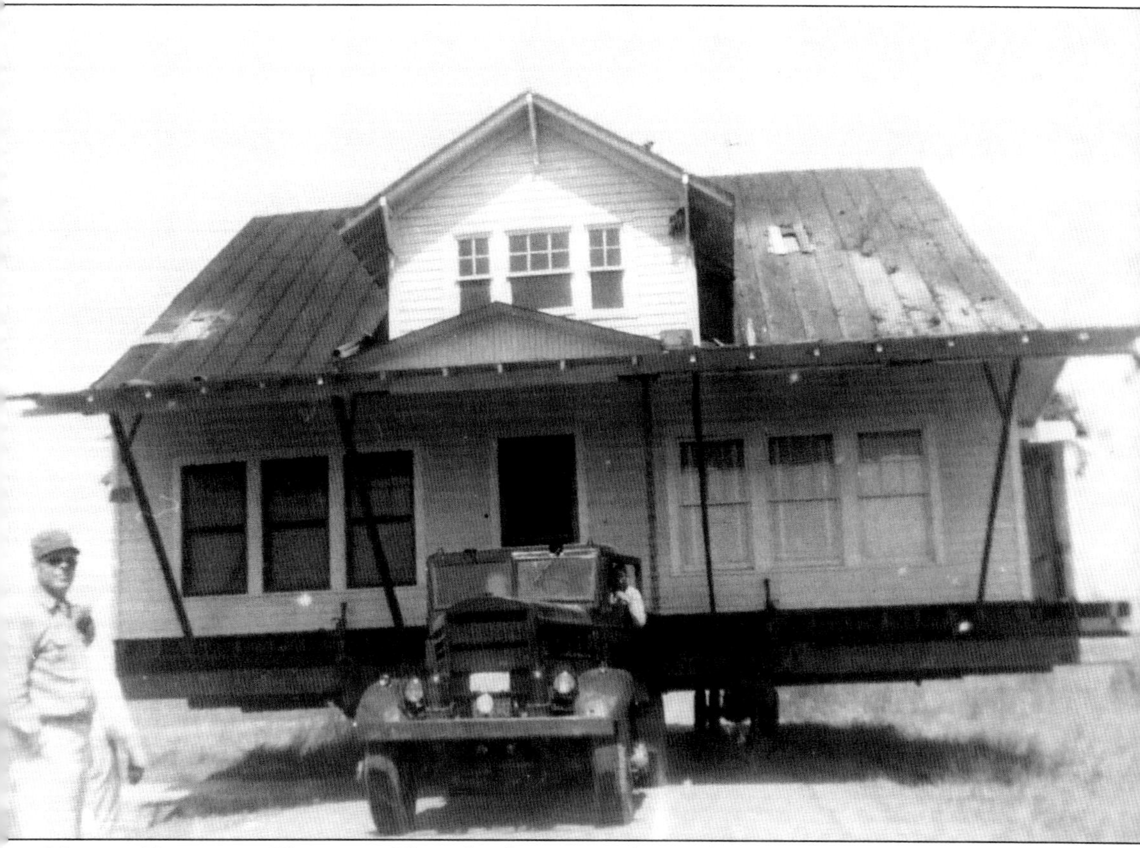

MOVING DOWN THE HIGHWAY. The job of moving a house down the narrow roads of rural Barnwell County was no easy task. The task took a lot of coordination from a number of people in order to successfully accomplish the job safely and without doing damage to the houses.

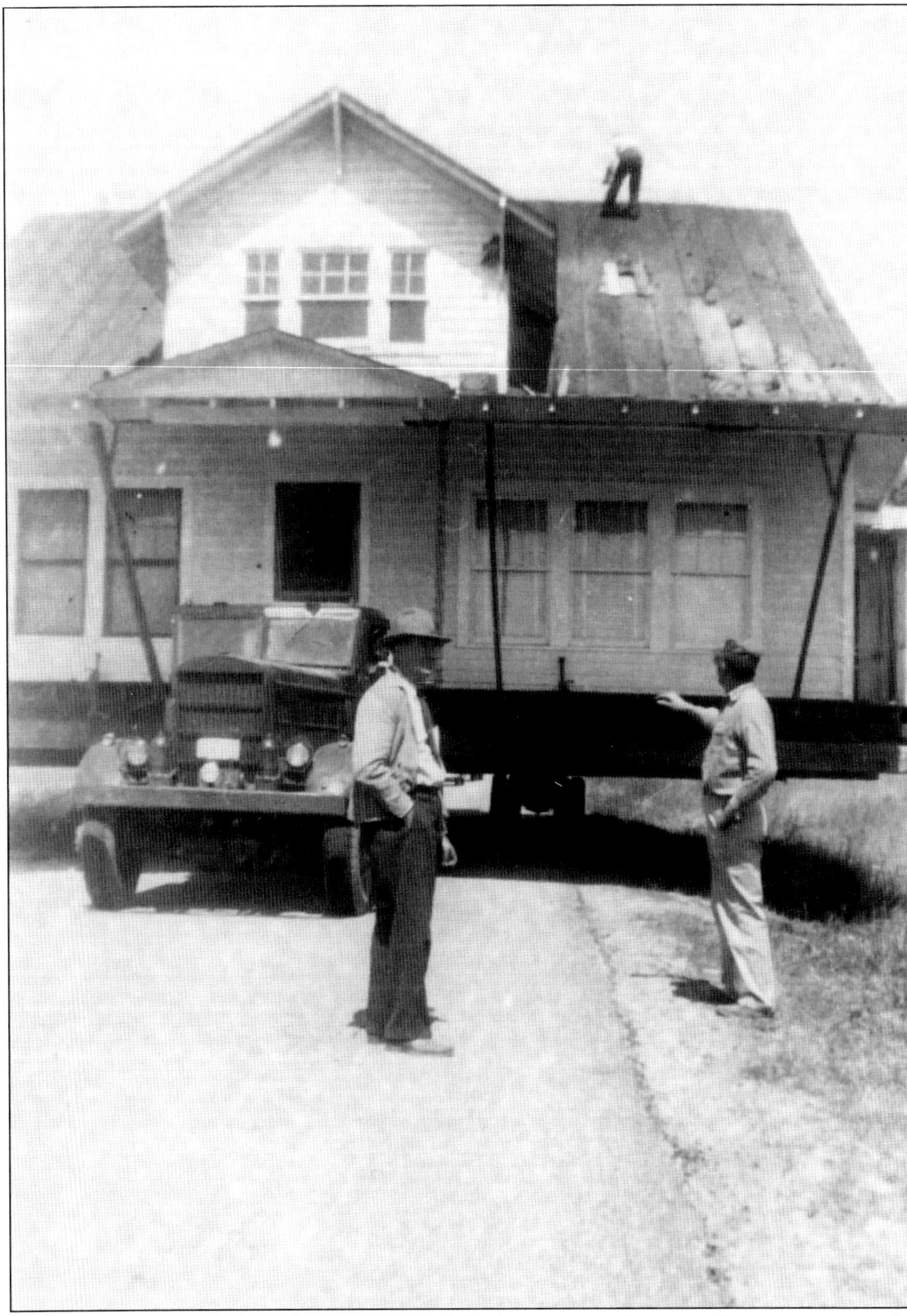

MOVING WIRES. Rural electrification provided the biggest impediment to house moving as the homes of Dunbarton were dismantled and relocated elsewhere. Someone had to ride the peak of the house down the road in order to lift the electric light wires high enough to allow the structure to pass underneath.

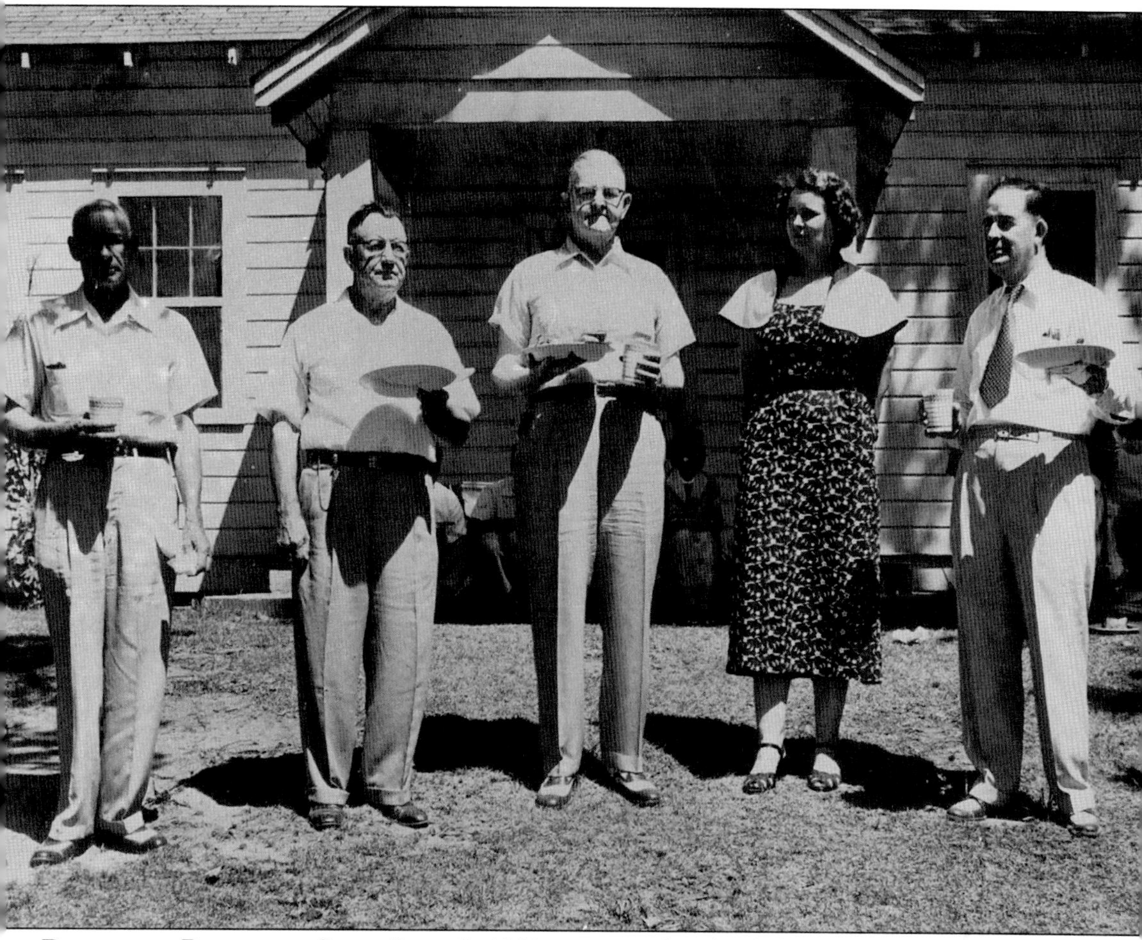

DUNBARTON REUNION AT STATE PARK. In 1953, one year after they left, the displaced residents of Dunbarton rented the Community Building at Barnwell State Park for a reunion of those who endured the evacuation of their town. Pictured here are city officials H.H. King, C.H. Beatty, P.J. Hiers, F.H. Dicks, and clerk Margaret Anderson.

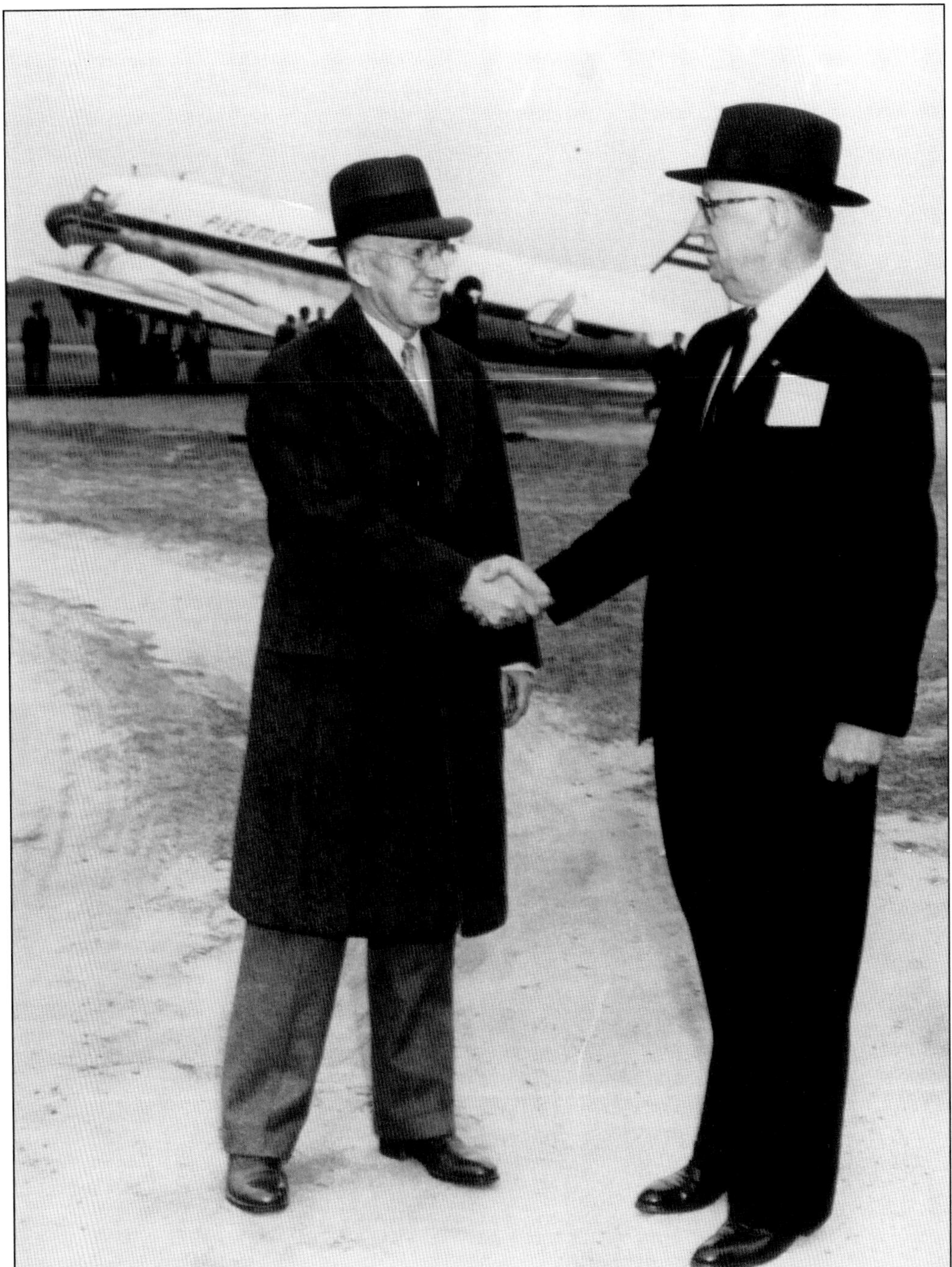

SENATOR BROWN GREETS MR. LITTLE. Senator Edgar A. Brown was perhaps the most instrumental factor in attracting Amerotron to Barnwell. After inviting Mr. Royal Little of Textron, Inc. to view the proposed site, he asked, "Now, what do we have to do to make this happen?" After Mr. Little outlined his requirements, Senator Brown immediately took him to WBAW radio station to make the announcement that a new industry was coming to town.

Nine

Amerotron Comes to Barnwell

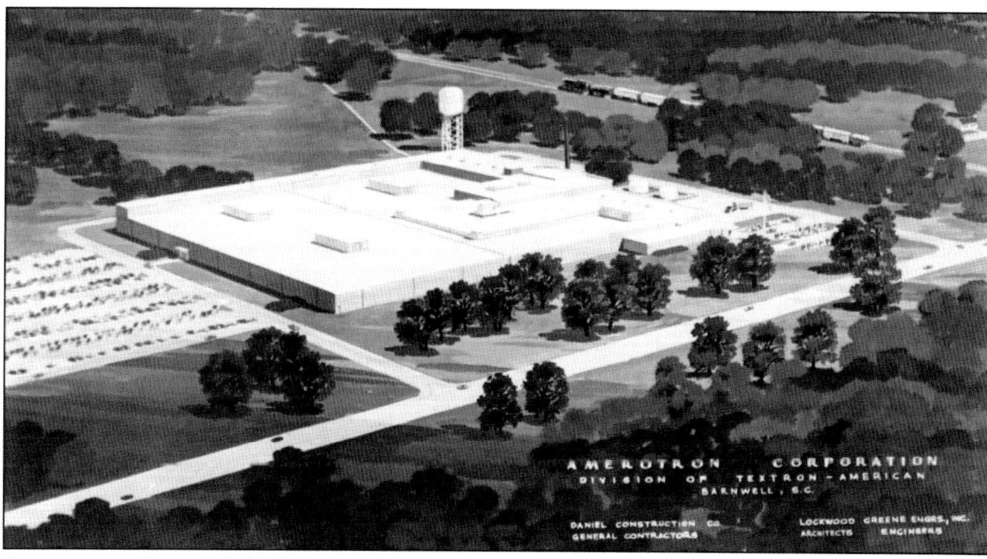

Amerotron Plant. The Barnwell Plant was dedicated on February 24, 1956, as the Woolen Division of Amerotron Corporation. Known locally as "the woolen mill," the product line consisted of staple fabrics for the womenswear dress and sportswear trade. Later, the market was expanded to wool writing materials for women and children and a line of quality menswear. The plant was the most modern integrated woolen operation in the world and was planned and equipped for the most current methods of manufacturing. In April 1963, Deering Milliken, Inc. acquired the Barnwell Plant, along with eight other Amerotron operations. Since 1963, several expansions and changes in equipment have taken place, converting the plant from the largest woolen manufacturing operation in the world to a highly complex and sophisticated dyeing and finishing plant. The well-trained work force strives to produce the highest quality fabrics that can be found on the market today.

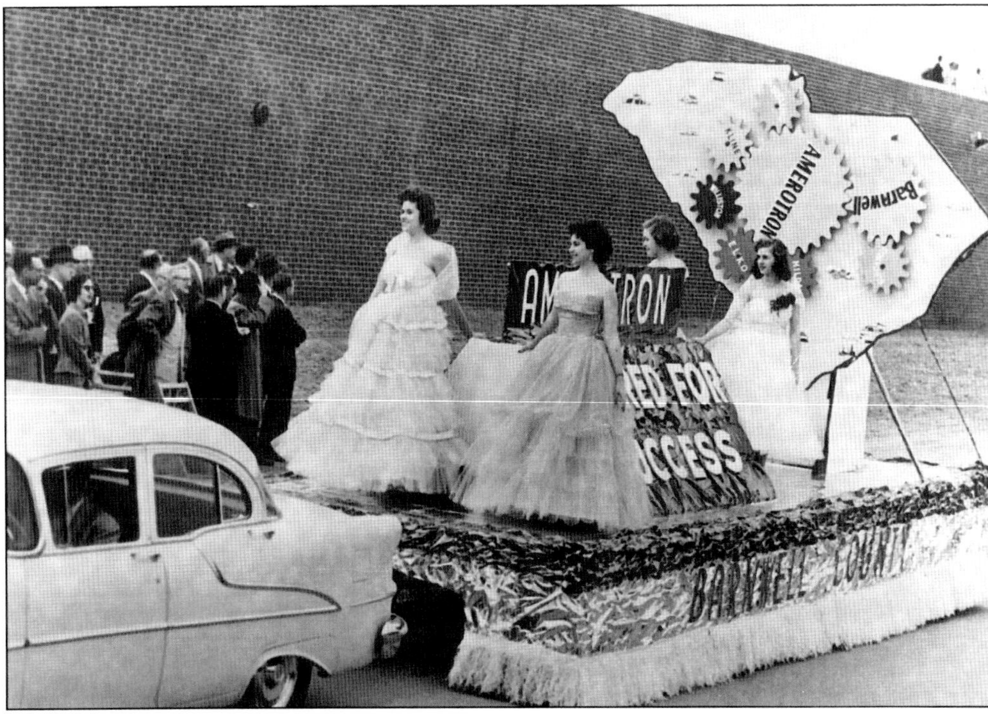

AMEROTRON PARADE. One of the events that marked the dedication of Amerotron was a large parade staged to call attention to the new industry. Fancy automobiles and pretty girls were featured as the townspeople participated in this festive occasion.

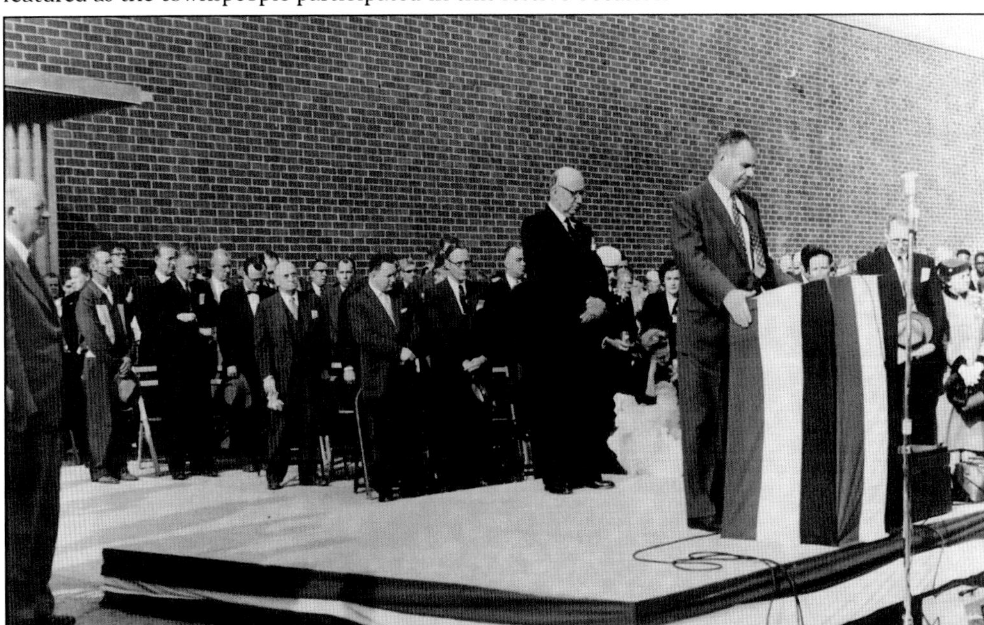

INVOCATION BY REVEREND WEBB. The minister of the Barnwell Baptist Church was asked to give the invocation at the impressive ceremony. Mr. Webb solemnly asked God's blessing on his community and the economic endeavor known as Amerotron.

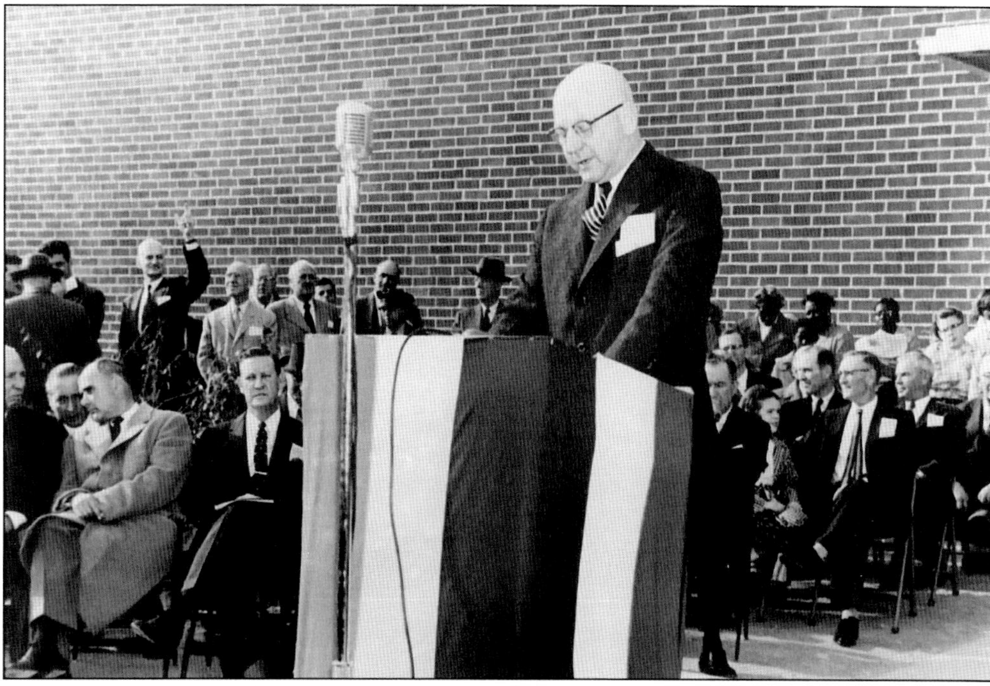

Speaker Sol Blatt Welcomes Amerotron. Although Senator Edgar Brown was probably the most influential politician to be involved in the addition of the new industry, he was supported wholeheartedly by his colleague, Speaker of the House Sol Blatt. Mr. Blatt added his congratulations to the host of others on that special day.

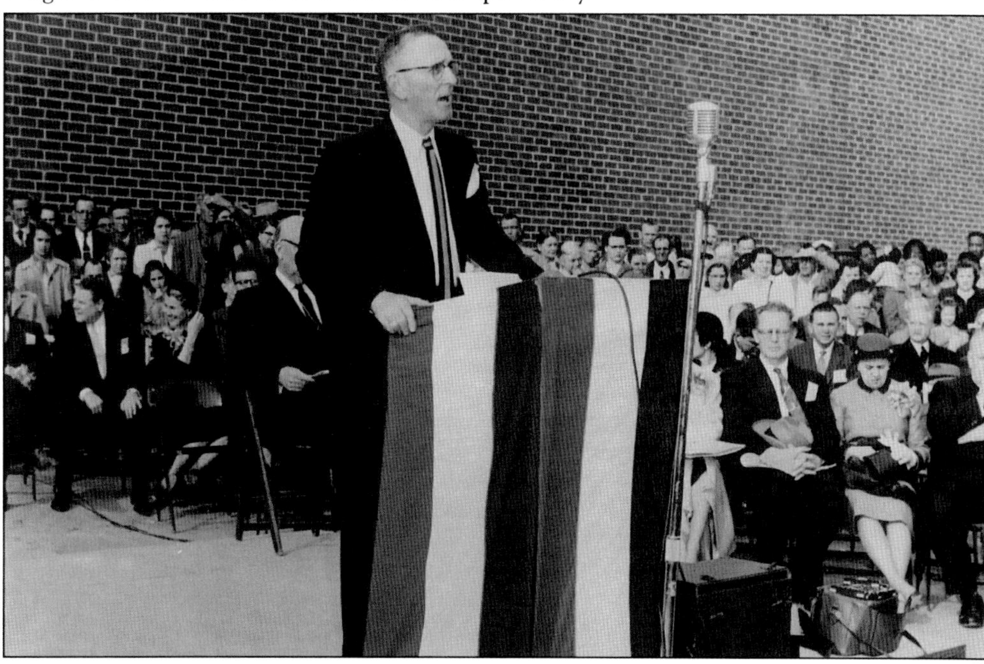

Mayor Mazursky Addresses the Crowd. Mayor Mazursky also lent his voice to those who praised the decision to bring Amerotron to Barnwell. His support in the endeavor was evident as he addressed the crowd gathered at the site of the new plant on Jackson Street.

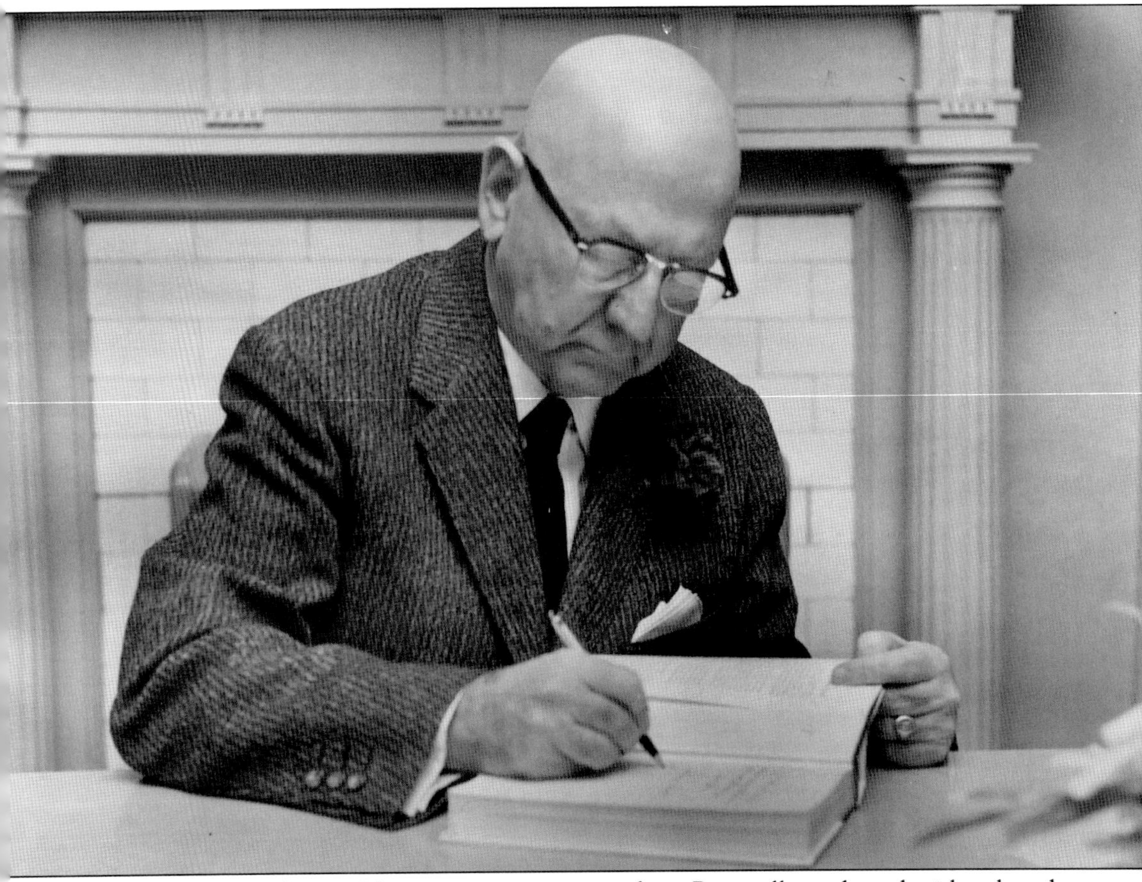

Sol Blatt. Solomon Blatt, renown statesman from Barnwell, graduated with a law degree from the University of South Carolina in 1917, to become the law partner of J.E. Harley, future governor of the state. Later, he joined Ira Fales to form one of the most influential law firms in the state. Mr. Blatt was a World War I veteran and a very successful public servant, having lost only one political campaign—his very first. After being elected to the South Carolina House in 1932, and speaker pro temp in 1935, he served as speaker of the house until 1973, with the exception of two terms in which he did not run for reelection.

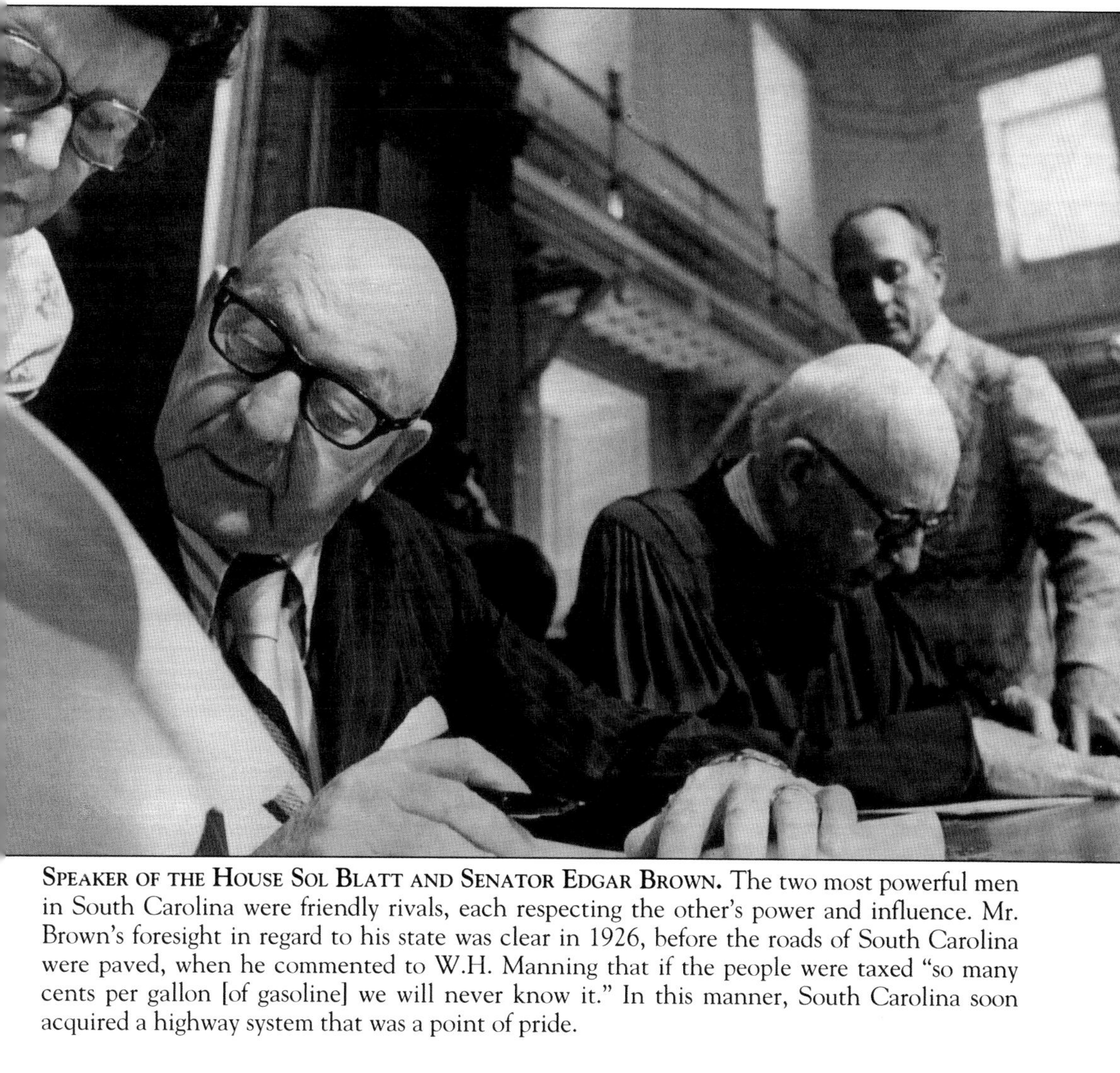

Speaker of the House Sol Blatt and Senator Edgar Brown. The two most powerful men in South Carolina were friendly rivals, each respecting the other's power and influence. Mr. Brown's foresight in regard to his state was clear in 1926, before the roads of South Carolina were paved, when he commented to W.H. Manning that if the people were taxed "so many cents per gallon [of gasoline] we will never know it." In this manner, South Carolina soon acquired a highway system that was a point of pride.

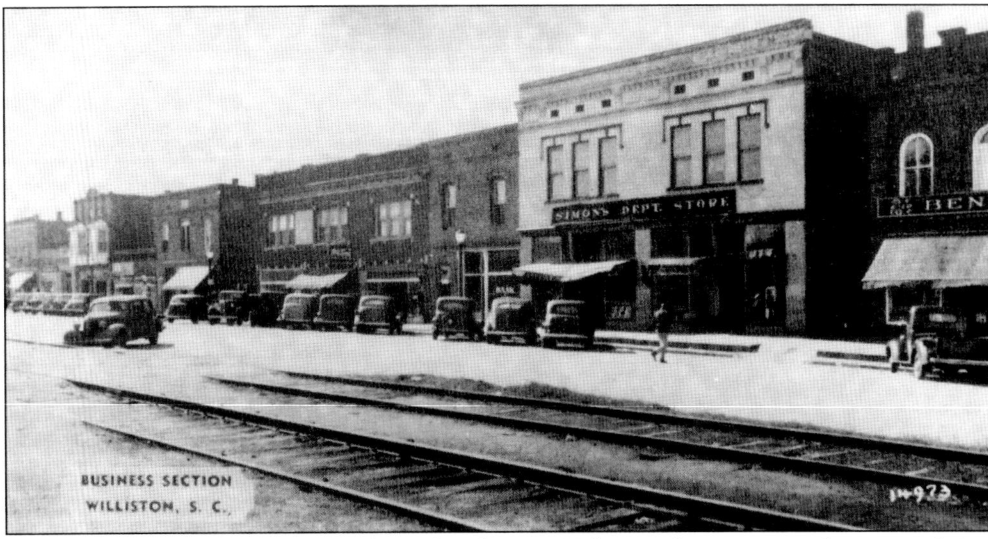

WILLISTON BUSINESS DISTRICT. The railroad gave Williston the economic boost needed to develop a well-defined business district. Like many Southern towns that grew up around the economy of the railroad, Williston had an opportunity to take advantage of the resources associated with the rail lines.

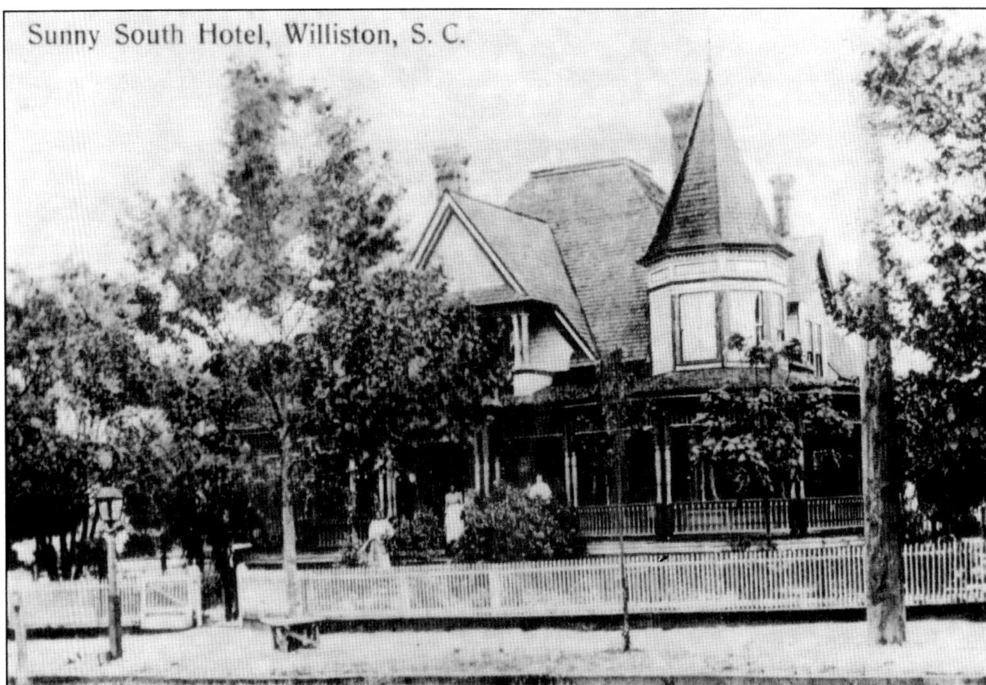

SUNNY SOUTH HOTEL. The Sunny South Hotel, shown here in a postcard printed in Germany and imported by Paul E. Trouche of Charleston, is an example of how many South Carolinians who owned property near the railroads took advantage of the opportunity to serve the many businesses thriving along the railroad line. Visitors to the Williston area were sure to be treated with respect and Southern hospitality during their stay in the community.

Ten

WILLISTON SOUTH CAROLINA

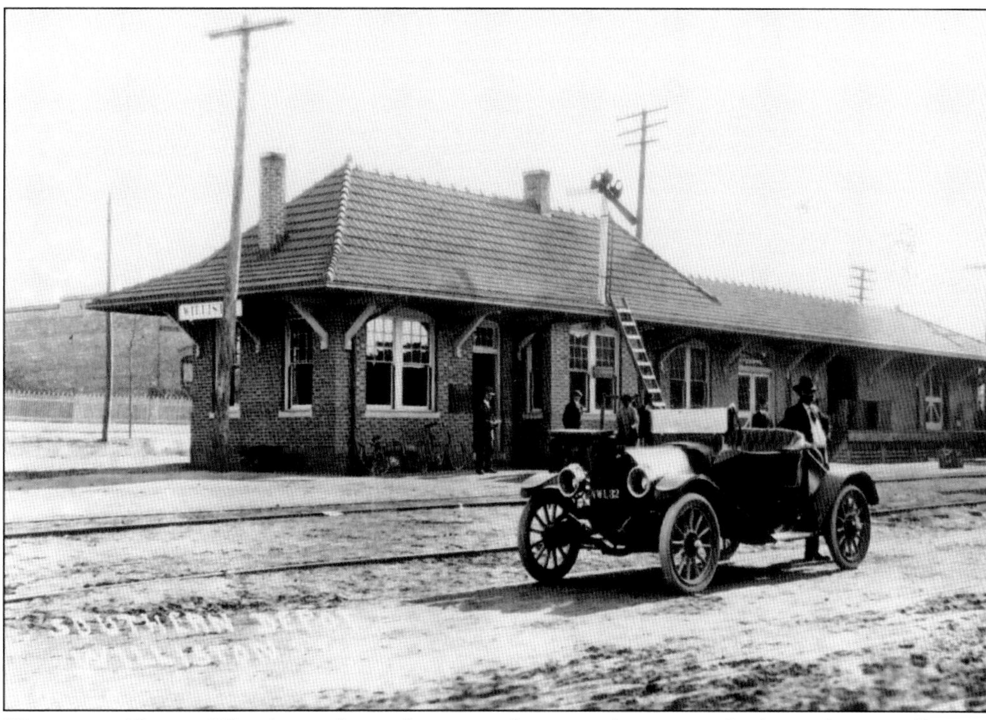

WILLISTON DEPOT. The depot shown here was the second structure built on this site. Erected in 1912, it was destroyed by a fire that originated on the loading platform on March 12, 1912. The fire spread to other buildings, and a large portion of the town was threatened. The brave action of the local fire department and assistance from nearby towns saved Williston from massive damage.

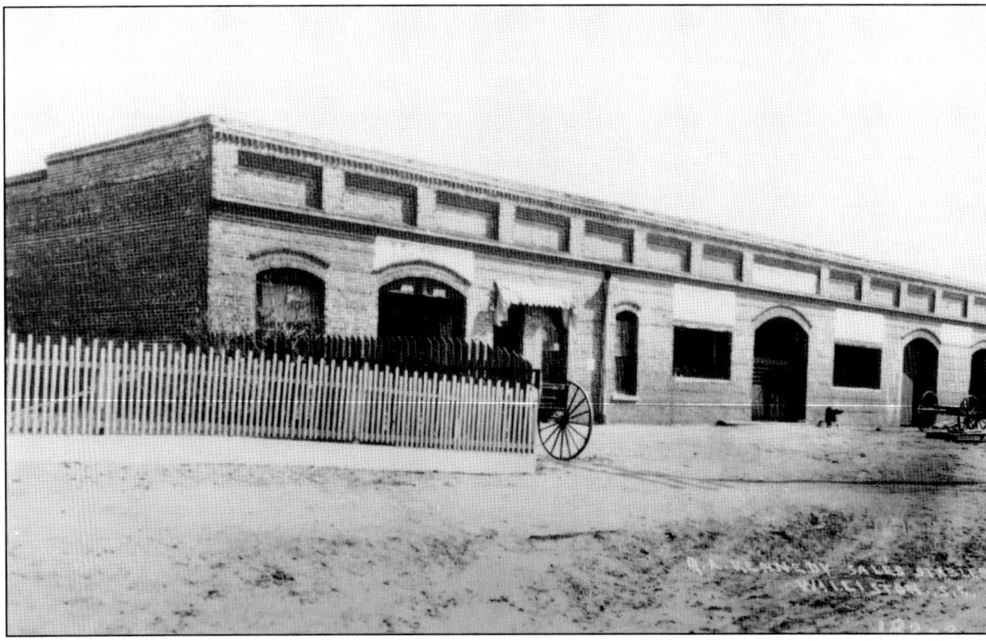

Kennedy Stables. Mr. Q.A. Kennedy's stables were located across the street from the Williston Depot and were destroyed in the same fire that consumed the depot.

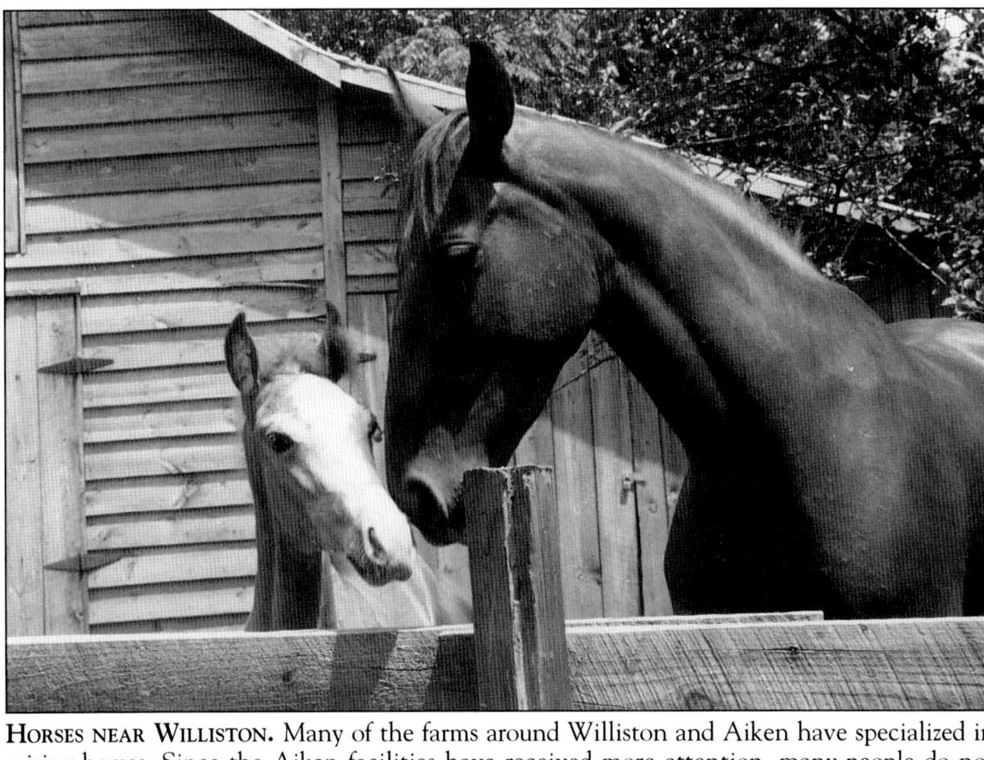

Horses near Williston. Many of the farms around Williston and Aiken have specialized in raising horses. Since the Aiken facilities have received more attention, many people do not realize the potential in Barnwell County.

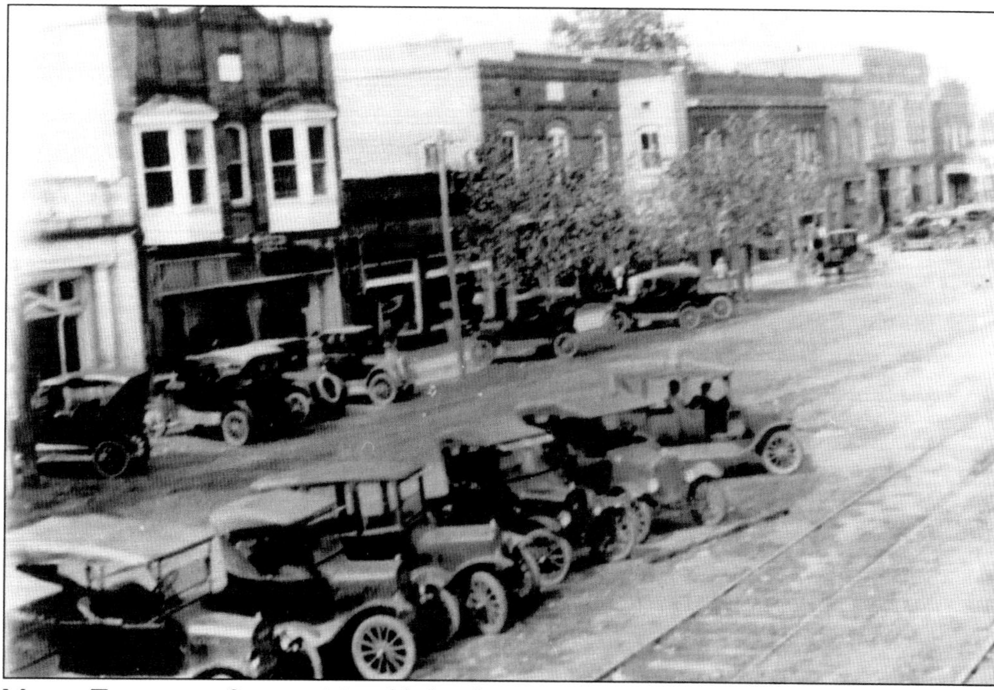

Model Ts on the Street. Most likely, this view of Williston was taken by a traveling photographer who made a decent living for himself by capturing the images of towns and selling them to the businessmen in the area.

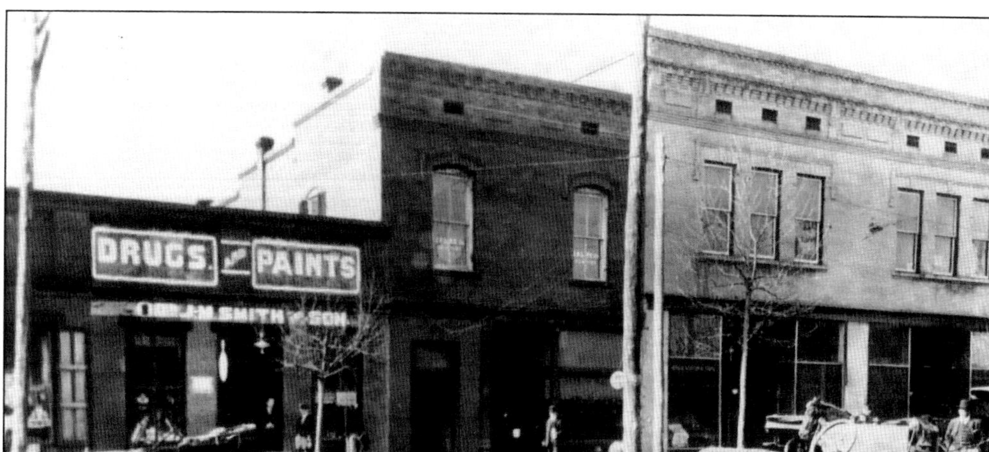

Smith Drugs and Paint. The Smith family has been involved with the drugstore business in the Williston area for a long time. The odd combination of "Drugs and Paint" shows how flexible small merchants had to be in order to give the community the kind of service it required.

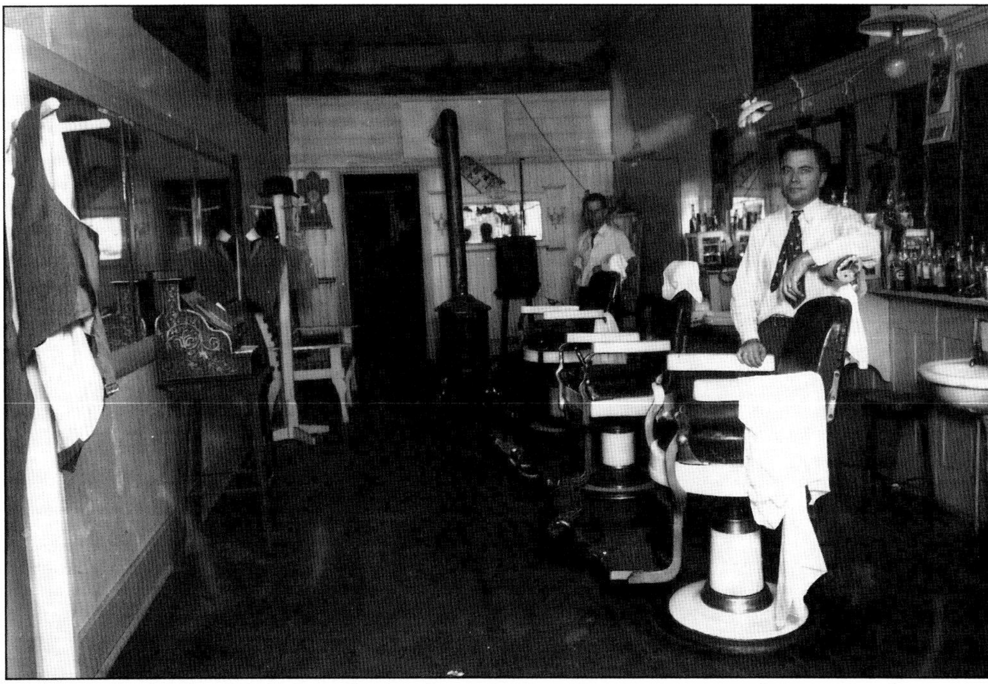

Barber Shop. Clem Boyleston's barbershop on Main Street was a popular stop for the men of Williston to "chew the fat" and catch up on the news of the day.

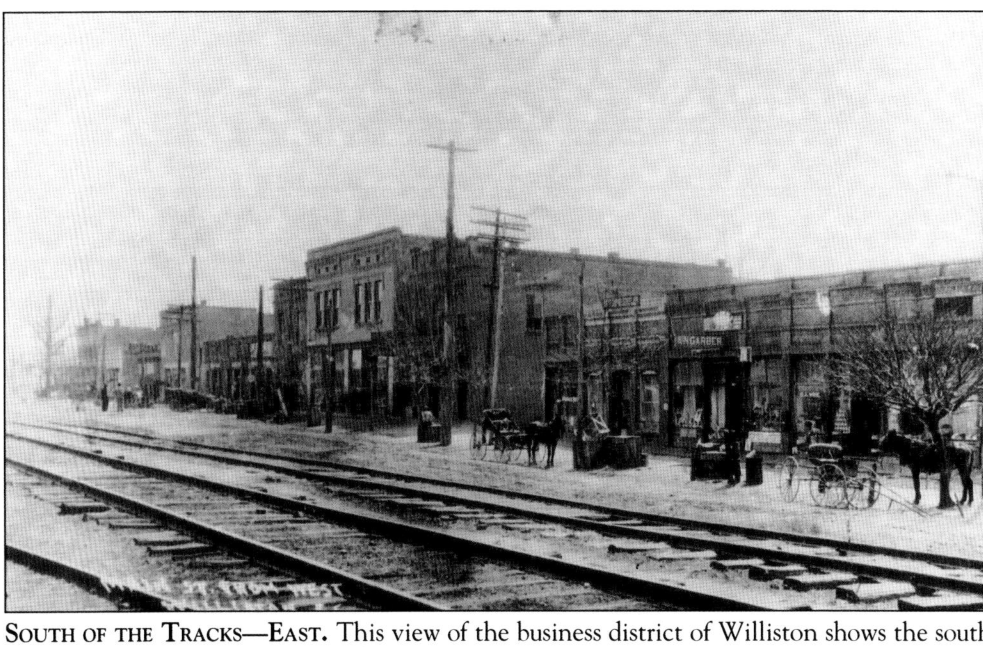

South of the Tracks—East. This view of the business district of Williston shows the south side of the tracks, looking eastward.

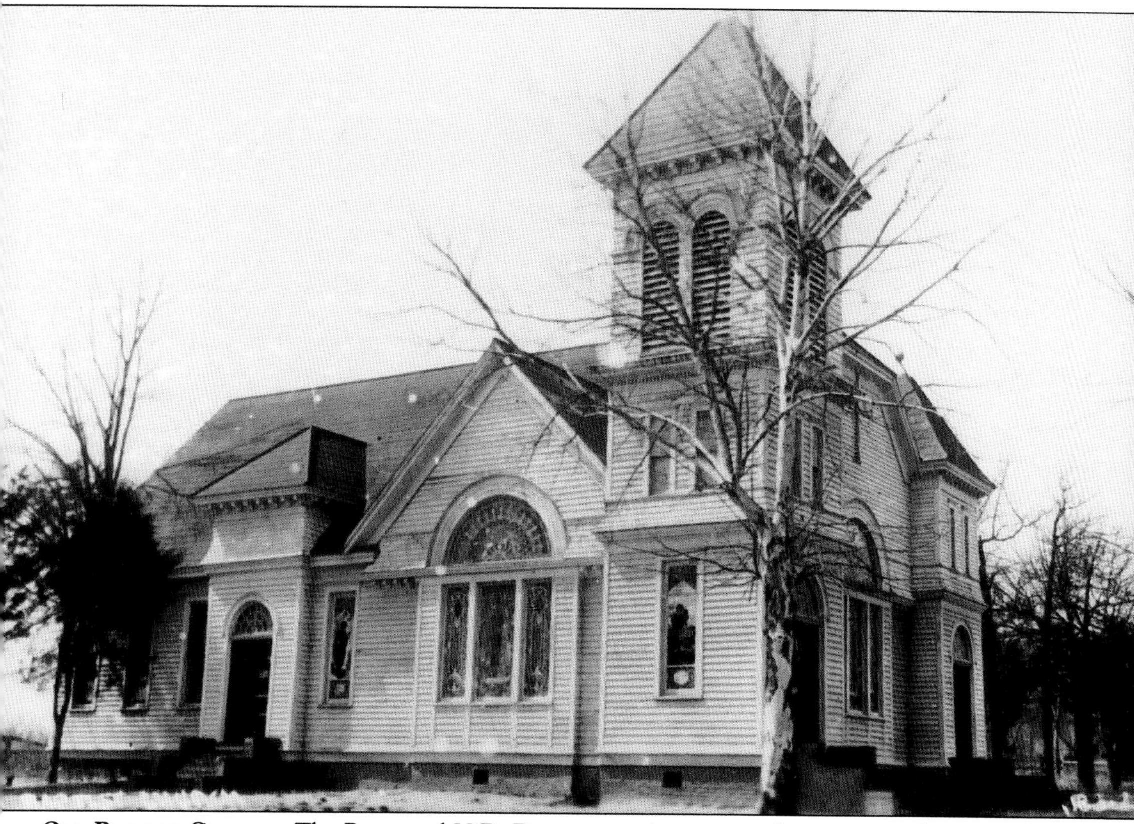

Old Baptist Church. The Reverend H.D. Duncan was instrumental in erecting the original house of worship. William F. Mathews and G.C. Mathews were the first deacons.

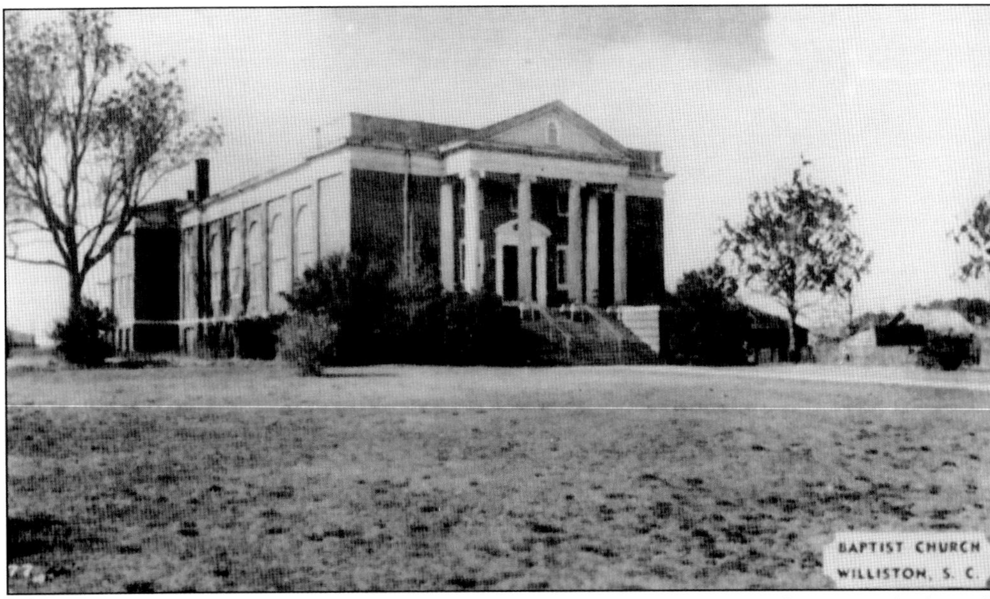

FIRST BAPTIST CHURCH. The Williston Baptist Church has seen tremendous growth through the years, serving many citizens as it coped with the influx of workers during the Savannah River Plant "boom," and later dealing with the issues of society and religion during the last half of the 20th century.

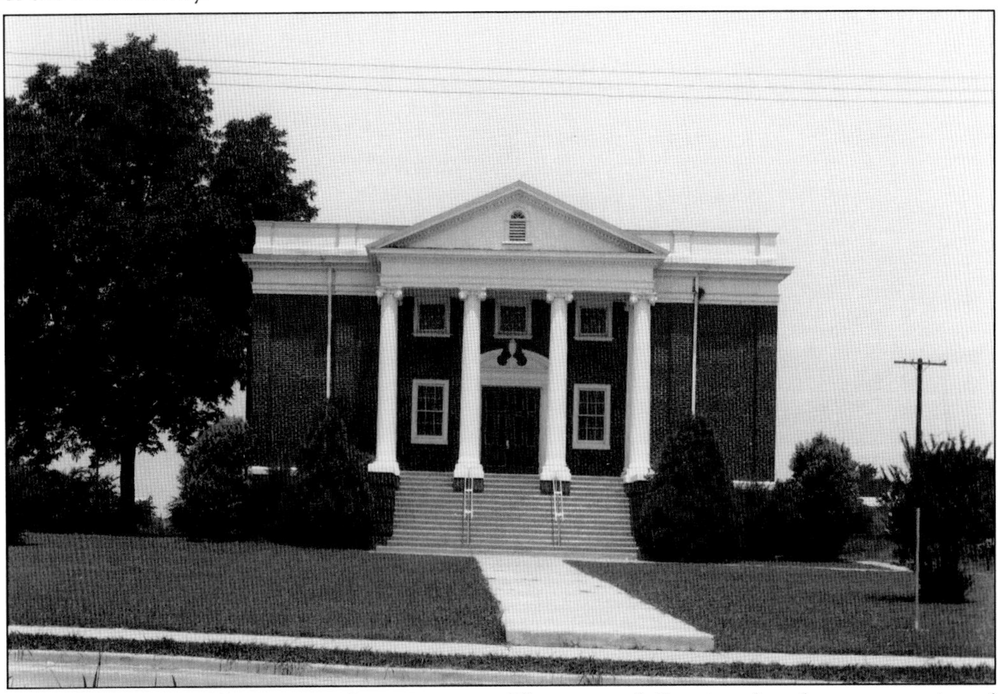

A CHURCH WITH HISTORICAL SIGNIFICANCE. The original Baptist church was constituted on September 5, 1857. In 1859, the church withdrew from the Savannah River Association and united with the Barnwell Association. In the late 1880s, a Women's Missionary Society was organized, and by 1924, the congregation had erected a third and final structure for their worship. In 1936, there were 535 members, and in 1962, the congregation grew to 884.

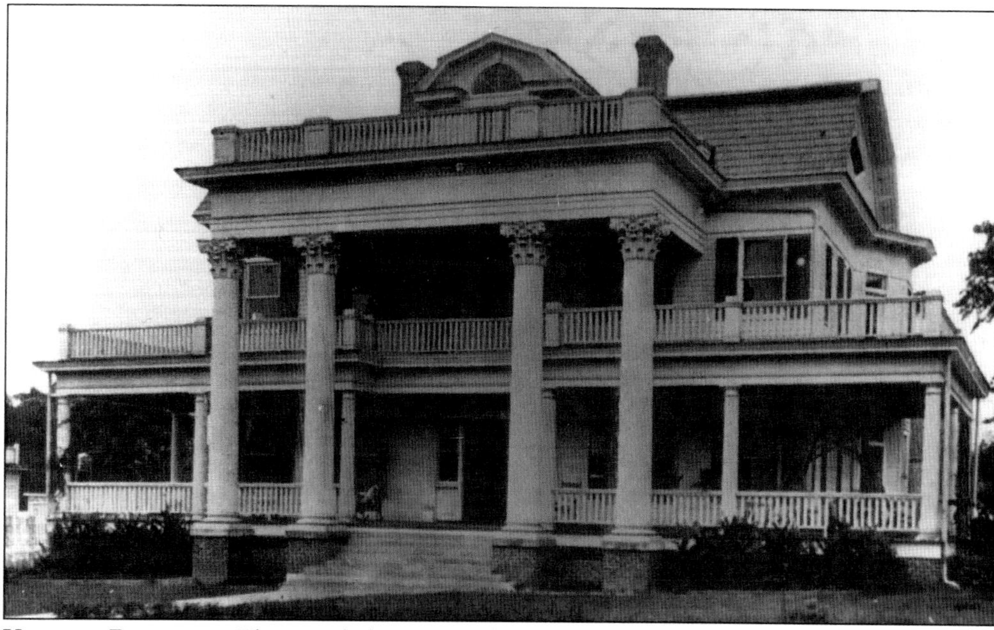

Kennedy Residence. This stately home was the residence of Mr. Q.A. Kennedy. It was filled with exquisite antique furniture.

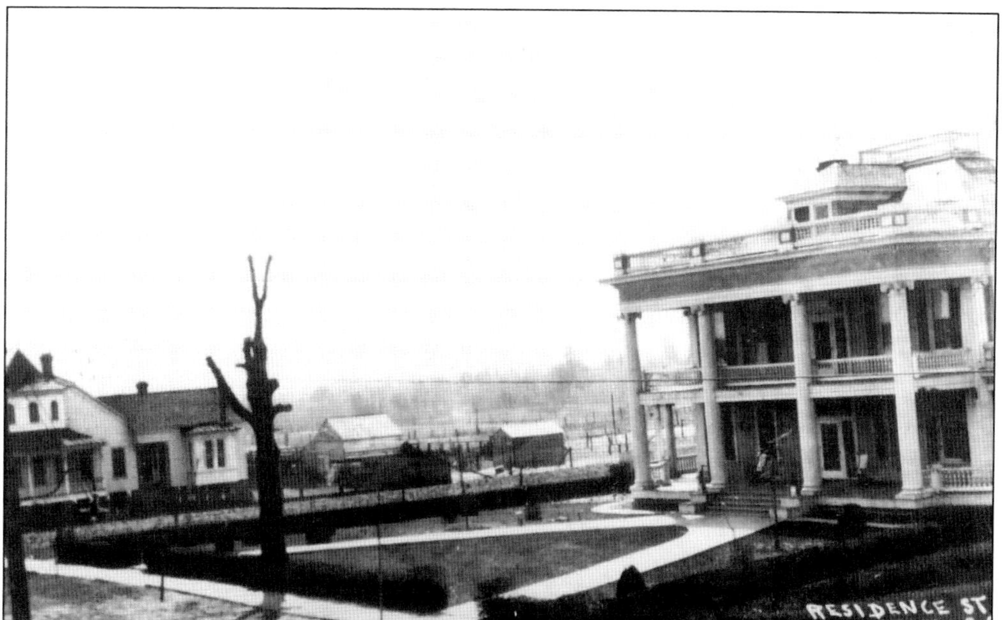

Residential Street Scene. This view of a Williston street has completely changed since this photograph was taken; the only structure still standing is the Ponder residence in the background. Mr. Q.A. Kennedy's home, visible in the foreground, is the site of the Whittle Motor Company's parking lot, and a Hardee's restaurant now stands in the middle ground.

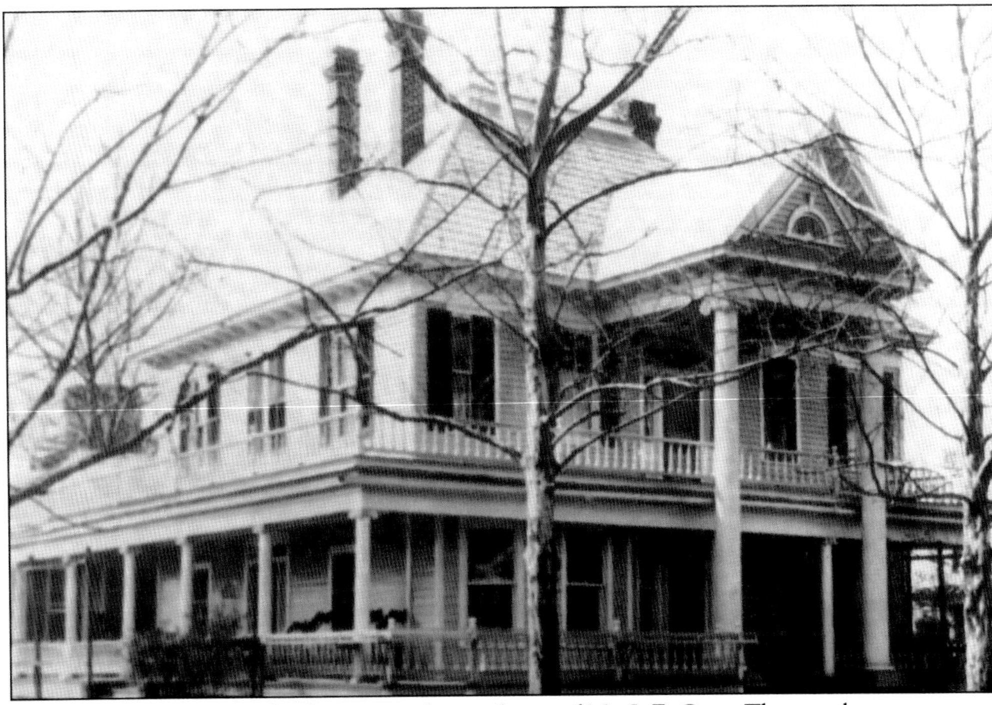

WILLISTON RESIDENCE. This home was the residence of Mr. L.E. Gree. The stately entrance was a focal point of this well-kept house.

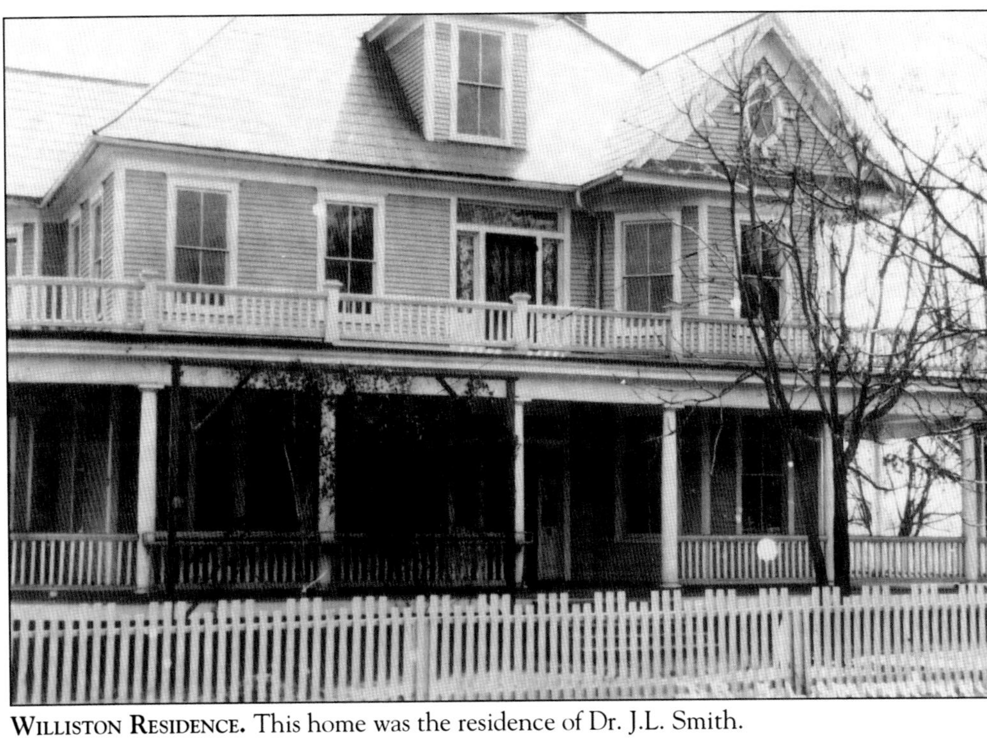

WILLISTON RESIDENCE. This home was the residence of Dr. J.L. Smith.

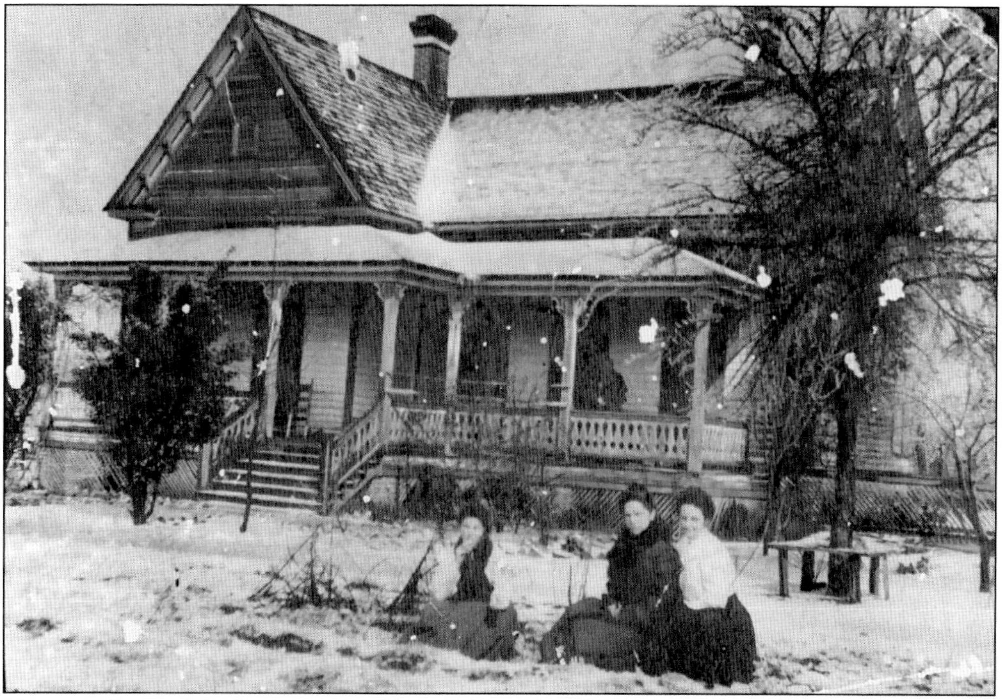

TROTTIE HOUSE. The home pictured here belonged to three sisters, the eldest of whom married Mr. Ike Trottie. Today, this house is the home of Jack Gray, who shows respect for his Southern ancestors by flying the Confederate battle flag daily.

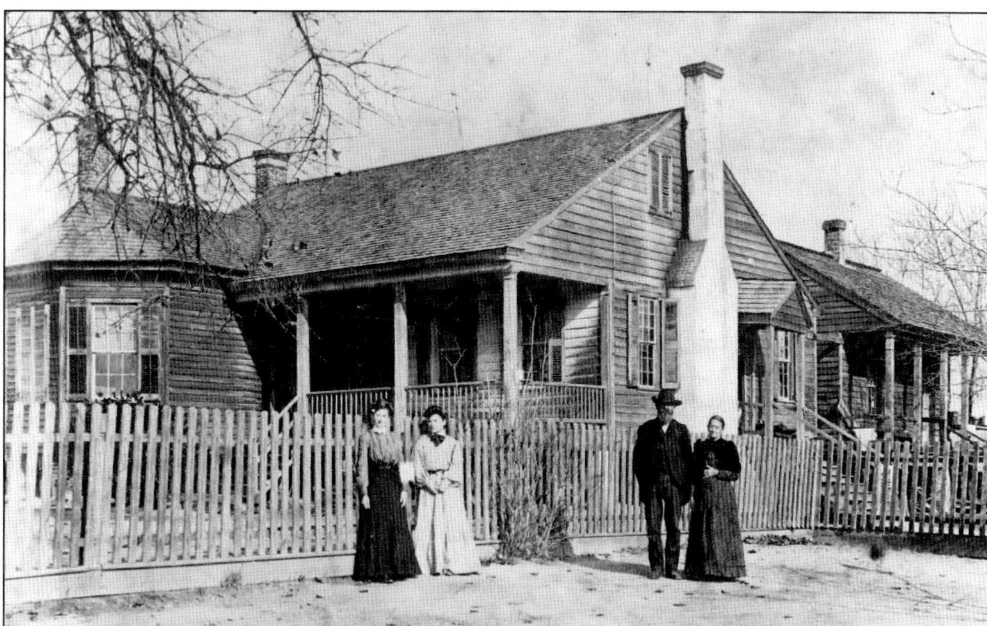

RESIDENCE. This house is thought to have been a model for the Trottie house. Although the exterior treatment is slightly different, the floor plan is essentially the same.

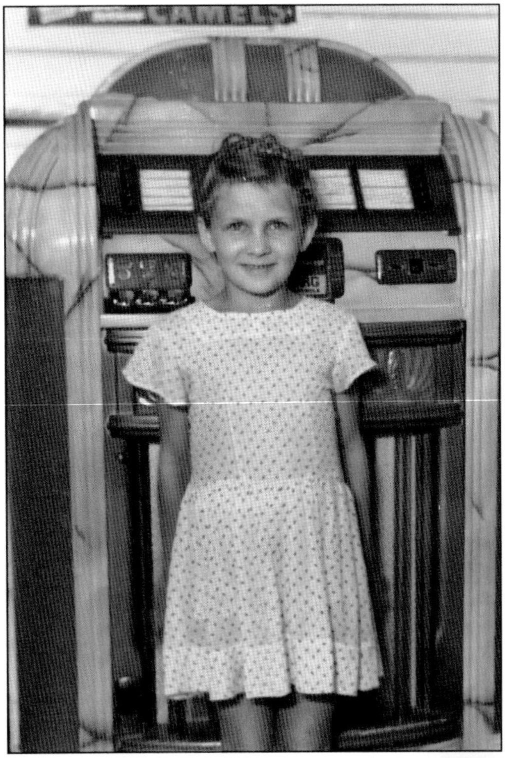

POSING WITH THE JUKE BOX. Young Peggy Halford poses in front of a juke box that was near her father's store. Mrs. Halford was known for her tasty sandwiches that she sold to the residents of Williston.

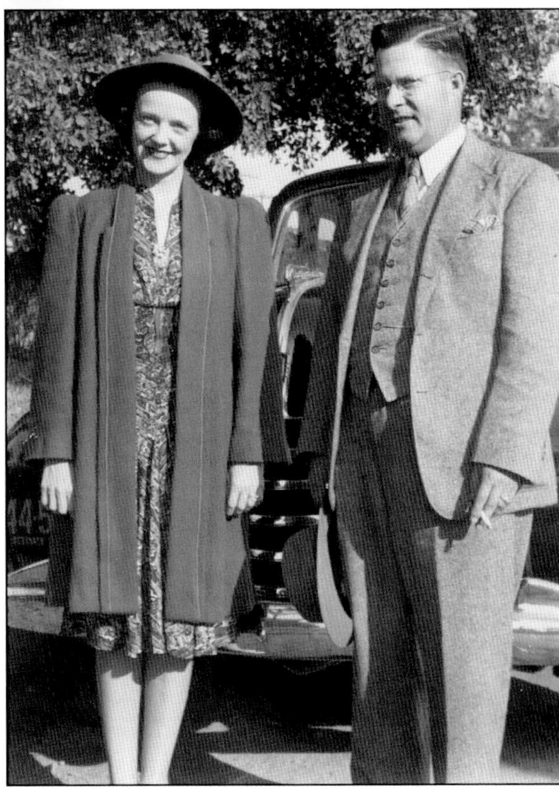

DR. TROTTIE. Dr. C.J. Trottie, who was a dentist, and his wife are pictured here as they appeared in the 1940s.

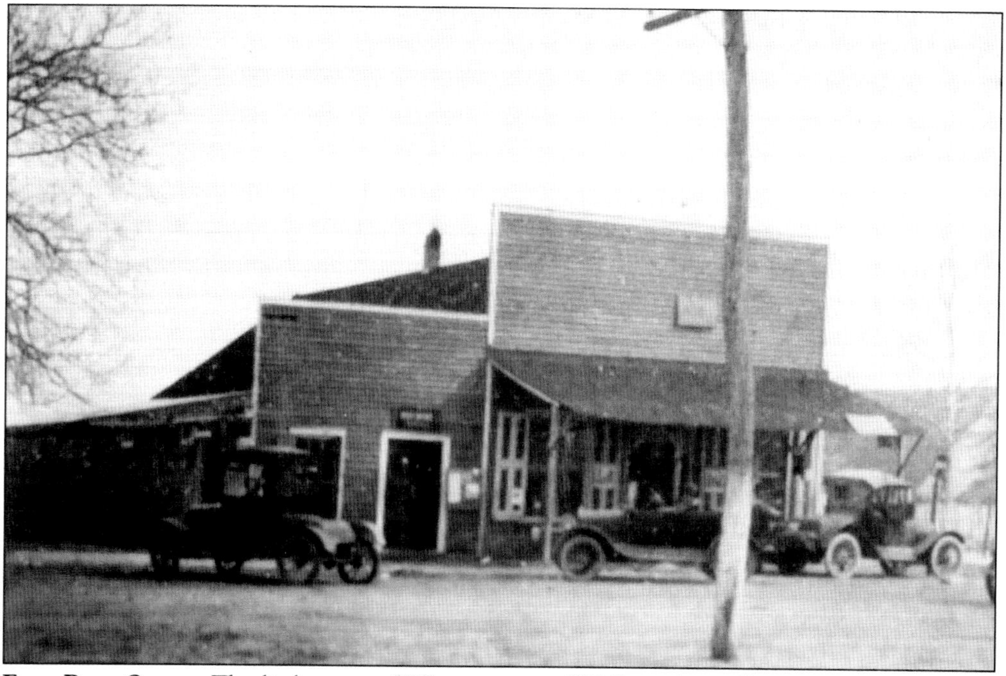

Elko Post Office. The little town of Elko was one of Williston's satellite communities. Being situated along the railroad between Williston and Blackville gave residents the convenience of not only living near a larger town, but also enjoying the simple pleasures of the country.

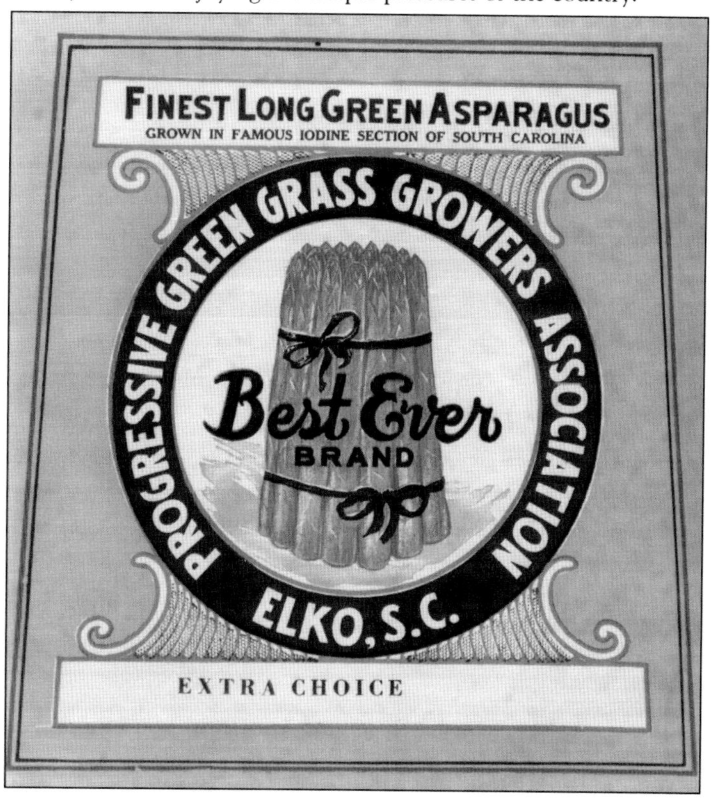

Asparagus Label. The Green Lumbar Company supplied many of the boxes that received these labels in the heyday of asparagus farming in Barnwell County. Before agricultural economics squeezed the farmers out of production, the Williston-Elko region was the capital of asparagus production in the world.

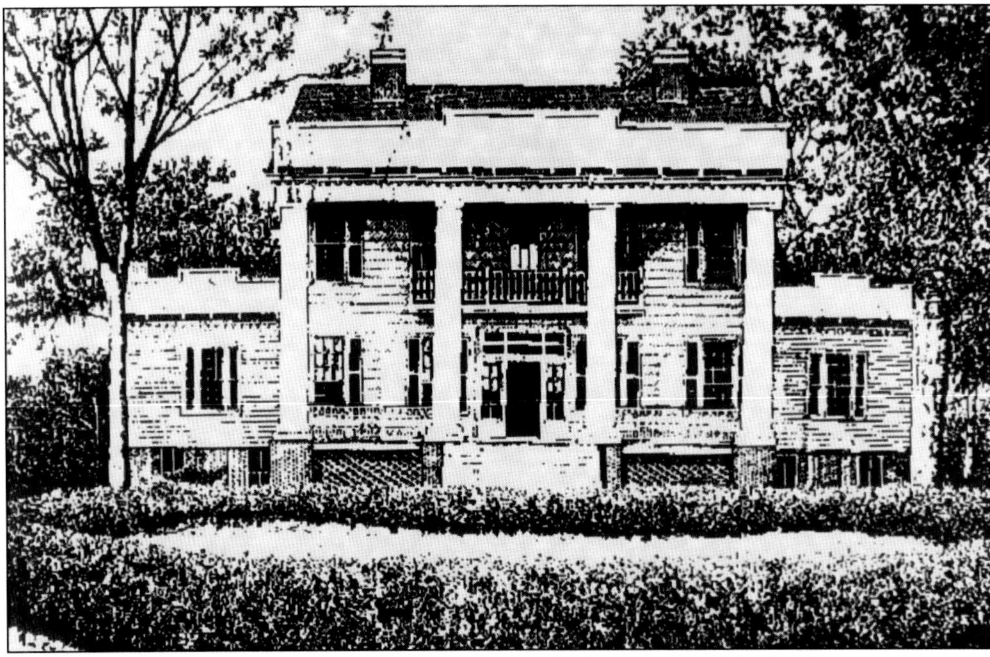

First House in Blackville. Records indicate that the first house in Blackville was constructed by Cornelius Tobin in the late 1700s and named Fairmont. The plantation house was designed with a hallway running from the front door through the back. The interior had wainscot paneling, with large glass windows in each room. The front of the house was placed on a circular drive and surrounded with a garden. Blackville Country Club is now located on the old Fairmont property.

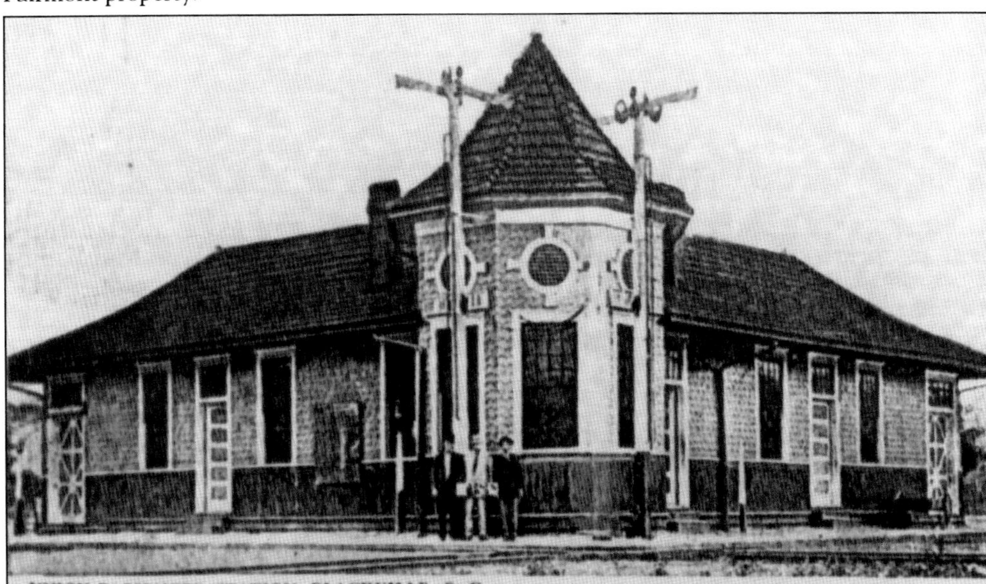

Union Passenger Station. The Victorian-style Union Passenger Station was located at the intersection of the two railroads running through Blackville. The structure has been moved from its original location to the grounds of the old Blackville High School, and is now serving as a library for the community of Blackville.

Eleven

BLACKVILLE SOUTH CAROLINA

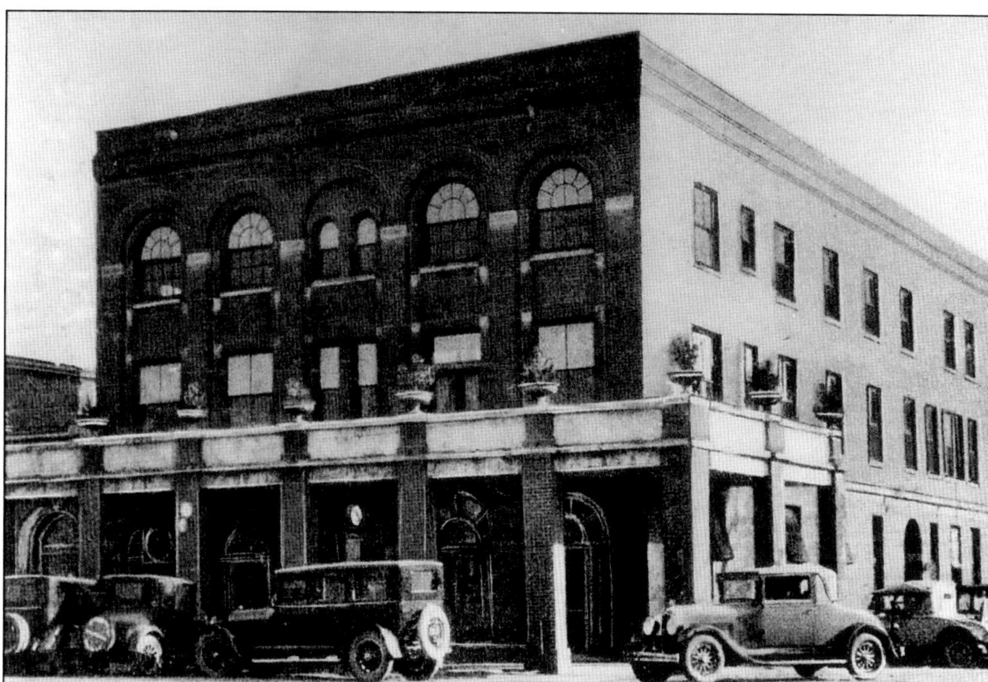

SHAMROCK HOTEL. The Shamrock Hotel has been a landmark in the Blackville area since 1912. Many residents remember the days when the hotel was in its prime. Some even remember gasoline being sold from the bottom floor of the hotel! The remains of the old Shamrock have become a political issue as citizens fight to save the old landmark from being torn down.

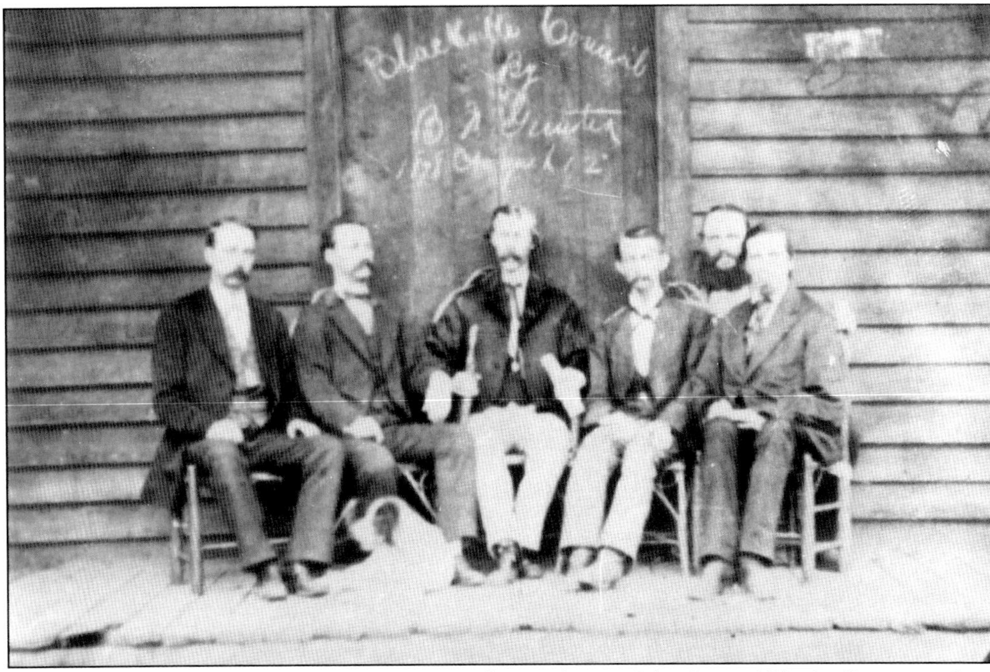

Blackville City Officials. The wardens and intendants of the City of Blackville appear here in the late 1870s as they pose against a backdrop of a local cobbler's shop.

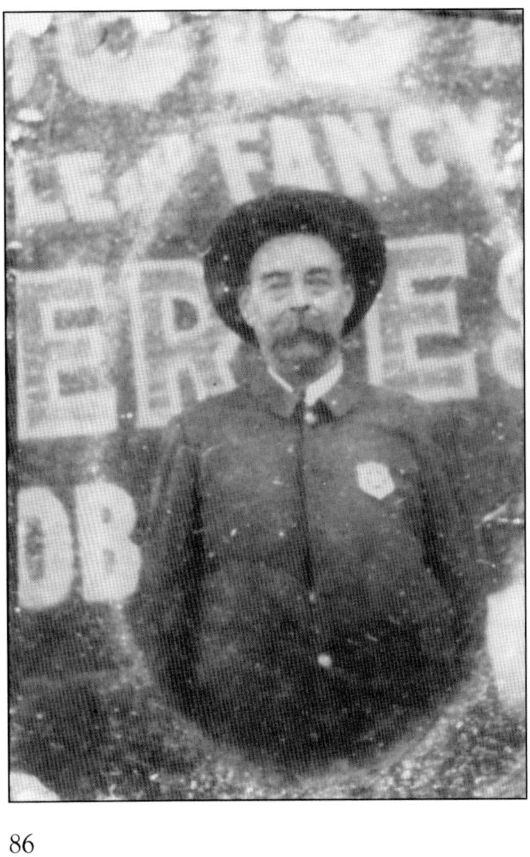

Blackville City Marshall. In the 19th century, Blackville had a city marshall. Pictured here is Marshall Owen Dyches posing against a side wall of a downtown building in about 1887. One of his responsibilities was to light the kerosene streetlights each evening.

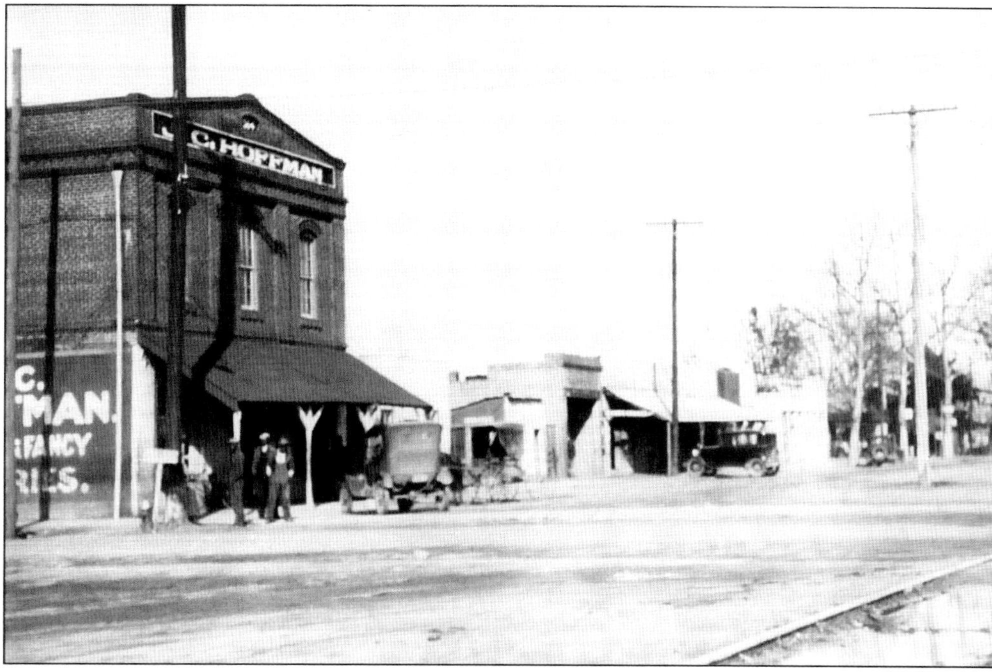

GINGER ROW. The area in the background, near the site of the present post office, was known as "Ginger Row." The top of Hoffman's Store had a large white arrow painted on it to help guide the WW II pilots who trained with Doolittle at the Barnwell County Airport.

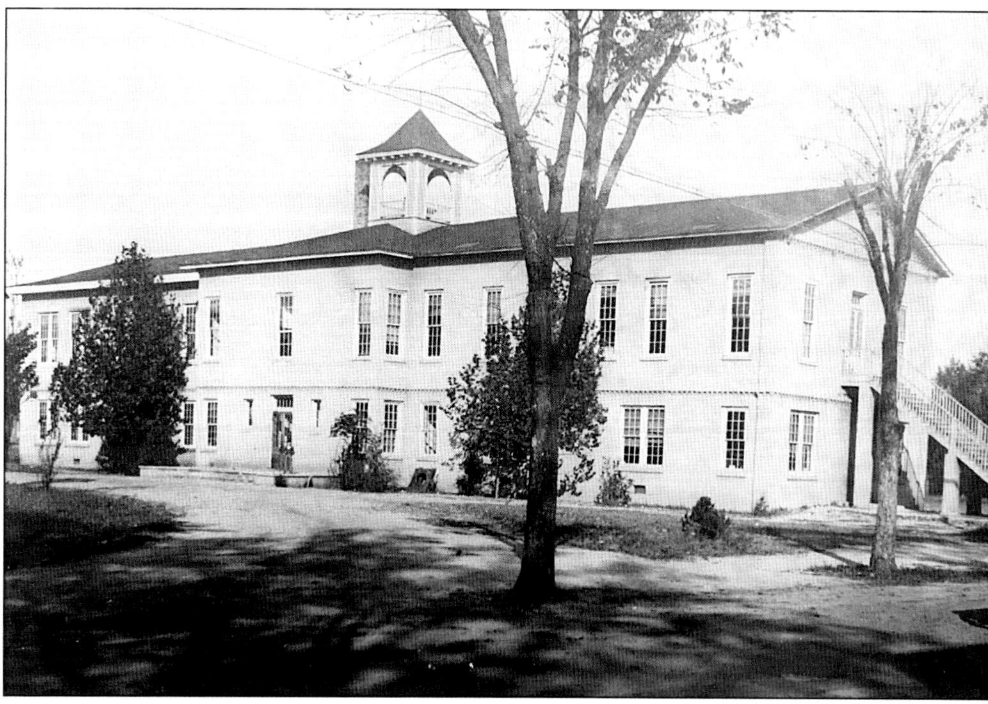

OLD COURTHOUSE. Compare this view of the old courthouse to the one on page 108.

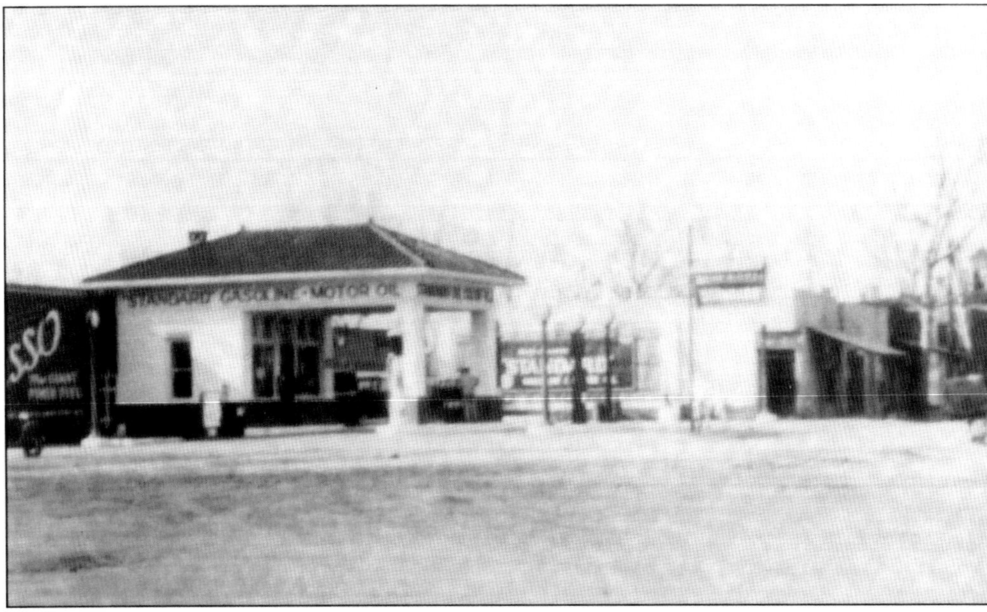

ESSO STATION. This location was the site of Fickling's Esso station, which for years was a fixture in downtown Blackville. Mr. Fickling was active in civic affairs, serving as mayor of Blackville for two terms, twice elected to the city council, and serving on the school board for 17 years. Mr. Fickling also served as magistrate for the Blackville Township. His service station handled the complete line of Standard Oil products.

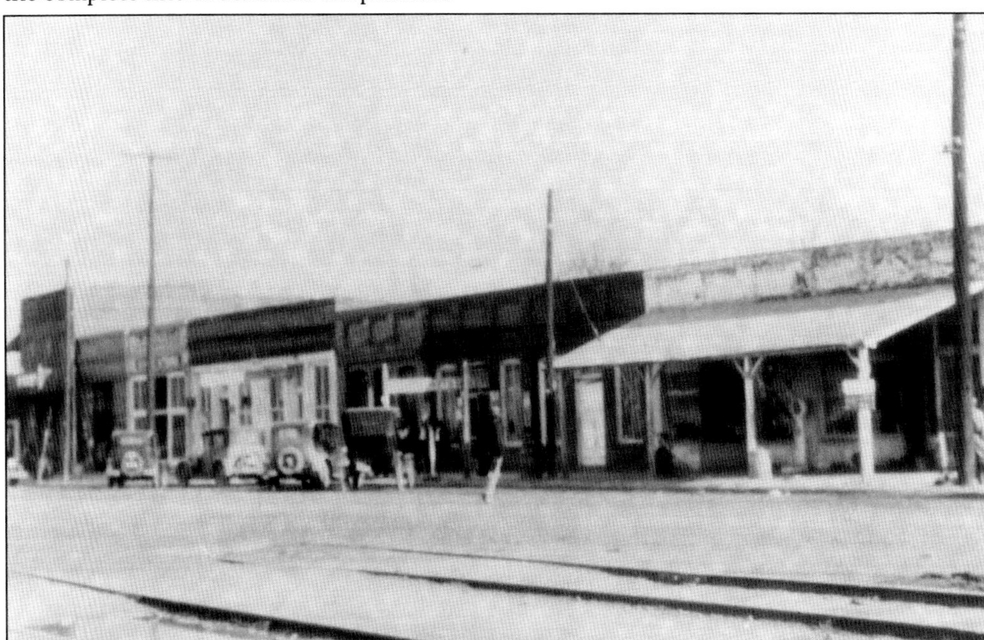

RAILROAD AVENUE 1920S. This view of downtown covers an entire block, from Clark Street to Lartigue Street. Captain J.L. Buist's store is pictured at the right corner. In the 1950s, this store became McDonald's Supermarket. Both depots that occupied spots near the tracks had been destroyed by fire at the time of this photograph.

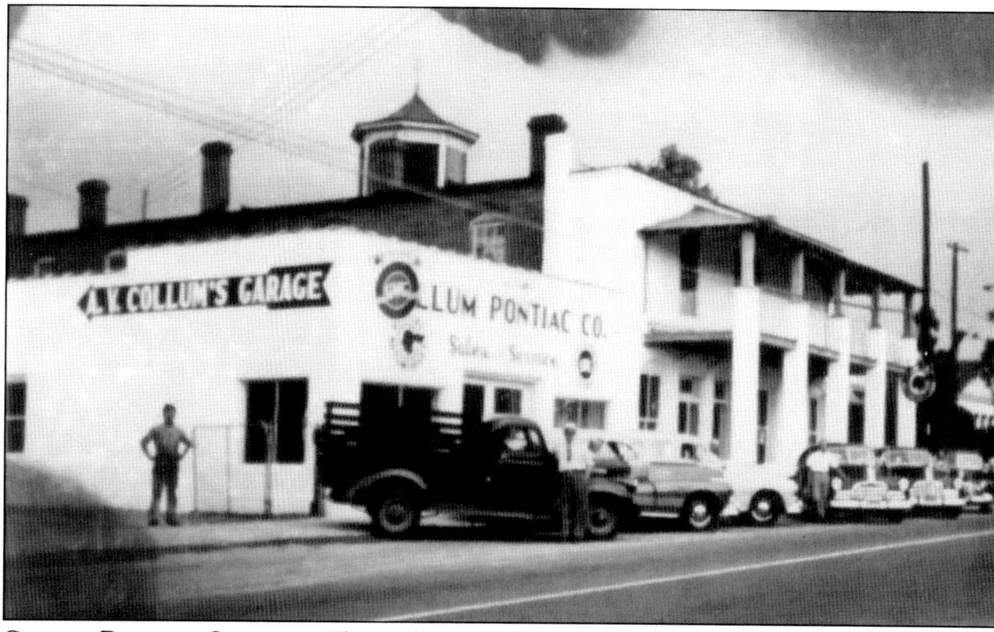

Collum Pontiac Company. The Collum Pontiac Company, established in 1936, was one of Blackville's most active and successful businesses. Mr. Collum was a well-known figure in Blackville since he served as the Southern Railway Ticket Agent and Telegraph operator for 20 years. The business employed trained factory mechanics and repaired all makes of automobiles, as well as provided service to Pontiac owners in the community.

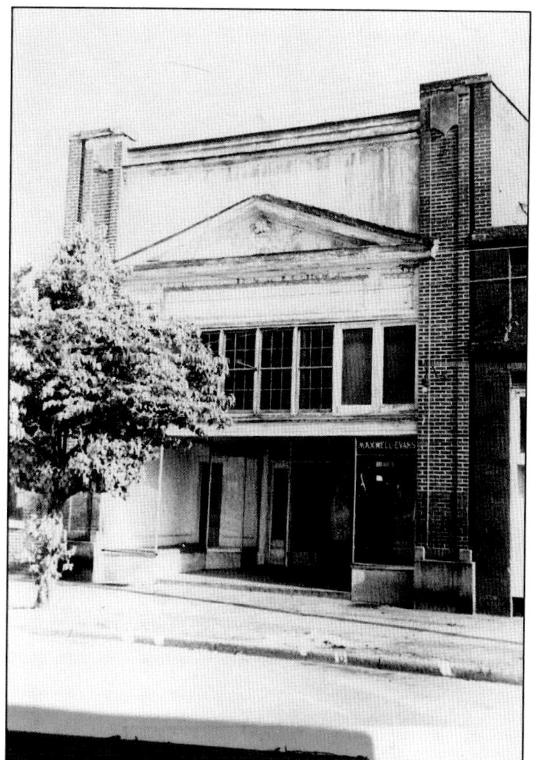

Successful Businesses in Blackville. This building contained the Maxwell-Evans Company, which was Blackville's contribution to a successful chain of Georgia-South Carolina stores. The store was managed by H.A. Evans and featured a line of nationally known merchandise.

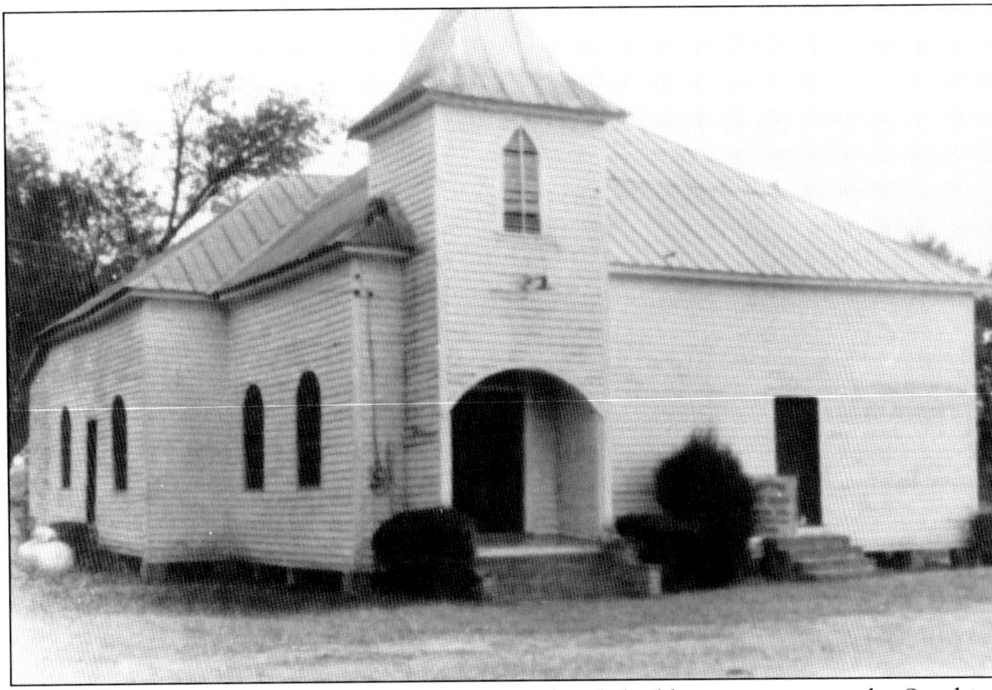

SUNSHINE BAPTIST CHURCH. The second Baptist church building was given to the Sunshine Baptist Church and is located on the old Charleston to Augusta highway.

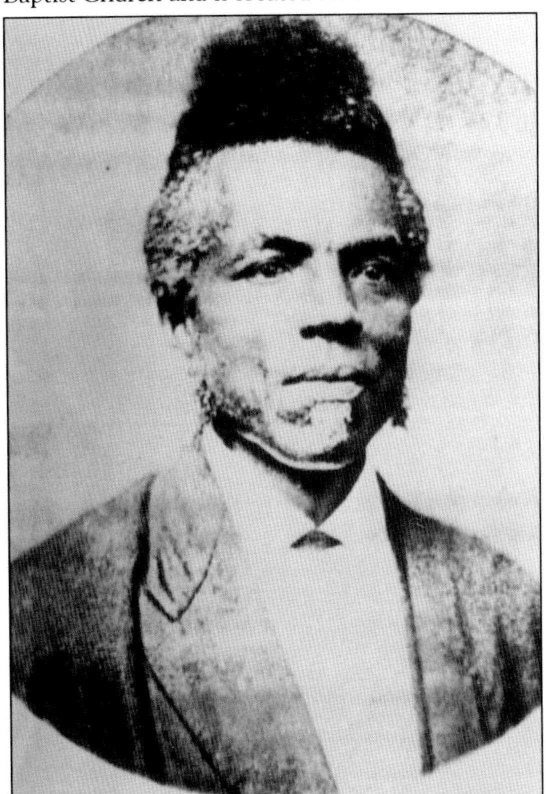

THE REVEREND JAMES TOLBERT. The Reverend James Tolbert was an influential early leader of the black community around Blackville, South Carolina. Local sources indicate that he walked barefoot to Blackville from Augusta, Georgia, and subsequently founded the First Macedonia Baptist Church.

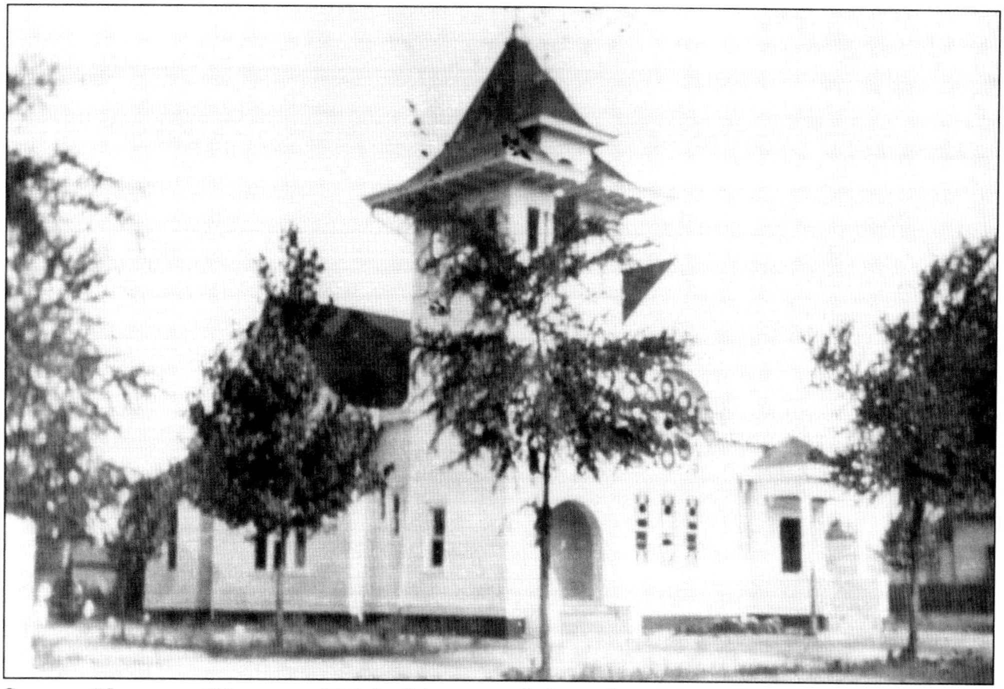

SECOND HOUSE OF WORSHIP. This building was dedicated on November 20, 1898, during the pastorate of Reverend A.P. Turner. The sermon was preached by Reverend Josiah H. Dew of Louisville, Kentucky, who took his text from Psalm 137 with the theme, "The Christian's Love for the Church."

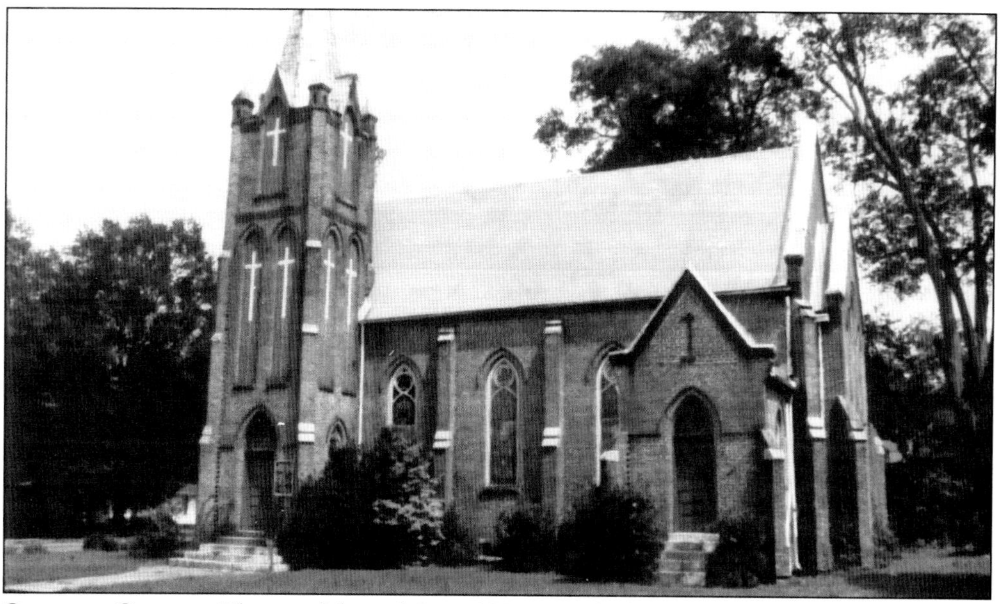

CATHOLIC CHURCH. The wood-framed Sacred Heart Catholic Church burned in 1887 and was replaced in 1898 by the sturdy brick Gothic-styled structure shown in this 1908 view. Located at the corner of Lartique and Dexter Streets, the building and its impressive design makes it a nostalgic landmark in the Blackville community. Services are no longer held on a regular basis, making the future of this old church a bit uncertain.

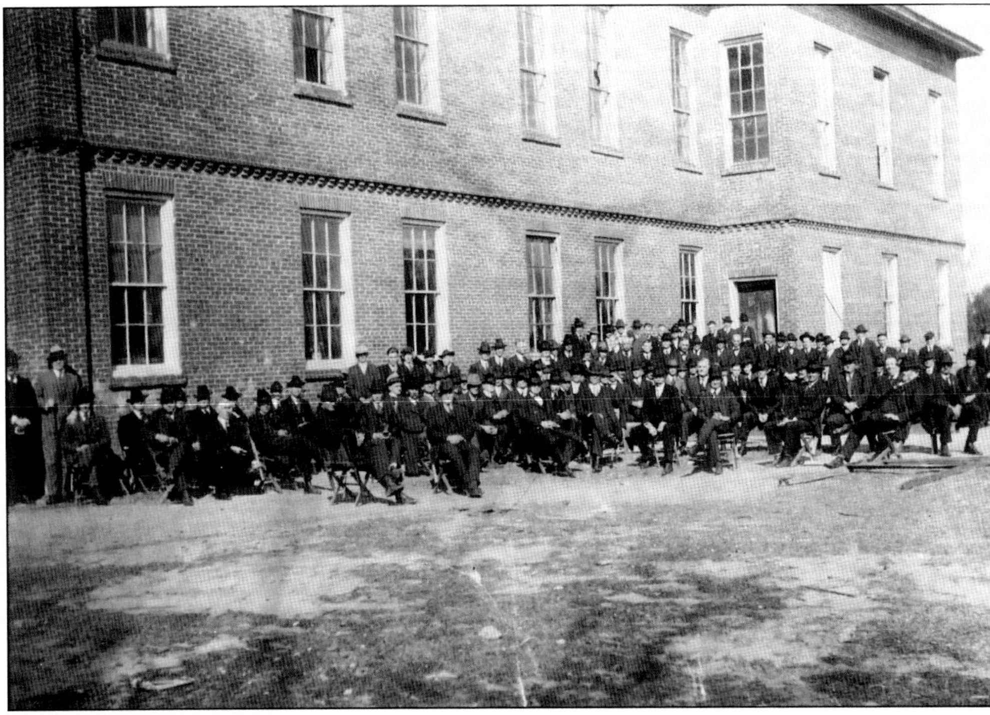

MEN OF THE CHURCH. The men's Sunday school class posed outside the church sometime near the turn of the century for their official portrait.

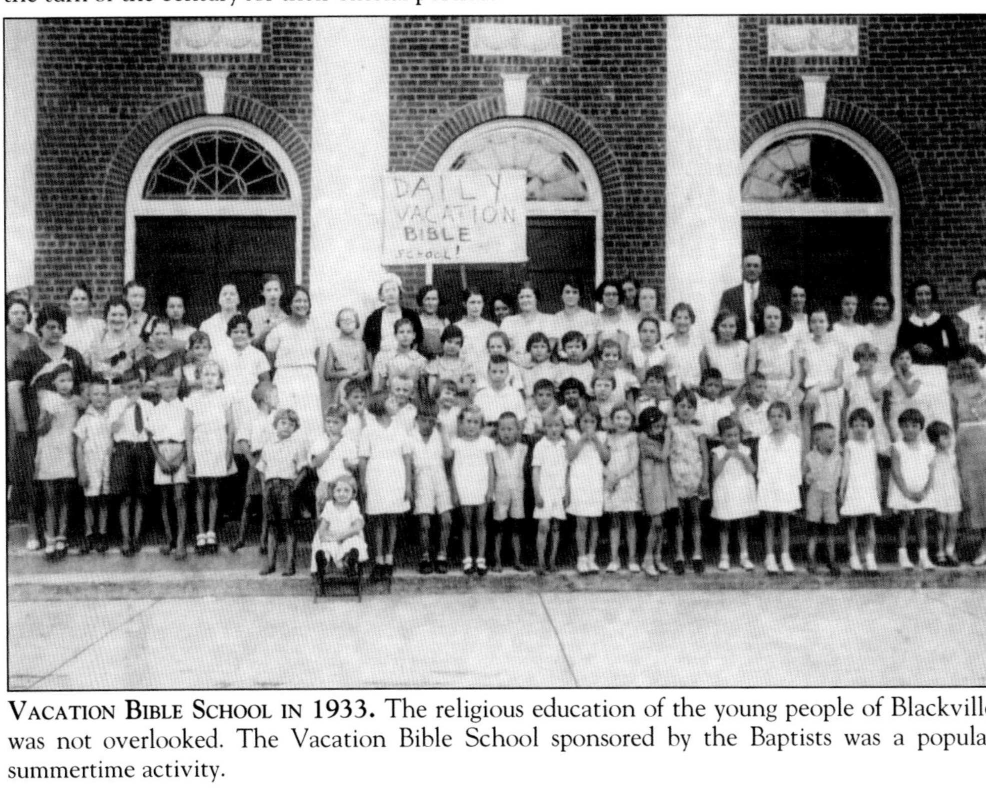

VACATION BIBLE SCHOOL IN 1933. The religious education of the young people of Blackville was not overlooked. The Vacation Bible School sponsored by the Baptists was a popular summertime activity.

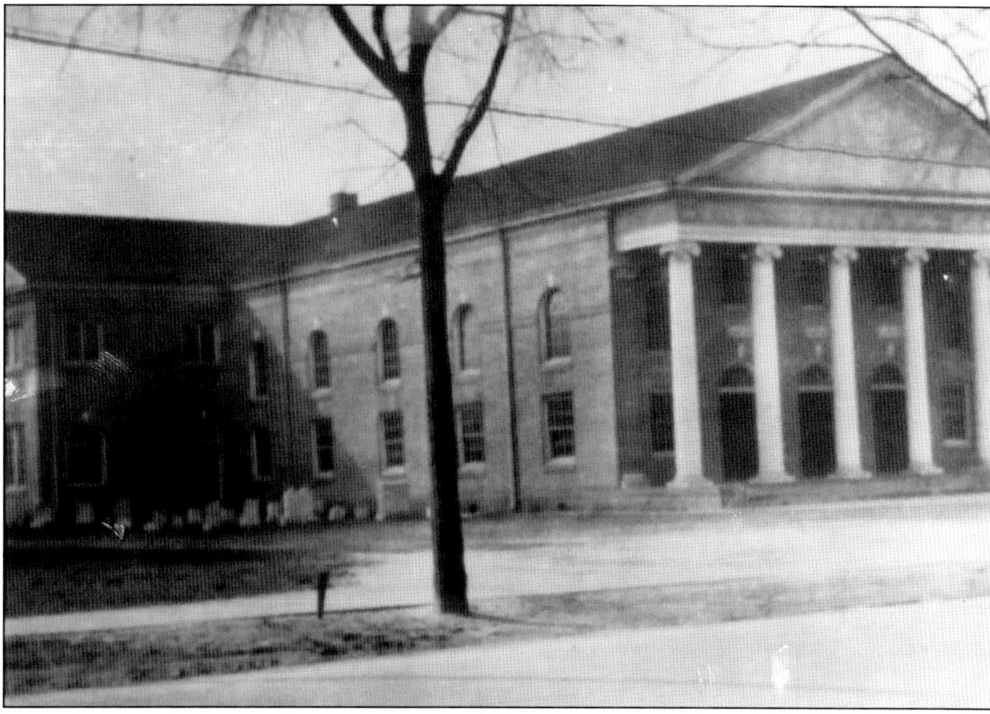

First Baptist Church. The congregation of the First Baptist Church worked hard to provide this beautiful sanctuary to meet their growing needs.

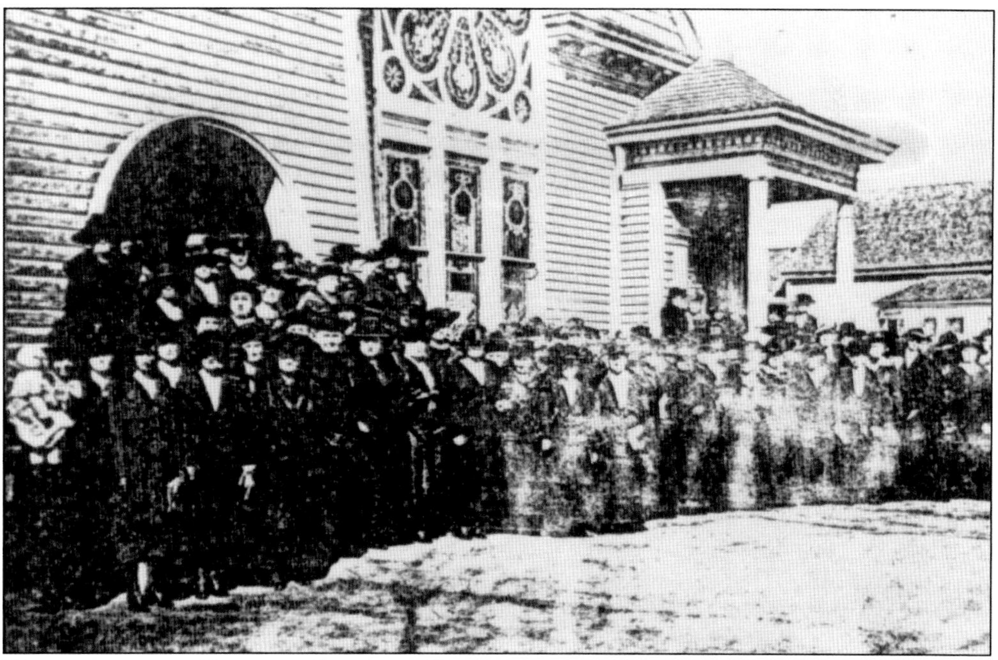

Women of the Baptist Church. The women of the Baptist Church pose outside their sanctuary.

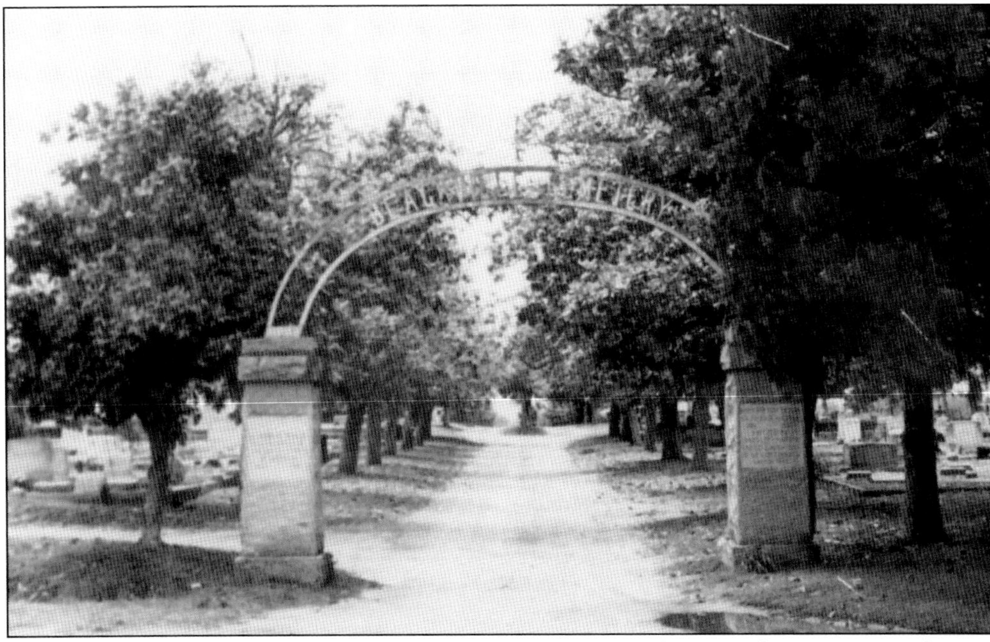

Blackville Cemetery. This cemetery, with its impressive archway at the entrance, is located just south of Blackville. The dignified, well-kept, sacred grounds are a model of what a properly attended cemetery should be.

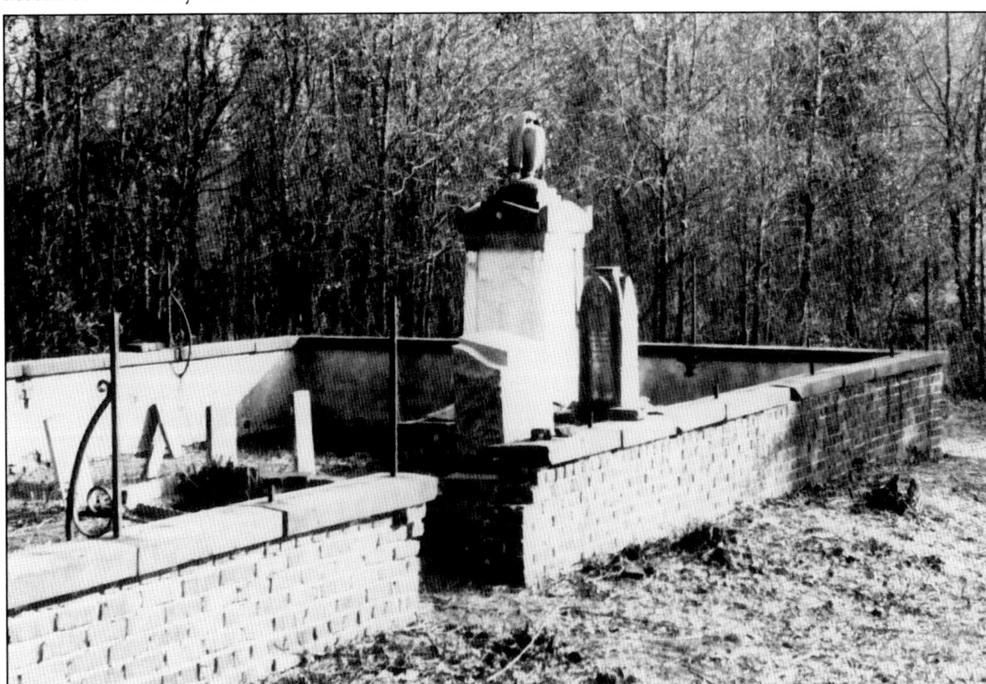

Peeples Family Cemetery. Scattered throughout the county are quite a few small family cemeteries that are still maintained by either the family or interested citizens. Darling Peeples's marker is the most prominent in this cemetery; it lies across from the Edisto Experiment Station.

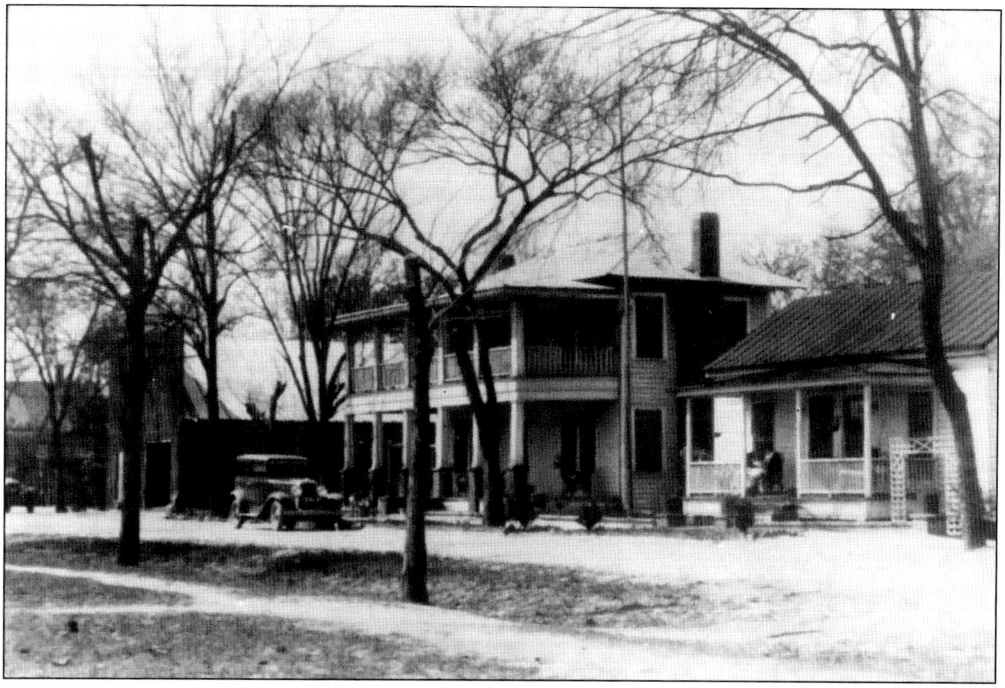

Nevils Homeplace. This two-story house was the home of James Nevils, whose family donated the property for the First Baptist Church. Conveniently, his mechanic shop was located next door.

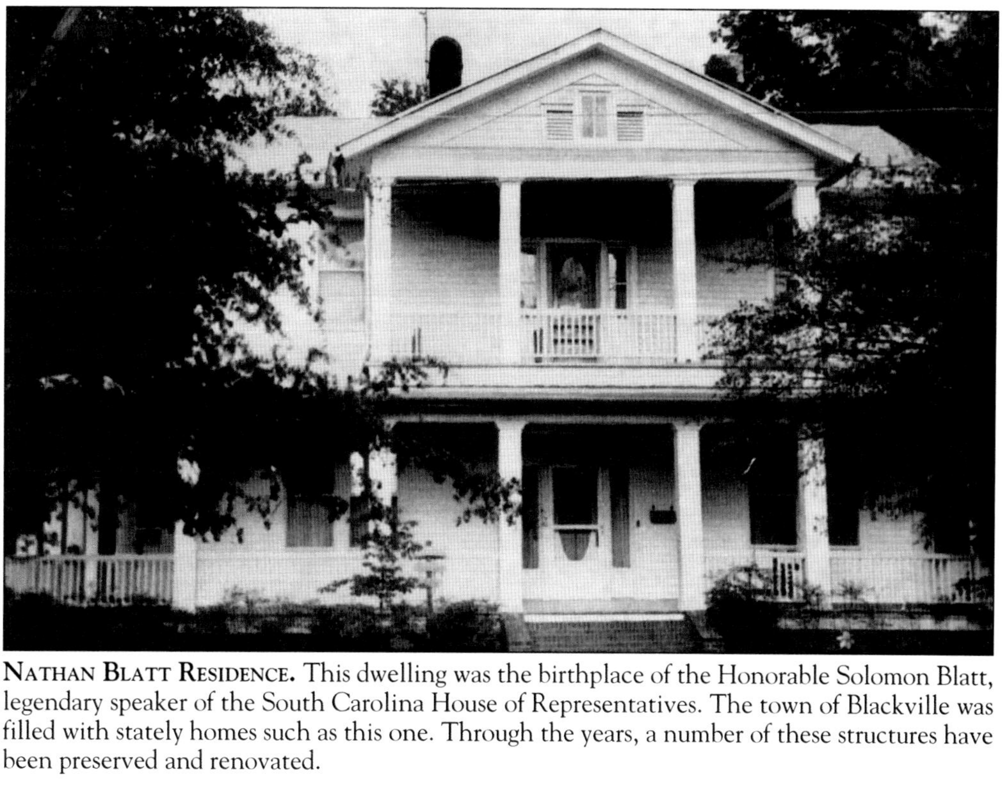

Nathan Blatt Residence. This dwelling was the birthplace of the Honorable Solomon Blatt, legendary speaker of the South Carolina House of Representatives. The town of Blackville was filled with stately homes such as this one. Through the years, a number of these structures have been preserved and renovated.

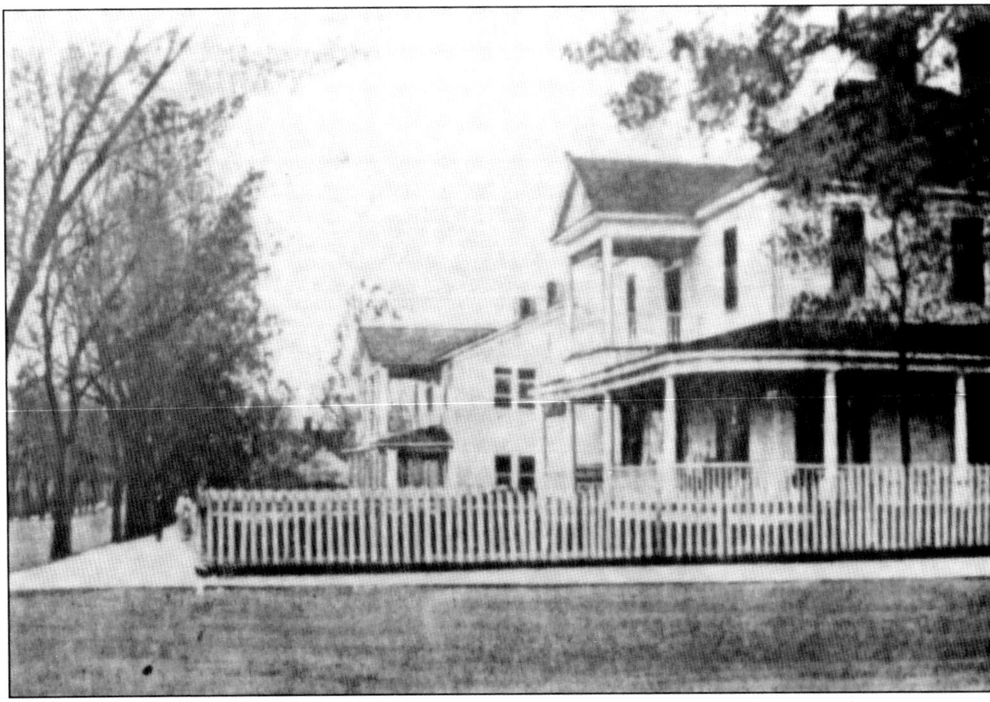

Blackville Residence. This street corner shows another example of the typical views around Blackville in the days when the railroad meant prosperity for the town. This photograph shows the northeast corner of South Boundary and Clark Street.

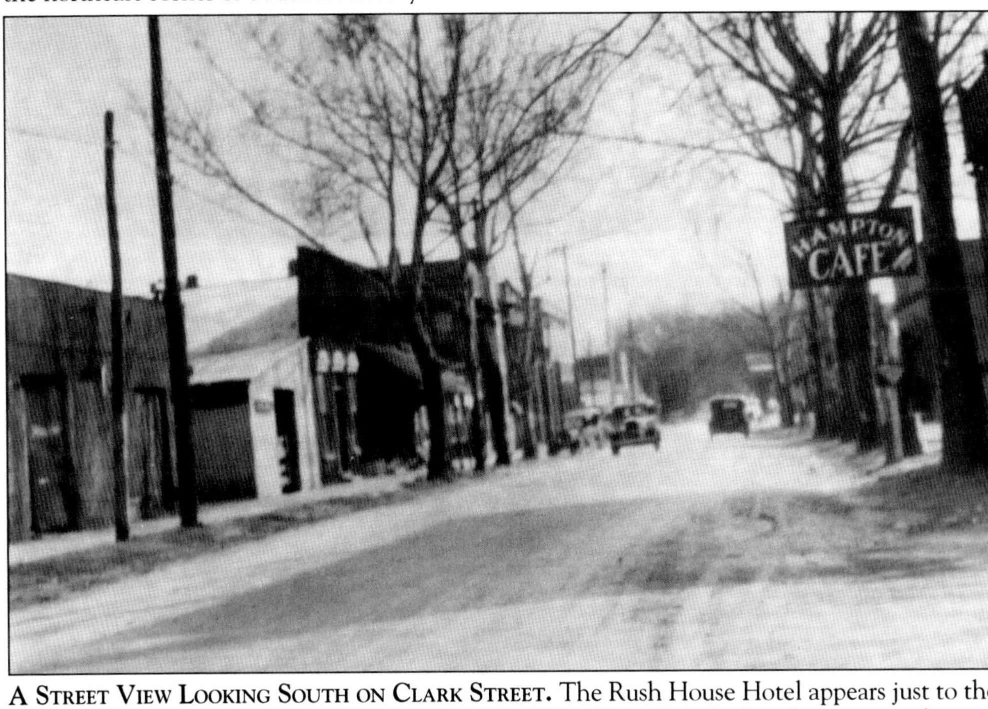

A Street View Looking South on Clark Street. The Rush House Hotel appears just to the right of this photograph. The Hampton Cafe, which was located in the hotel, was a popular spot for the citizens of Blackville for many years.

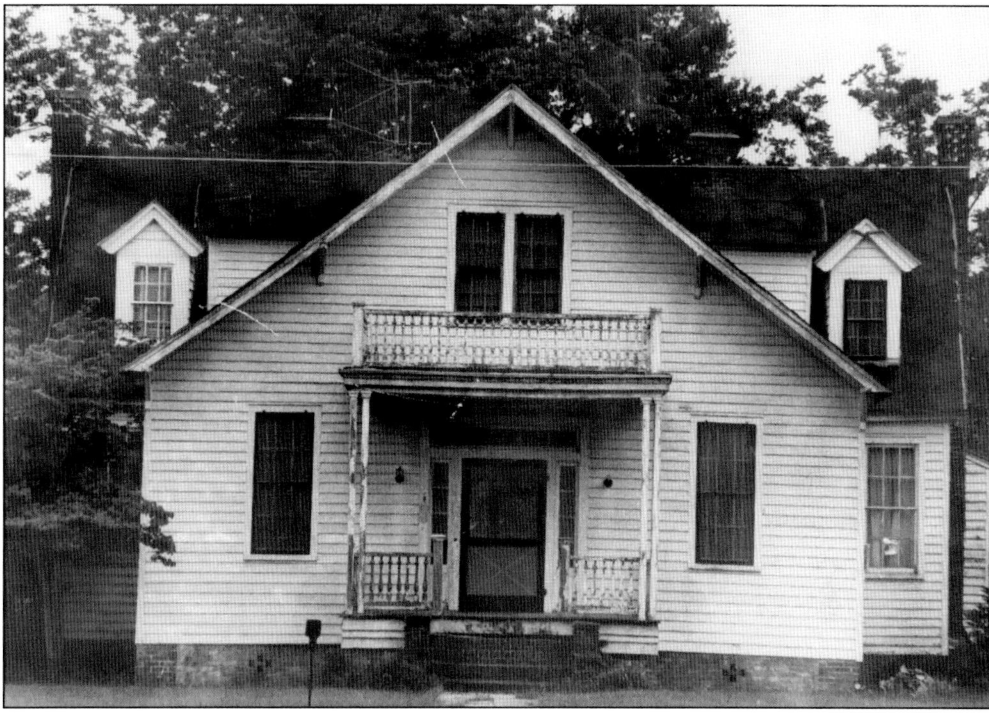

Former Carrol Residence. At one time, this home was the residence of the last members of Blackville's well-known Carrol family. It is located next to Dr. Hammonds's home on Main Street.

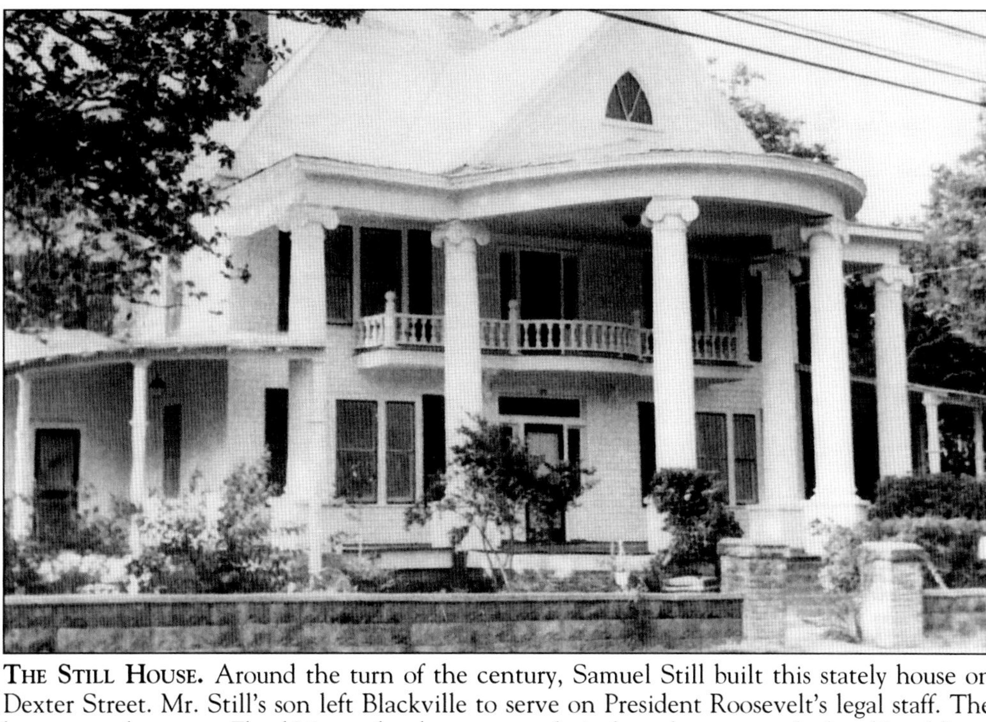

The Still House. Around the turn of the century, Samuel Still built this stately house on Dexter Street. Mr. Still's son left Blackville to serve on President Roosevelt's legal staff. The home, now known as Floyd Manor, has been restored nicely and serves as a bed and breakfast.

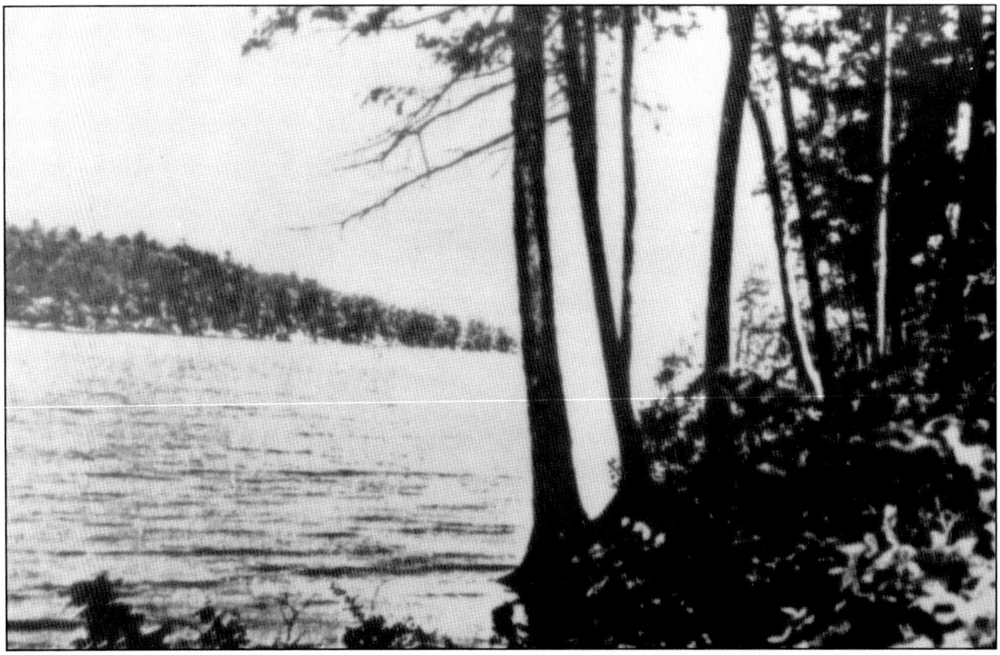

Barnwell State Park. The Barnwell State Park, located approximately 3 miles south of Blackville, was another Civilian Conservation Corps project during the 1930s. Designed to provide recreational areas for the public, the park became a popular spot for fishing, boating, and swimming.

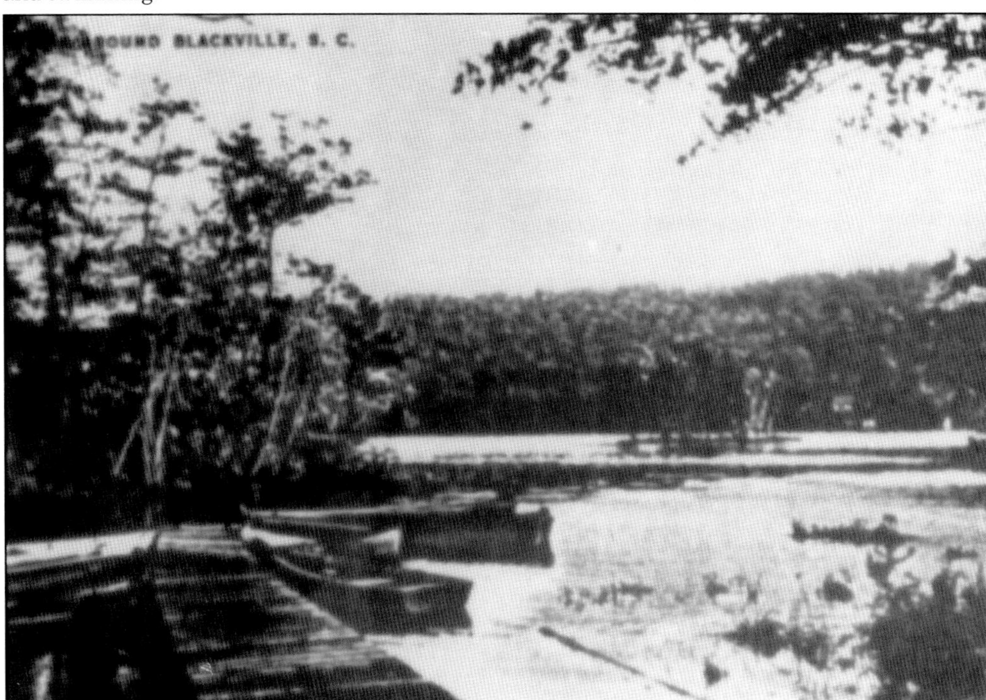

State Park Dam. In order to prepare the area for the public use, a dam was built to form the new lake, and buildings were erected for a bathhouse near the swimming area.

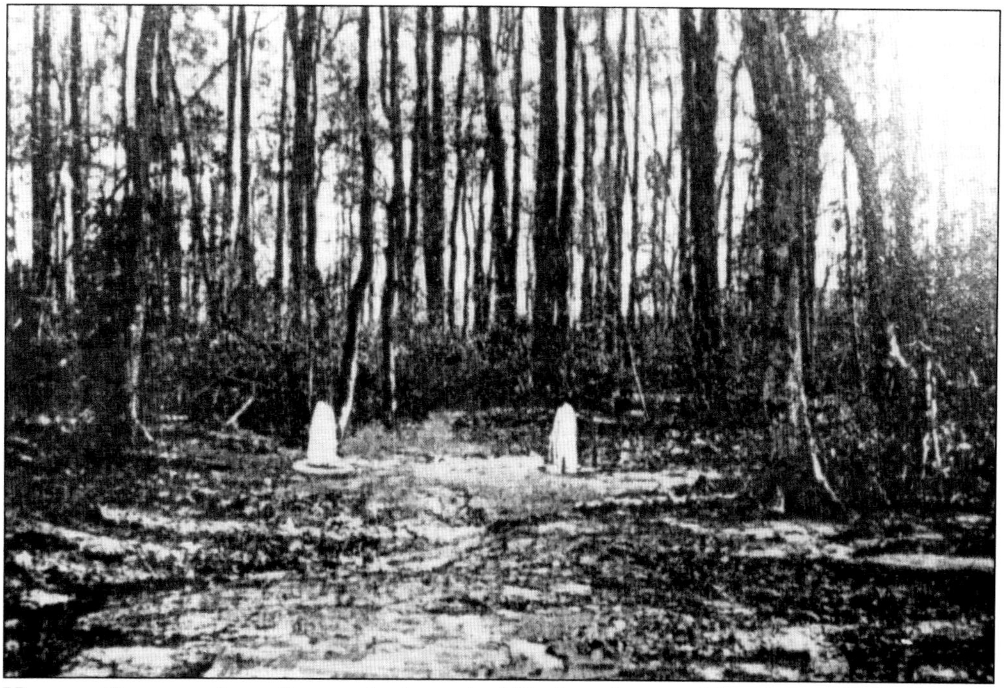

HEALING SPRINGS. According to the legend of Healing Springs, Native Americans living in the area showed the springs to Nathaniel Walker. The springs were considered to be sacred because of the healing powers of the mineralized water. To this day, the springs have retained that reputation, and many local residents and visitors come to fill containers full of the cold, clear water.

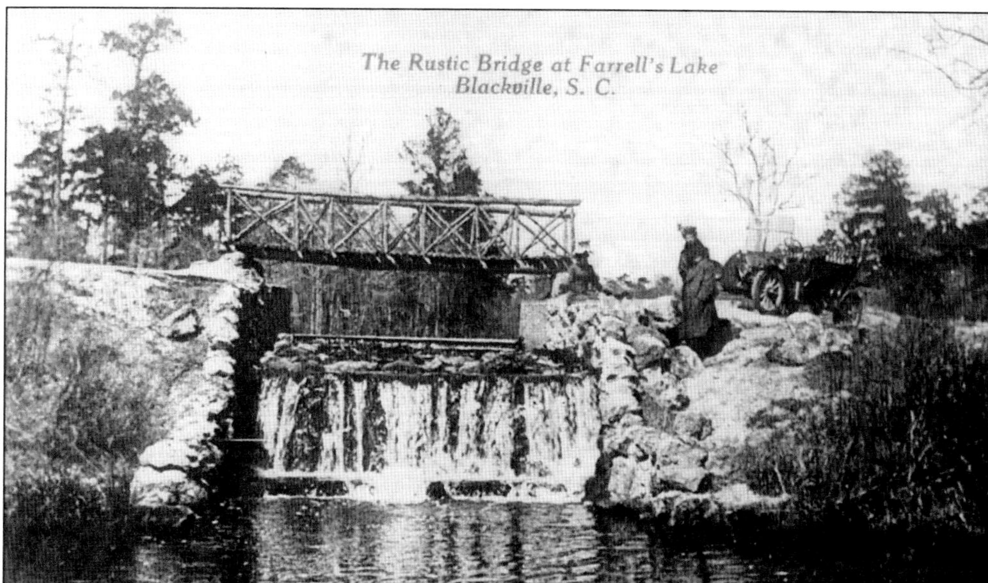

FARRELL'S LAKE. Early in this century, Farrell's Lake was a very popular spot for Barnwell County residents. Motorists brought their friends and families out to the lake for an afternoon of enjoying the breezes, a cool dip in the water, or dropping a line and hook in hopes of catching a bit of supper.

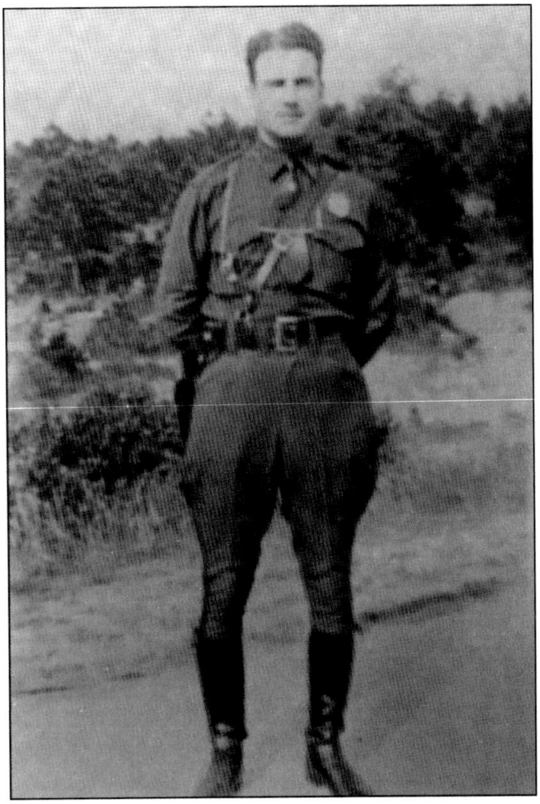

Highway Patrolman. Although it may seem to modern-day motorists that the South Carolina Highway Patrol has always been around, there was a time when they did not exist. Shown in the new uniform of the patrol, the proud patrolman, Officer Fanning, was in the first class of patrolmen to be trained.

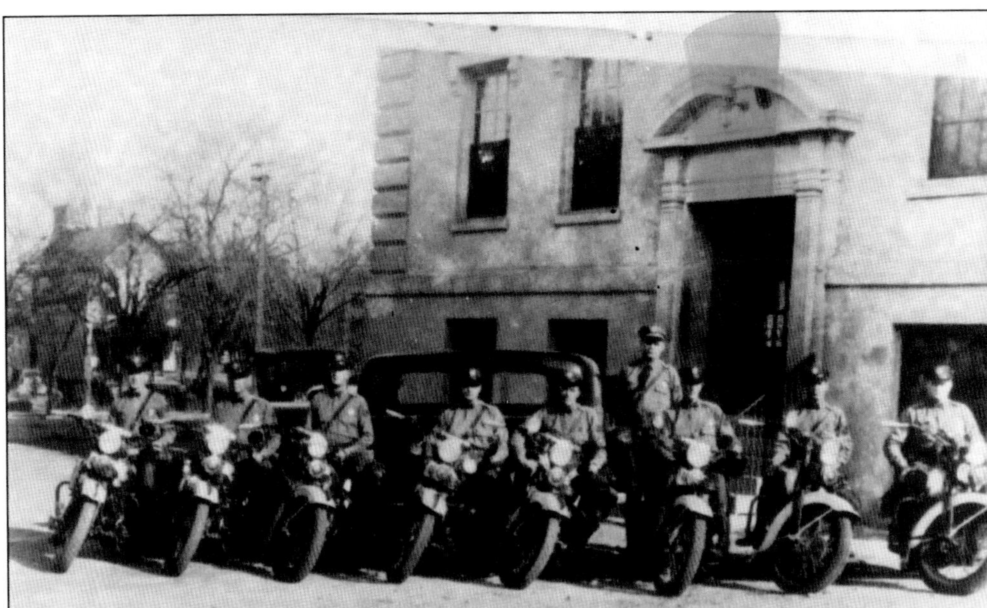

Patrolmen at Orangeburg. The first class of highway patrolmen trained in the city of Orangeburg, and then were assigned to various posts around the state. Pictured here is the first group to be given assignments.

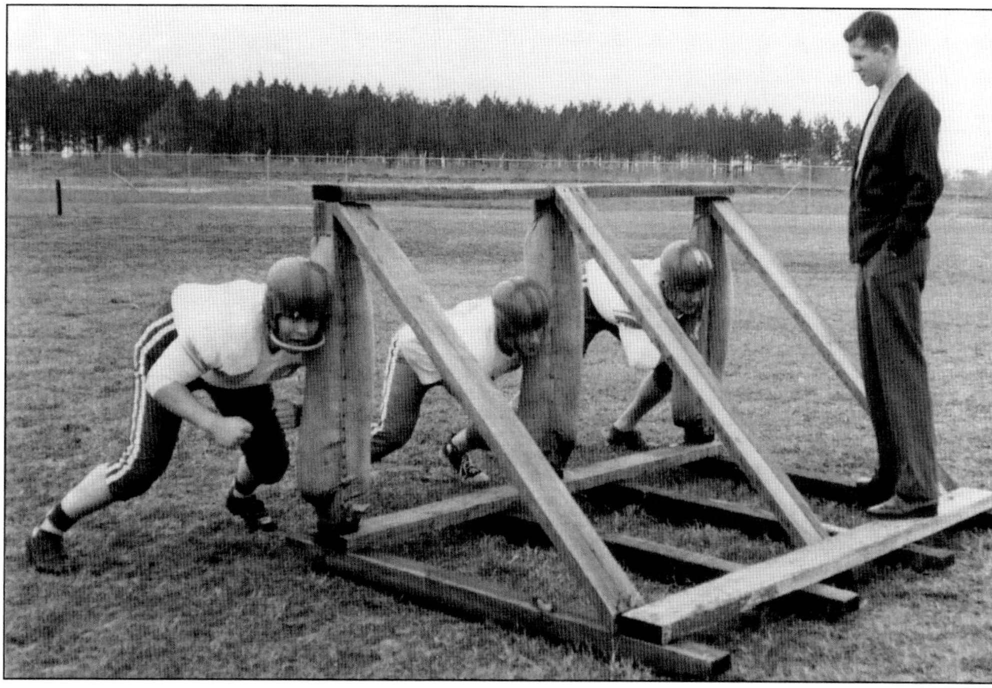

Coach Hughes and His Blocking Sled. Coach Chuck Hughes was a popular football coach in the late 1950s. Here, he encourages his players as they learn proper blocking techniques. Many of Blackville's young men learned the fundamentals of the game under the watchful eye of Coach Hughes.

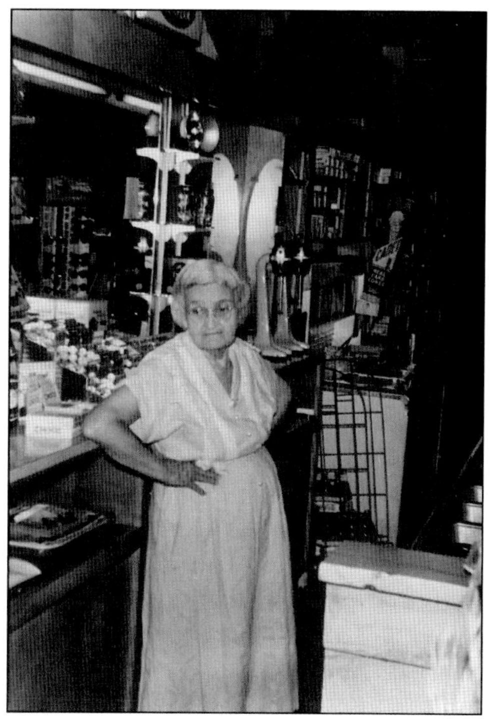

Mrs. Nellie Rush. Mrs. Nellie Rush was a mainstay around Rush's Pharmacy. She appears in this photograph, which was taken in the pharmacy in the early 1950s.

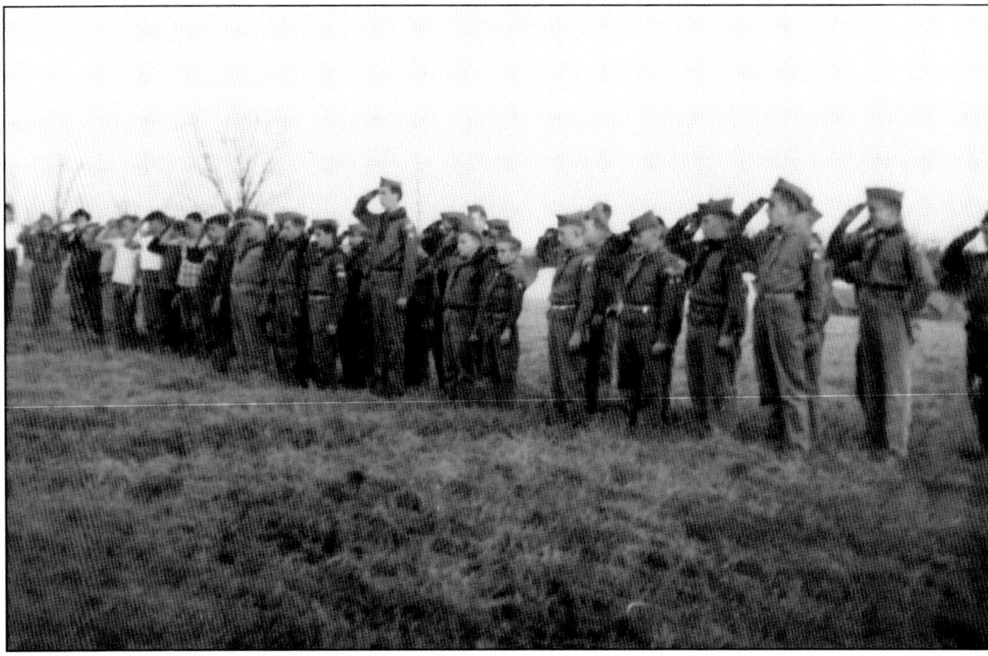

BOY SCOUT SALUTE. Look closely, now. Do you see yourself in this Boy Scout lineup? No matter what part of the county you hailed from, this gathering of Boy Scouts at their jamboree showed the unity of purpose displayed by this fine organization.

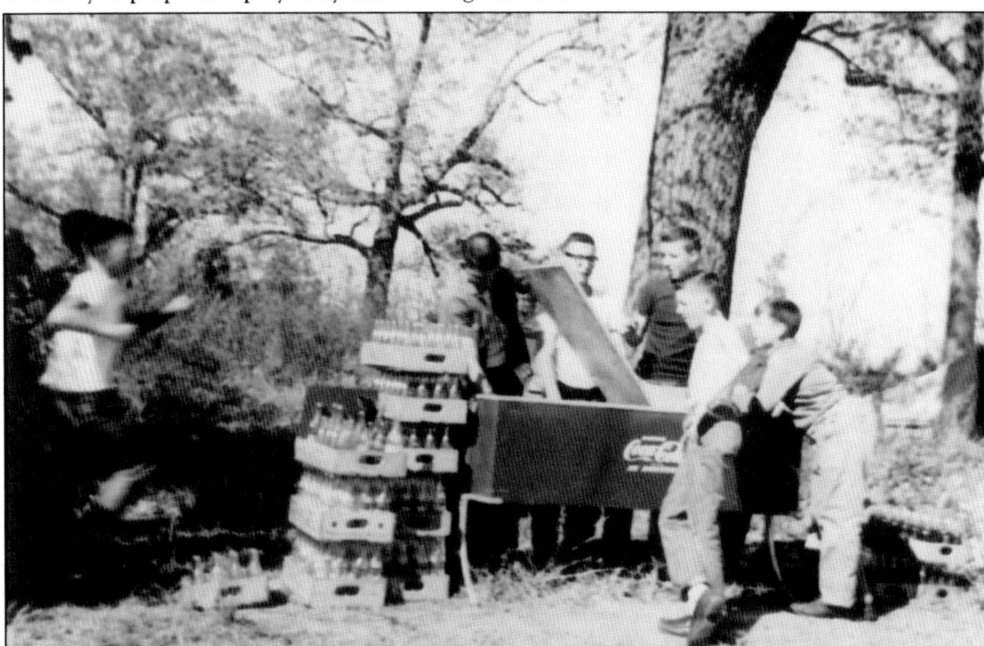

POSING WITH THE COKES. The Boy Scout troops were supported enthusiastically by the community. When the Boy Scouts got together, there was never a lack of food and drinks for them. The stacks of drinks shown in the background exemplify the support given by the adults who sponsored the various troops represented.

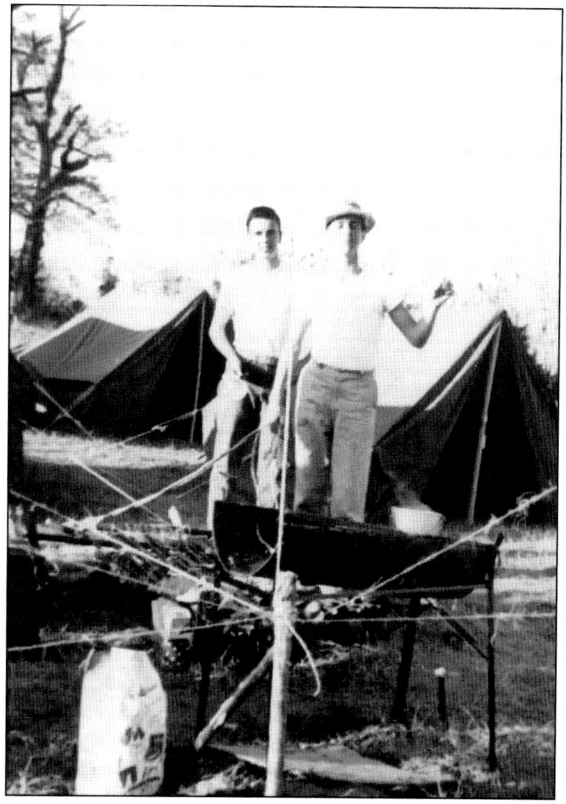

Cooking, Boy Scout Style. The Boy Scouts learned many skills, including how to prepare a quick meal over a fire. The Boy Scouts of Barnwell County enjoyed and took advantage of these opportunities.

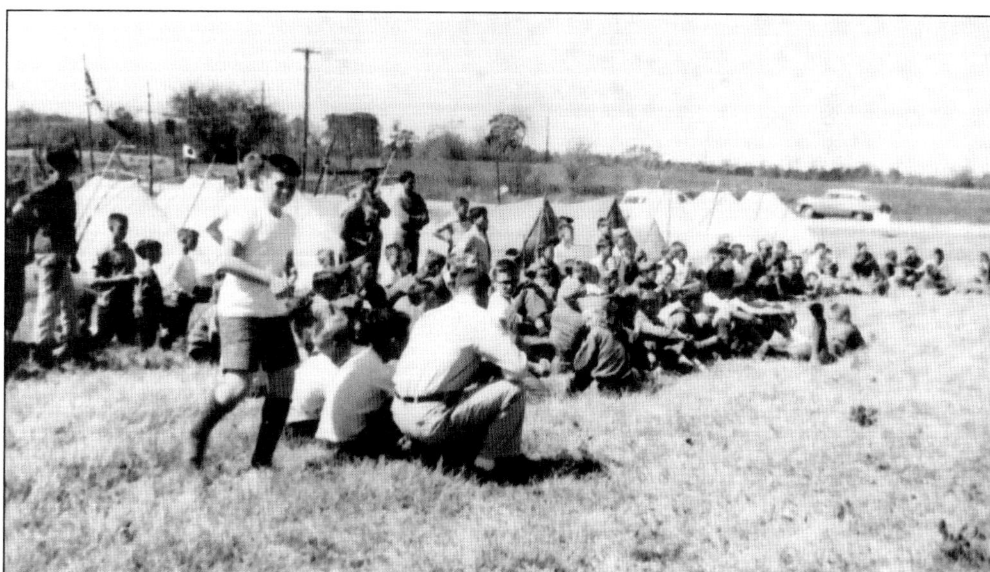

Tenting Tonight on the Old Campground. A county-wide jamboree was a sight to behold. Tent after tent was set up while friendships were renewed and new ones formed among the young scouts. This was one of the few times that county rivalries were put aside for a weekend, and the boys found time to socialize with others from Barnwell, Williston, and Blackville.

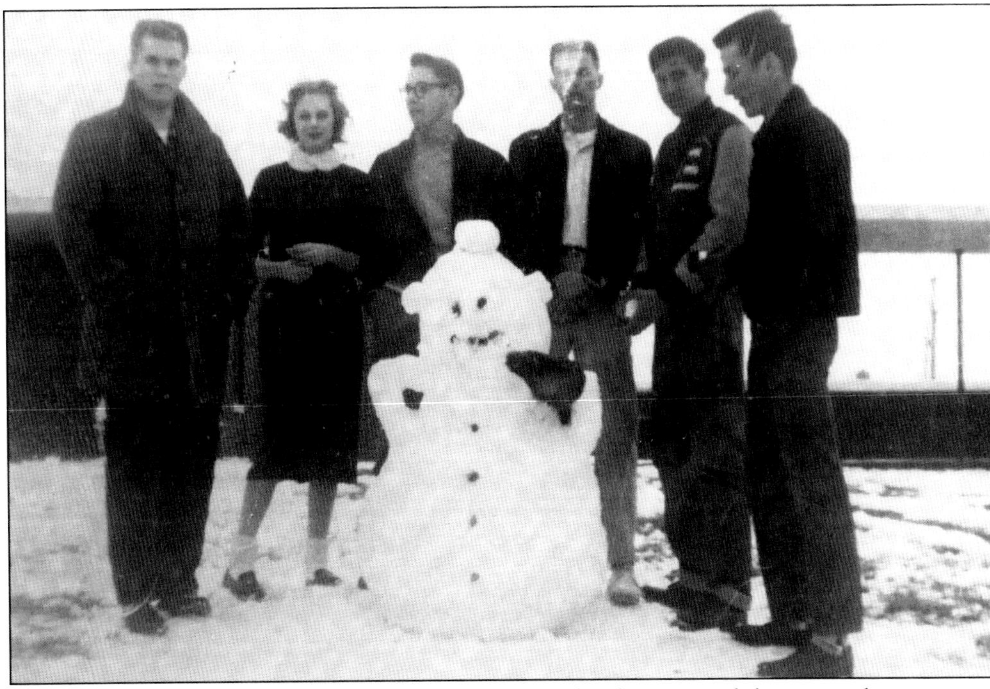

A Snowy Scene in the 1960s. Local teenagers took advantage of the unusual snow storm that left a few inches of snow on the ground in the early 1960s. The group here shows off their snowman, proving that there is a little of the child in all of us left no matter how old we are. It seems that Southern snow tends to bring this aspect out no matter when it comes.

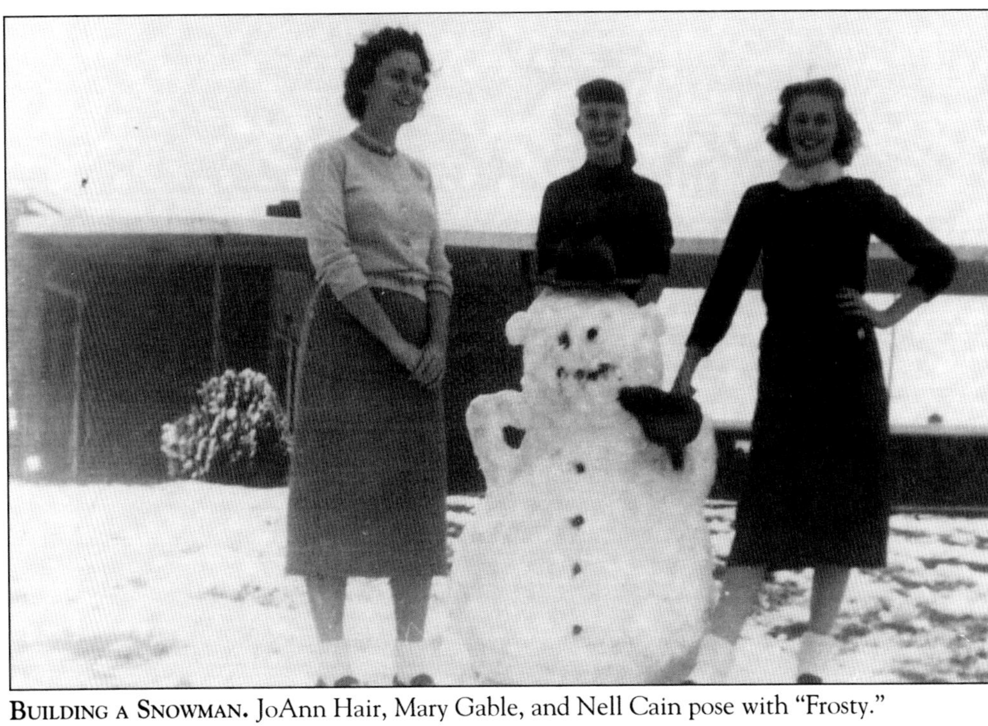

Building a Snowman. JoAnn Hair, Mary Gable, and Nell Cain pose with "Frosty."

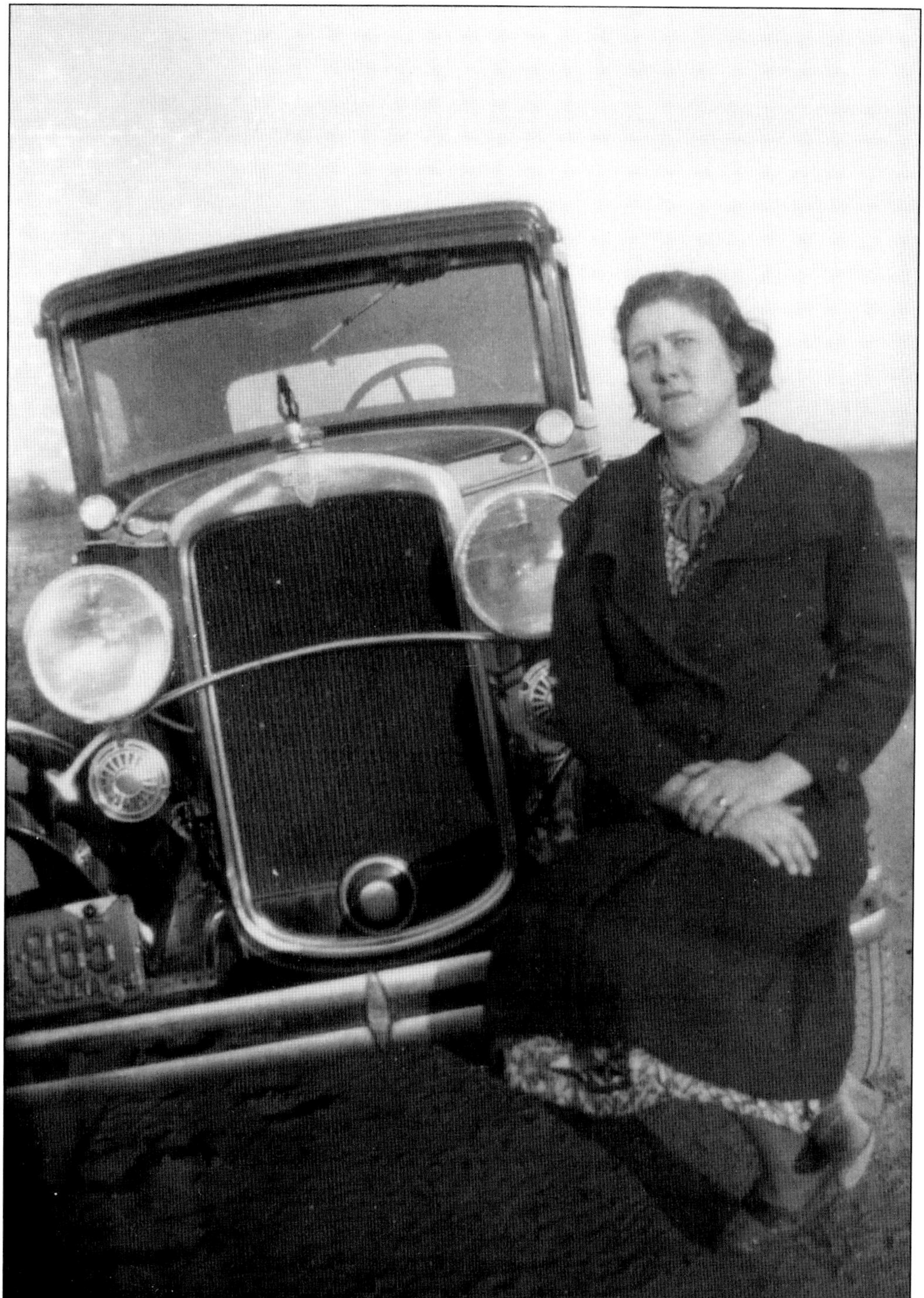

Alberta Cole. Mrs. Alberta Cole received her driver's license in a time when regulations were more relaxed. Hailing a passing highway patrolman, she inquired about procedures for obtaining a license. The patrolman then followed her a few miles, observing her driving. He pulled her over, commented, "I think you can drive," and wrote out a license for her.

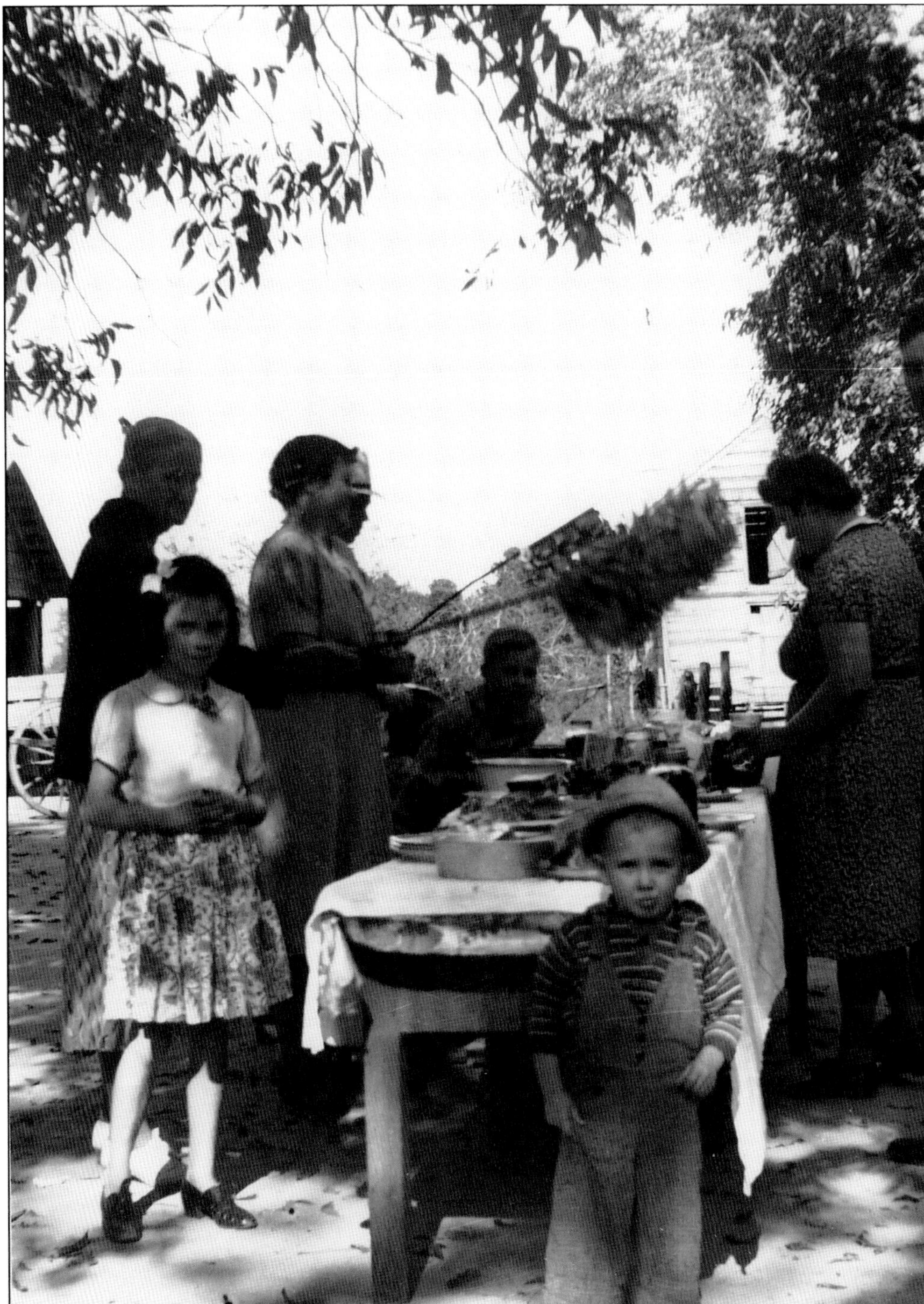

Black/Collins Reunion. Family bonds were strong among the Black/Collins family. Once a year, relatives would travel great distances—some from as far away as Texas—to gather and have dinner on the ground. The finest restaurants in the world could never match the taste of fresh-killed chicken, vegetables right out of the garden, and gallons of iced tea.

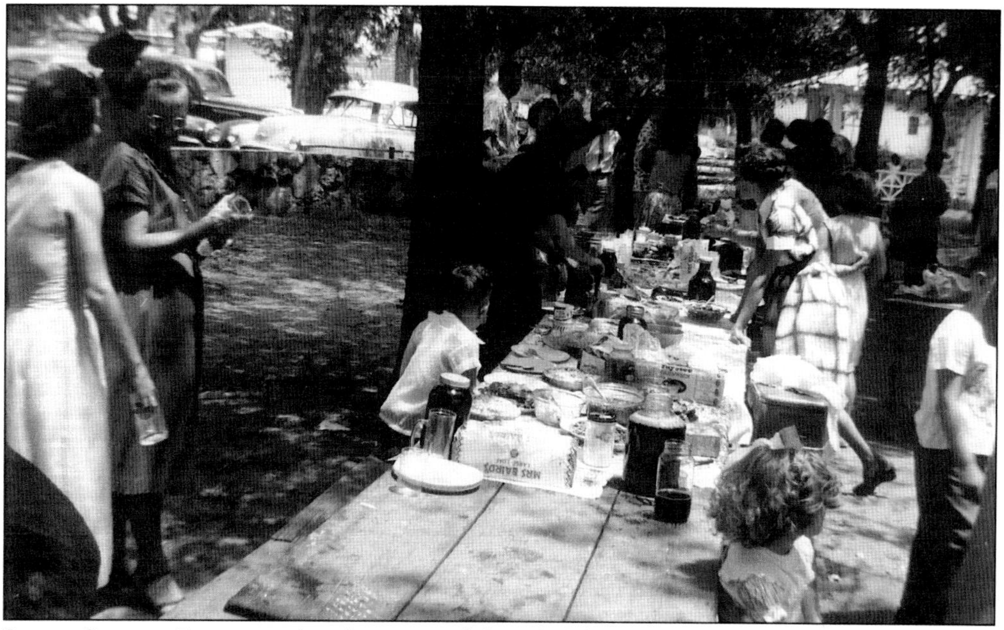

Black-Collins Reunion. Another view of the Black/Collins festivities during their reunion gives us an insight as to the closeness of the family. It is obvious that many people went to a lot of trouble to make the family affairs successful.

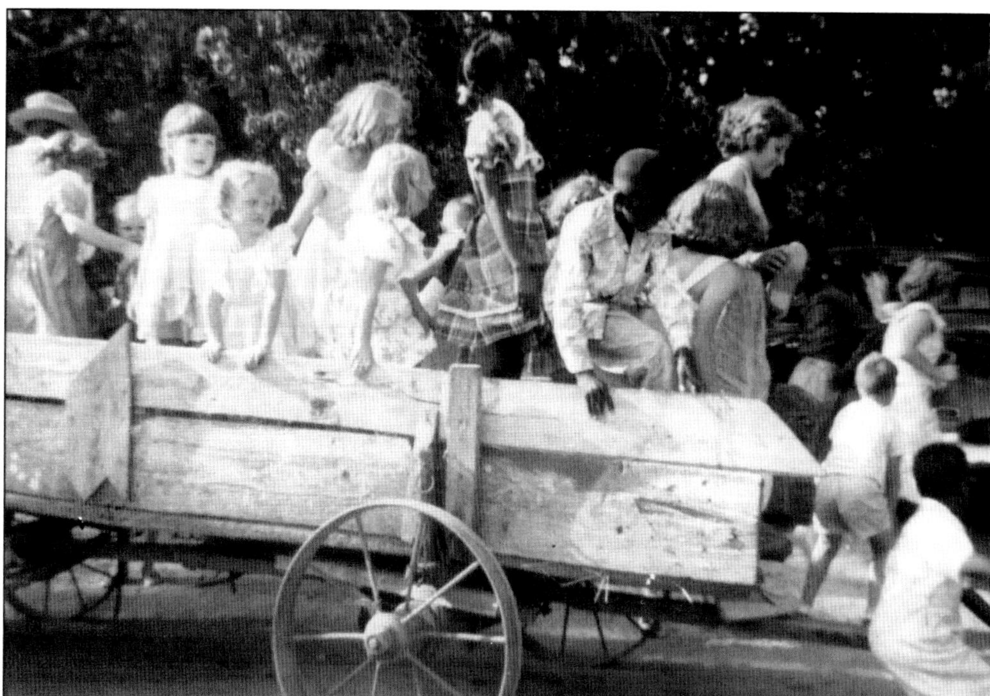

Wagon Ride. The annual Black/Collins reunions were opportunities for the young people of the family to get to know each other and form bonds that would last for a lifetime. Wagon rides were special treats that delighted the children.

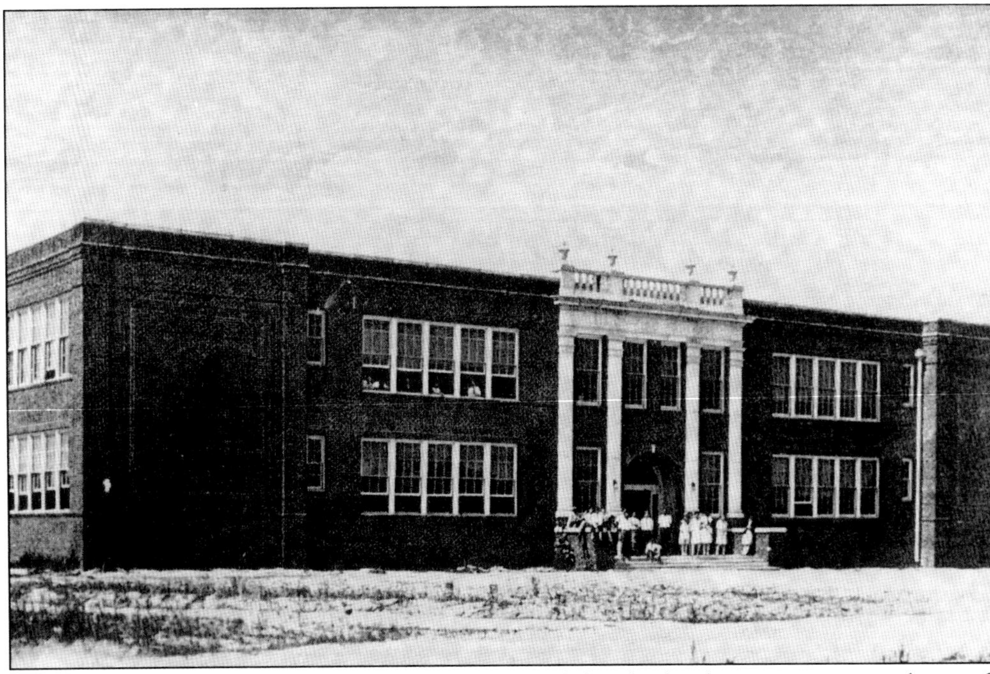

Williston High School. The arrival of the consolidated schools concept meant that each town would provide a school to which rural students would be bused. Williston's school was an attractive addition to the town.

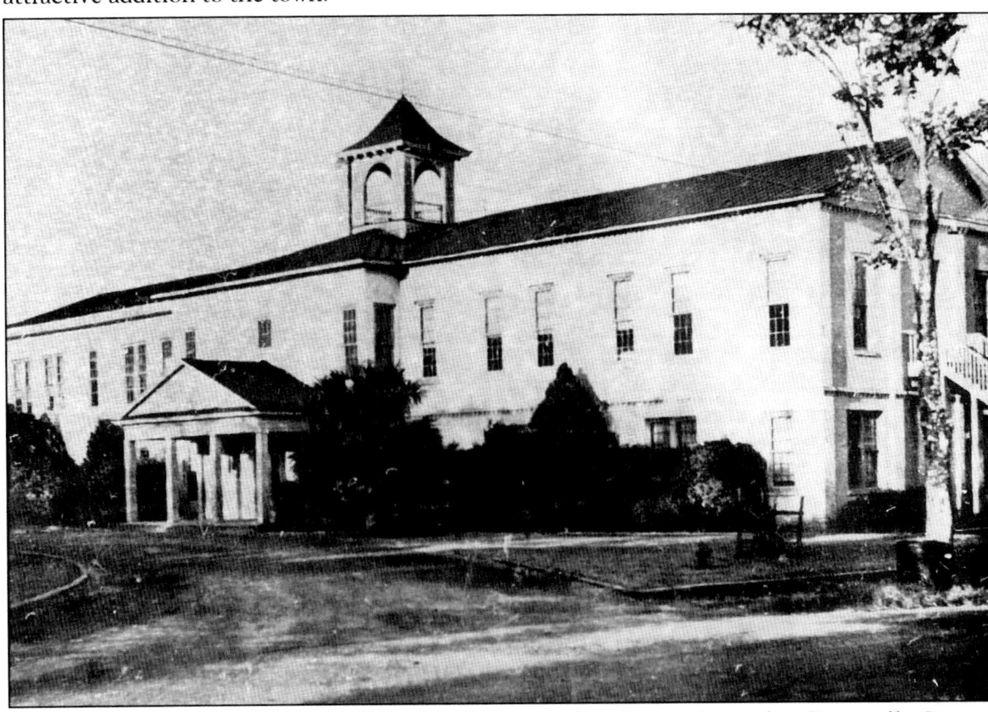

Blackville Graded School. This building was briefly used as the Barnwell County Courthouse before the county seat was moved to Barnwell and a permanent courthouse building was constructed.

Twelve

School Days

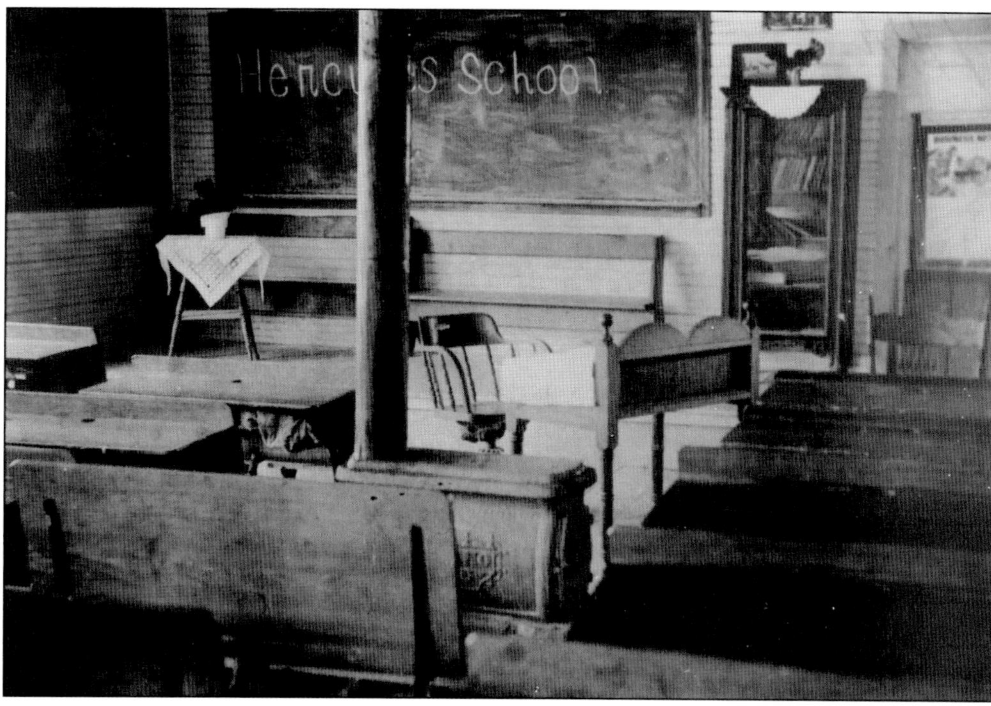

Hercules School. Before the consolidation movement of the late 1920s and early 1930s, education in Barnwell County consisted of instruction delivered in one-room schools located in the towns and scattered all over the countryside. This interior view of Hercules School is typical of the schoolhouses of the pre-consolidation era. In 1929, a special act of the legislature provided for centralized high schools, and by mid-century the one-room schoolhouses ceased to operate.

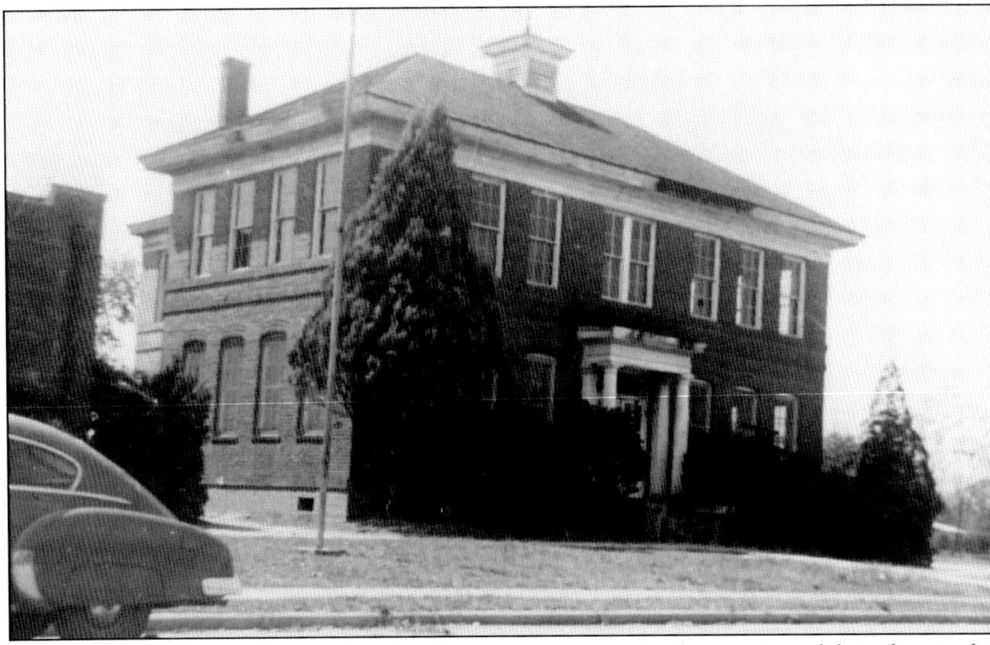

DUNBARTON SCHOOL. The people of Dunbarton have many fond memories of their days in this schoolhouse. The memory of the schools will live on in the photo albums and hearts of many.

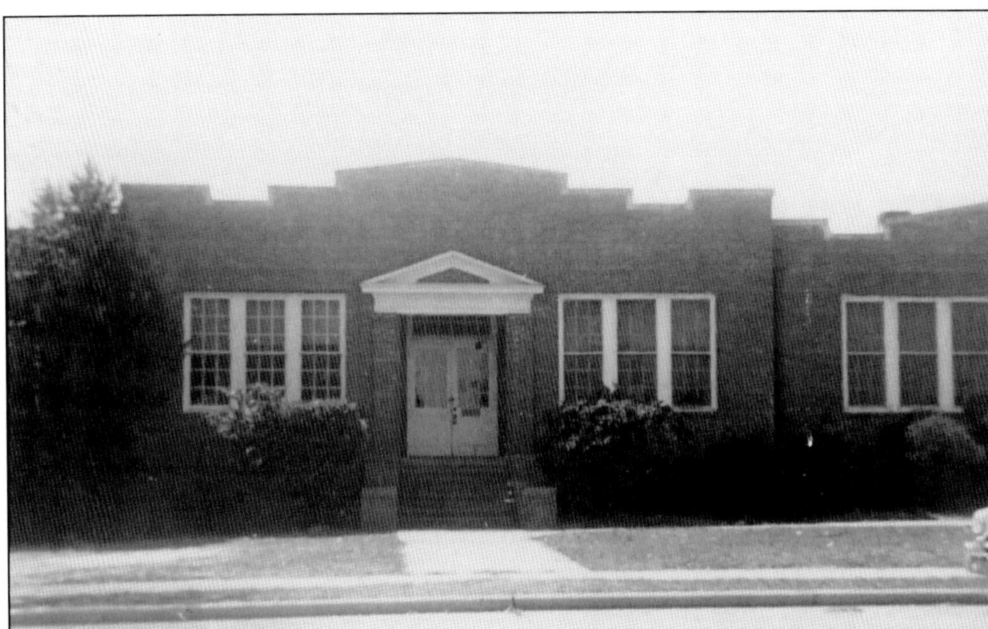

DUNBARTON HIGH SCHOOL. The distinctive architecture of this Dunbarton school made it a showpiece for the citizens whose taxes supported this school.

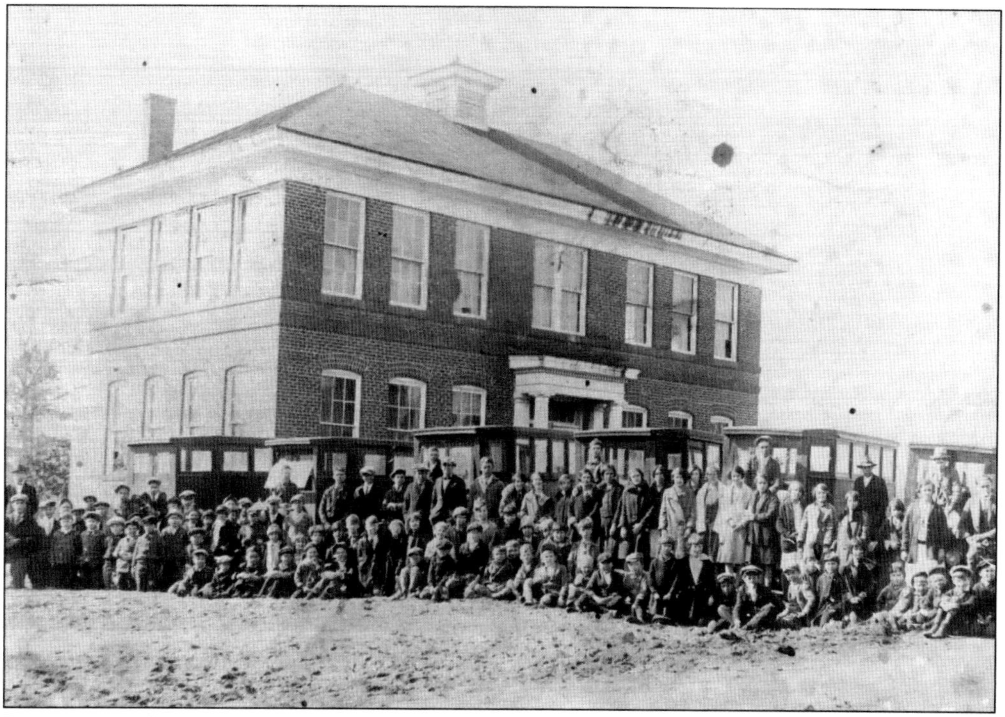

Dunbarton School and Buses. This unusual photograph not only includes the school and the children who attended it, but shows how they arrived there as well. The consolidation of the schools in the Dunbarton School District after the turn of the century made it necessary for the buses to be purchased.

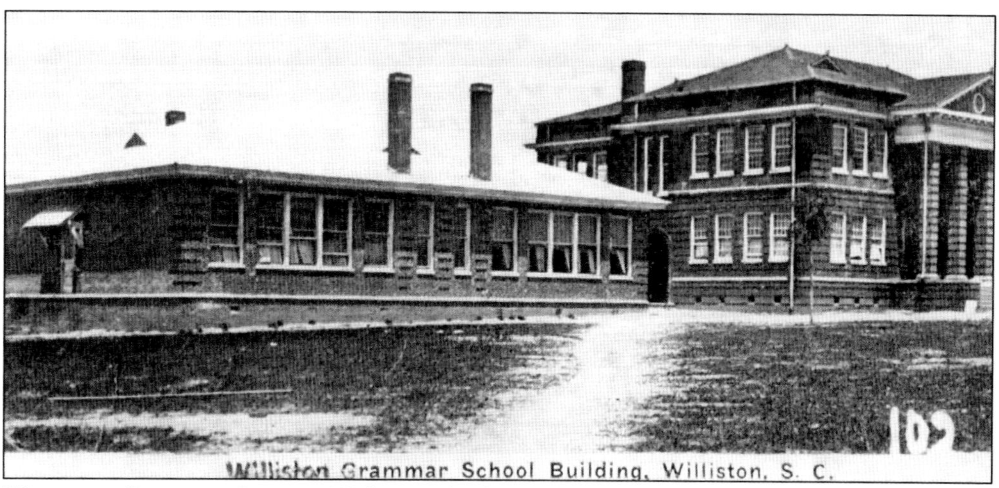

Williston Grammar School. Williston also boasted a handsome building in which to educate its students.

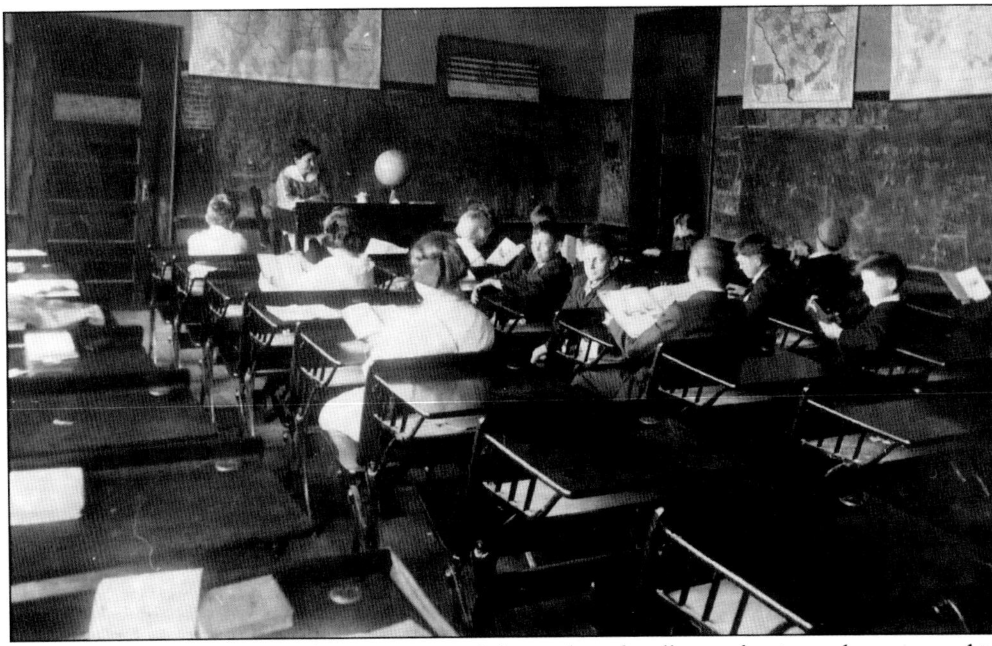

Unidentified Classroom. This rare postcard shows the schoolhouse furniture that was used in the 1930s and 1940s.

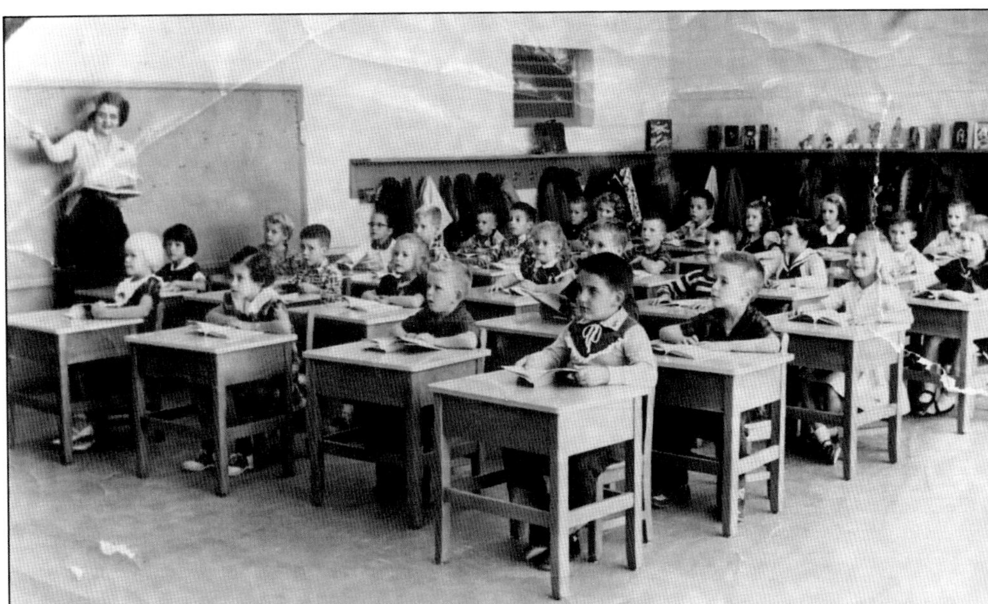

First Grade in 1954. The new elementary school was ready for occupancy, and Mrs. Carrie Turner was eager to take her group of pupils down the exciting road of discovery. The Class of 1966 would begin their journey here and see many changes throughout their years of education. The same year, the United States Supreme Court decision in *Brown v. the Board of Education* would make sweeping changes, and this group would see the effects before their departure from the Barnwell school system.

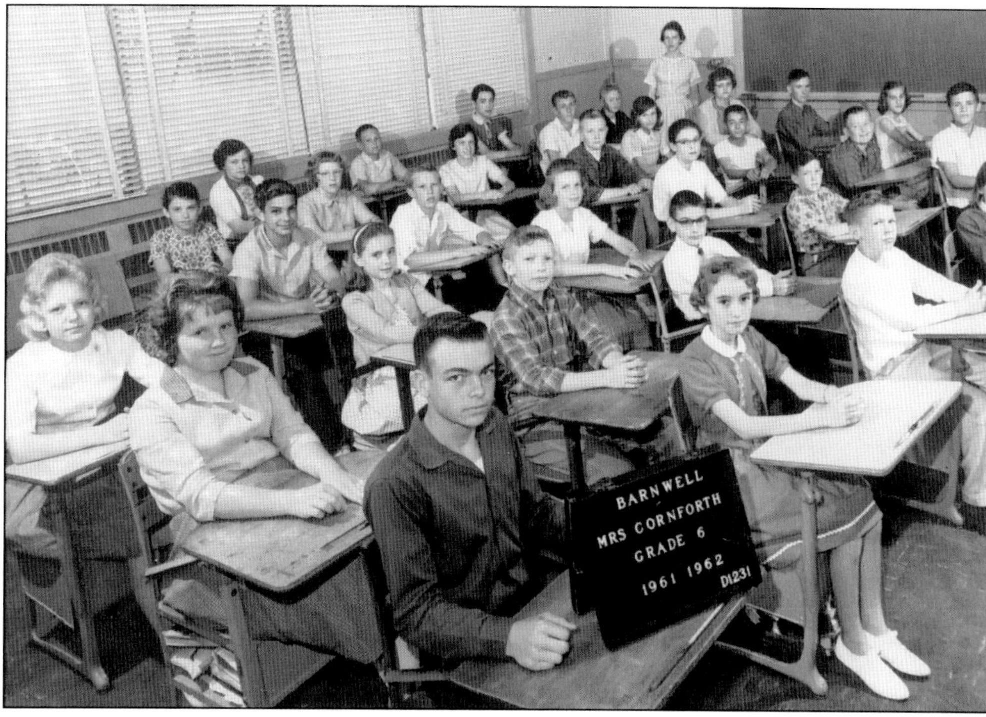

SIXTH GRADE IN 1961. The Class of 1968 sits quietly for their class portrait, unsuspecting that this decade would be one of turmoil and strife. The assassination of an American president and increasing military involvement in Southeast Asia would color these students' attitudes about our society.

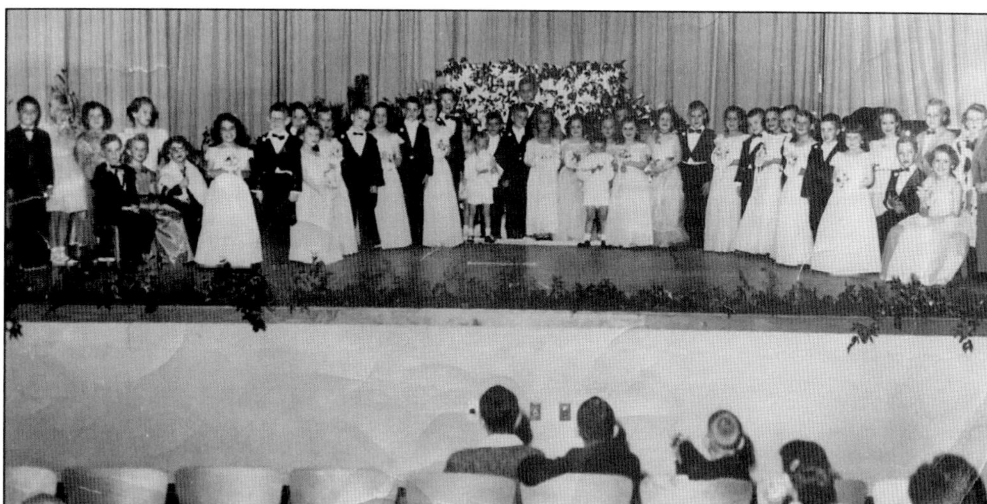

TOM THUMB WEDDING IN 1955. The rush of workers constructing the Savannah River Plant forced Barnwell to construct a new elementary school to accommodate the influx of students. One of the most useful features of Barnwell Elementary School was the new auditorium. First graders from the school took advantage of the new facility to stage a Tom Thumb wedding. The fledgling students dressed up in their finest outfits and thoroughly enjoyed this festive occasion.

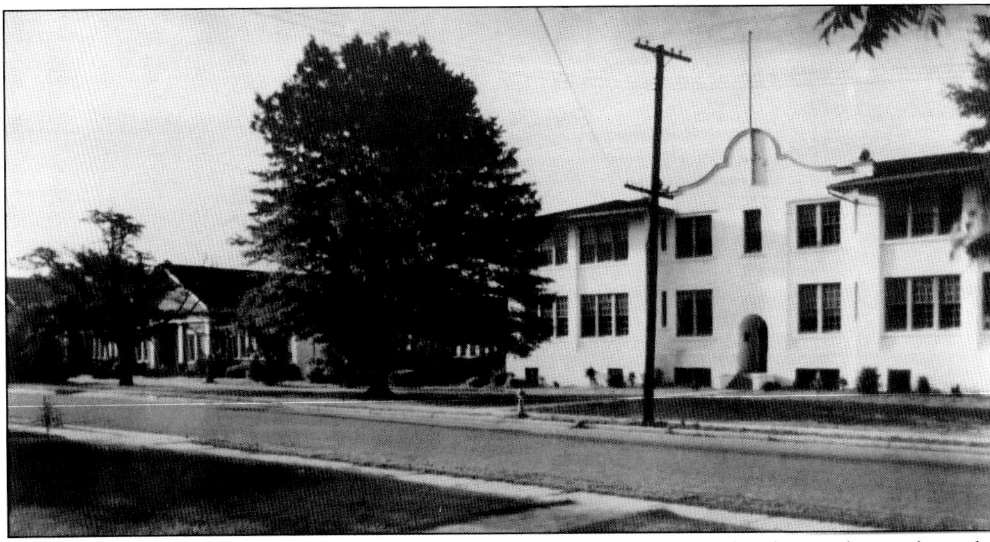

Hagood Avenue Schools. The high school and the elementary school were located on the south side of Hagood Avenue. After the new high school and gymnasium were constructed in the 1940s, the large white building which had been constructed in 1914 was no longer needed. It was torn down in the late 1950s.

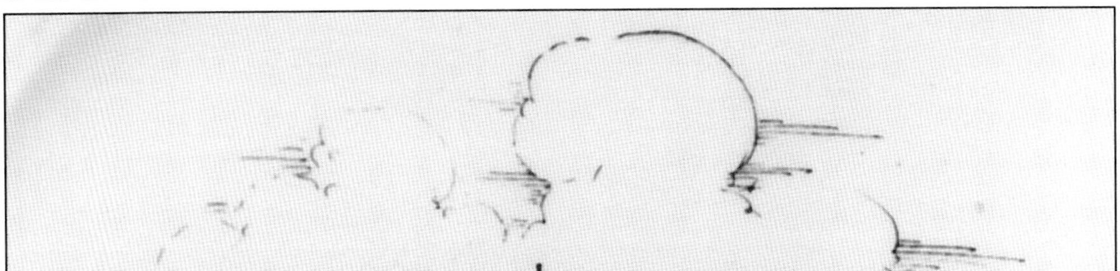

Plate for Hagood School. The community rallied around the school district and supported the rebuilding of the school on Hagood Avenue that had been destroyed. Apparently, one of the activities connected with this effort was the sale of decorative plates with a likeness of the school imprinted on them.

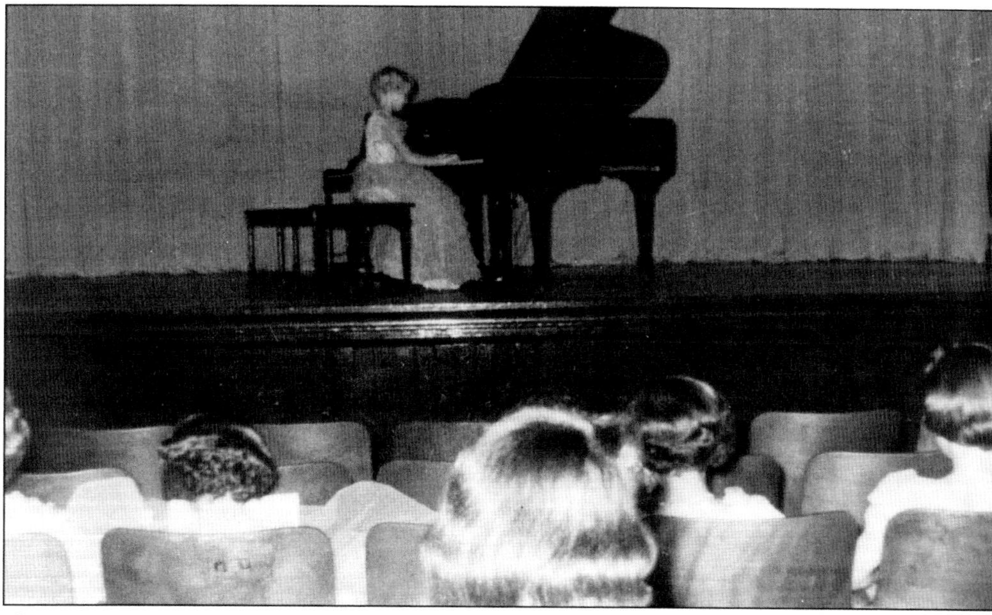

Hagood Avenue Auditorium Recital in the Late 1950s. The Hagood Avenue school had the largest auditorium of the Barnwell schools. Private music teachers were allowed to use the school's facilities to teach piano lessons and the auditorium for their pupils' recitals. In this photo, Mrs. Brandenberg's pupil, Marie Witt, presented her recital piece to an appreciative audience.

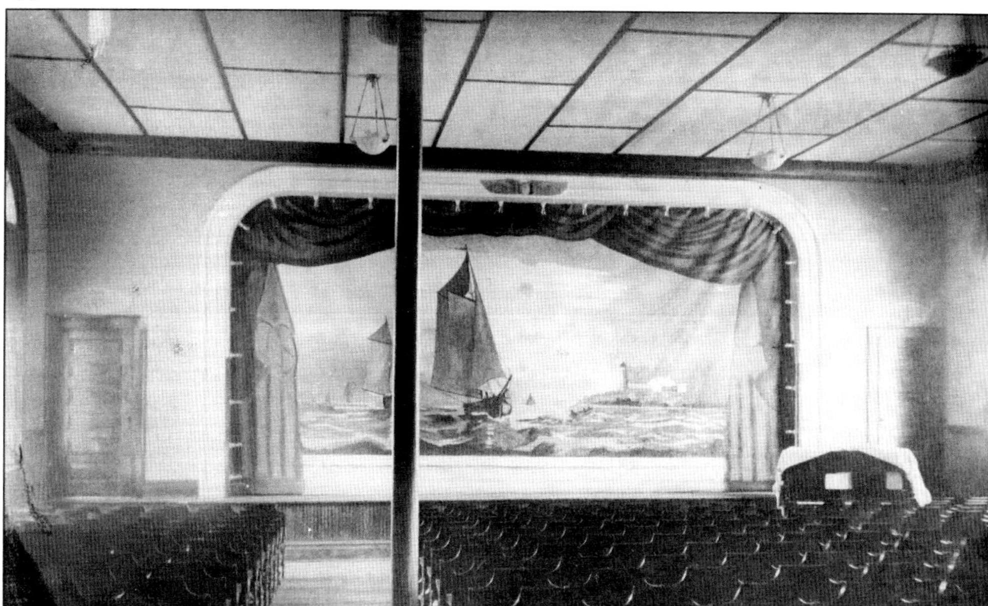

Hagood Avenue Auditorium in the 1940s. This view of the Hagood Avenue auditorium shows the structure before it was destroyed by fire in the late 1940s. When the auditorium was rebuilt, structural changes allowed the supporting pillars to be eliminated. It had a spacious backstage area and a back entrance that led directly to the stage area, as well as storage facilities downstairs.

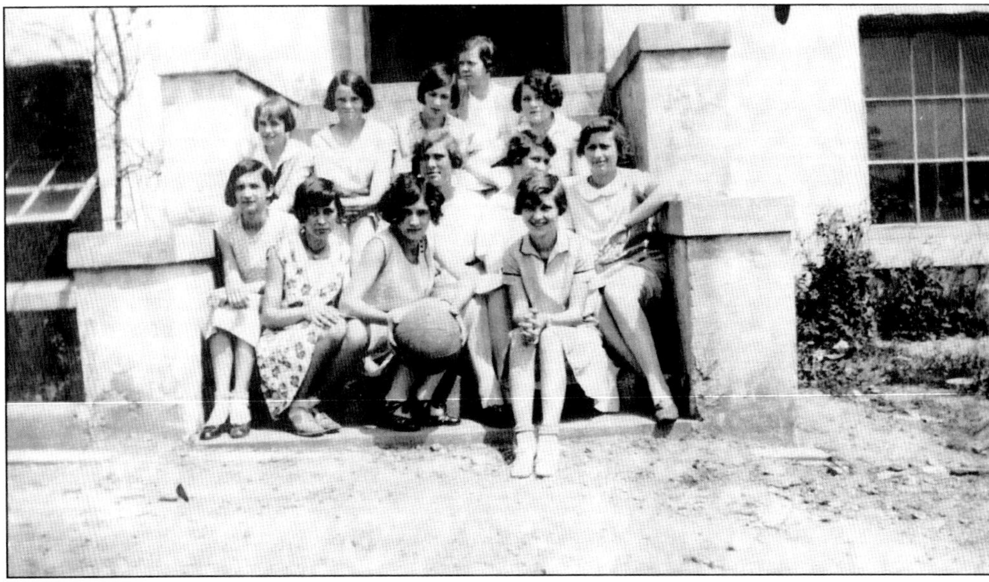

Barnwell Basketball Team. According to the caption accompanying the photograph in the school yearbook, Barnwell's 1929–30 girls basketball team was a distinct improvement over the teams of the preceding years. The girls' coach was Miss Margaret "Git" Free.

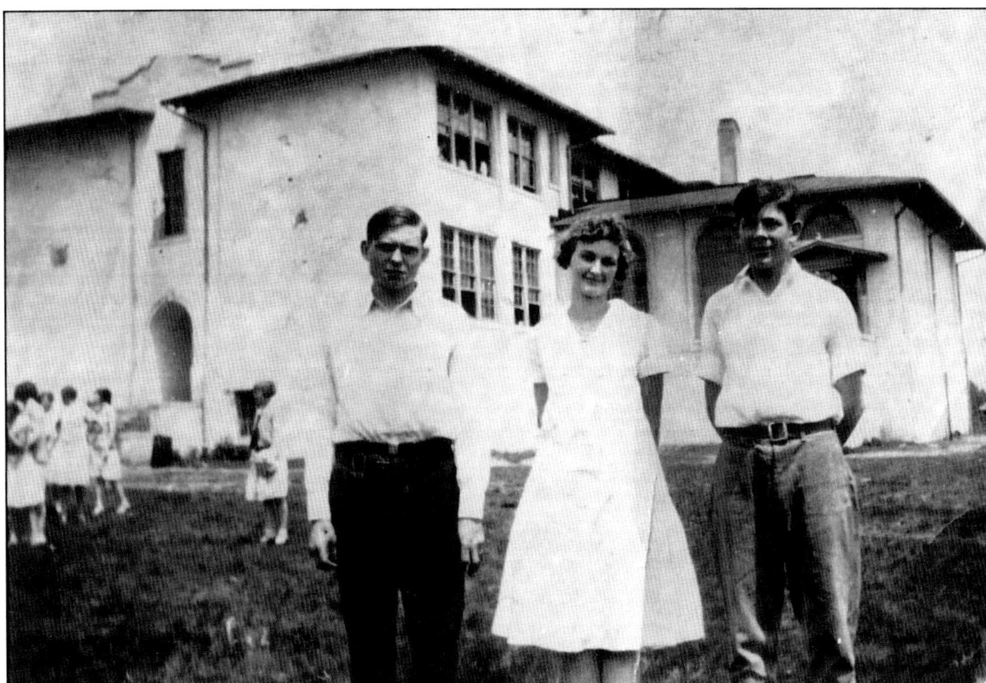

Dedication of the Yearbook. This photograph appeared on the dedication page of the 1930 Barnwell High School yearbook, the *Hurricane*.

HURRICANE YEARBOOK STAFF. The staff of the *Hurricane* are pictured beside the high school as follows: Editor-in-chief Fannie Cooper, Literary Editor Mildred Lewis, Athletic Editor Lois Cromer, Joke Editor Elizabeth Hagood, Snapshot Editor Claire Dicks, and Business Manager Elmer Grubbs. The advisor was Miss Virginia Kyzer.

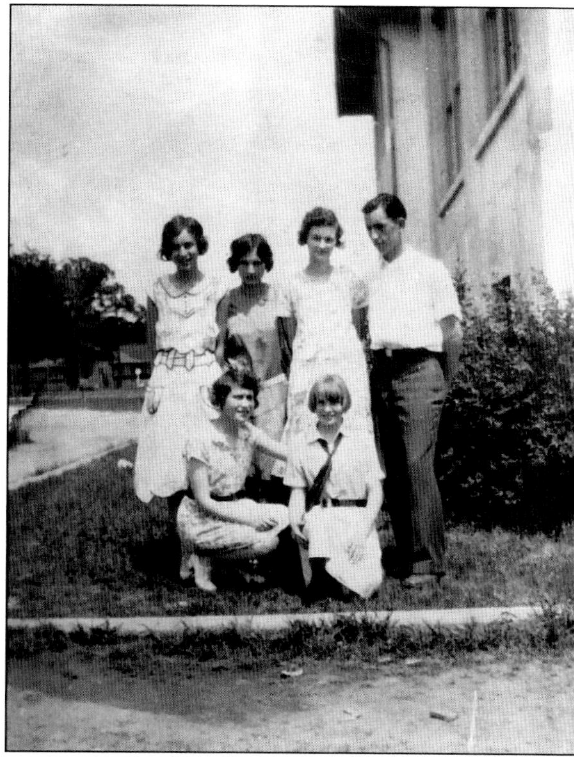

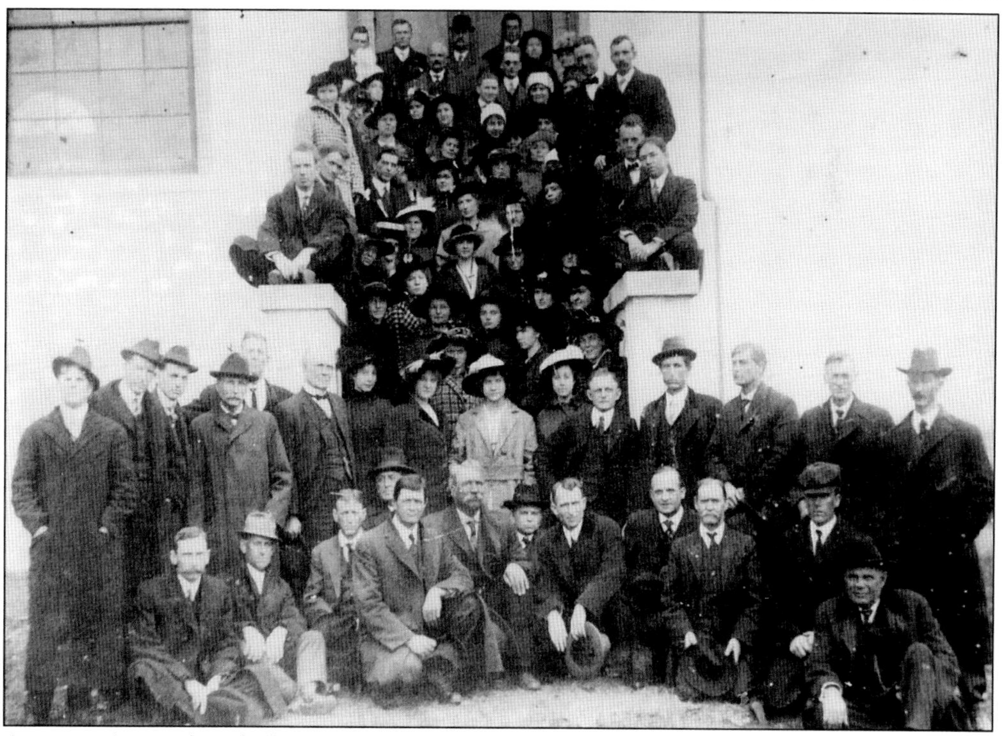

ALUMNI. An unidentified group of alumni poses outside the school building. Is there anyone out there who knows who these folks are?

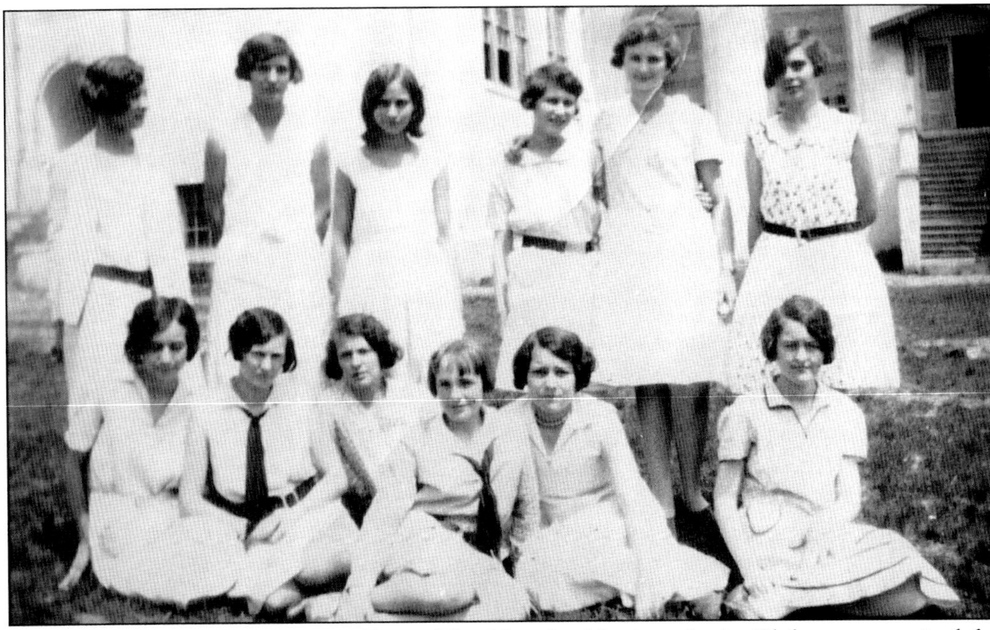

The Vestales Virgines Latin Club. The Vestales Virgines Latin Club was organized for the purpose of boosting interest in the study of Latin and presenting instructive programs in an interesting way. Its members consisted of those pupils who were studying Virgil. Honorary membership included the faculty.

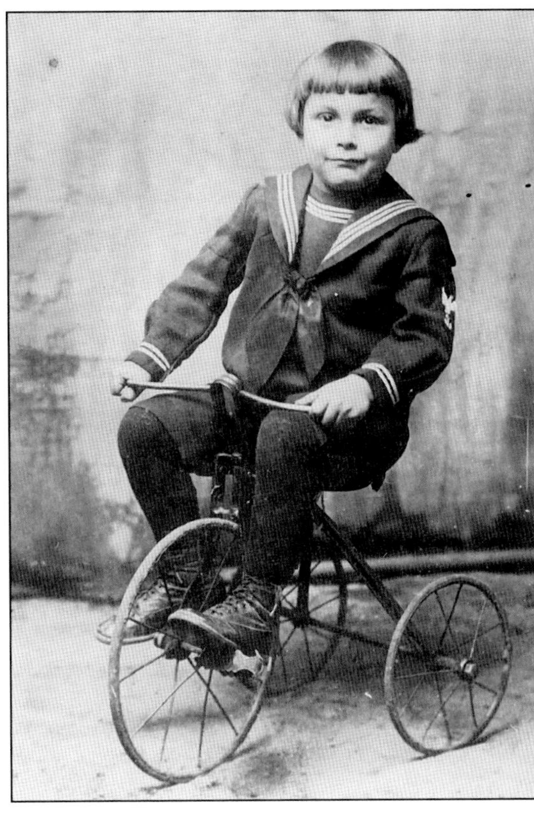

Typical school child in the 1920s.

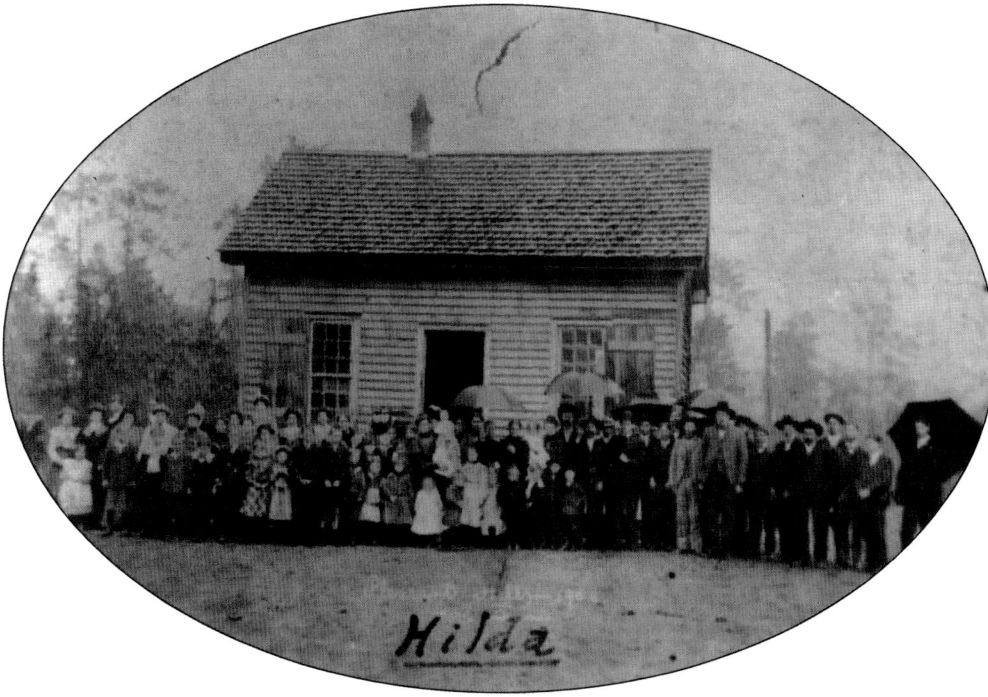

PLEASANT HILL. The faculty and students of Pleasant Hill braved the elements for their portrait.

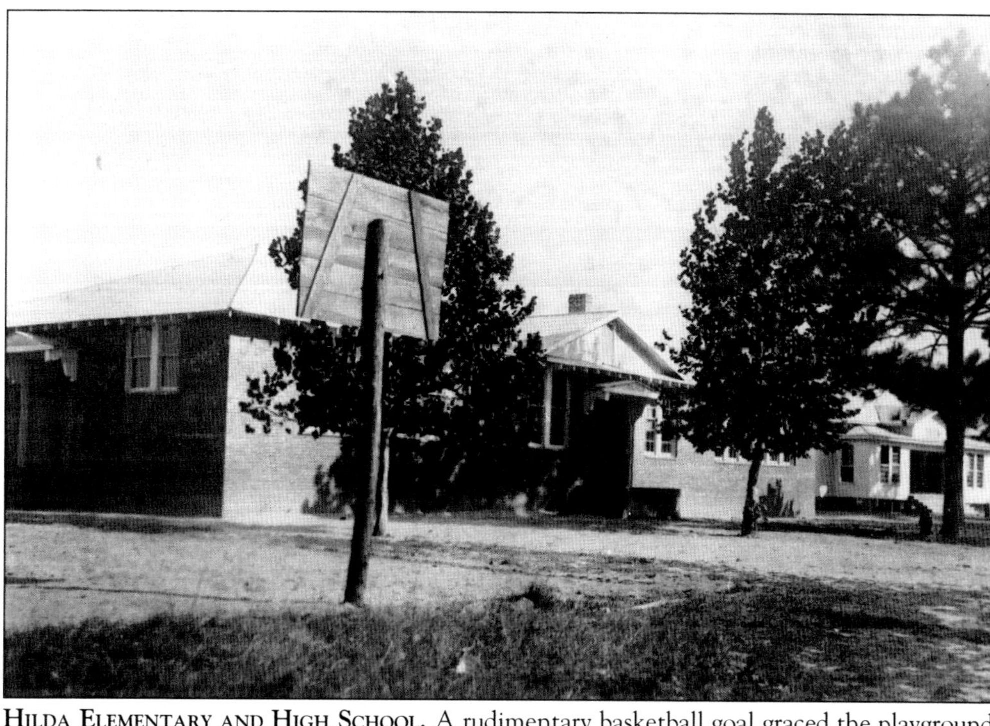

HILDA ELEMENTARY AND HIGH SCHOOL. A rudimentary basketball goal graced the playground of this combined campus.

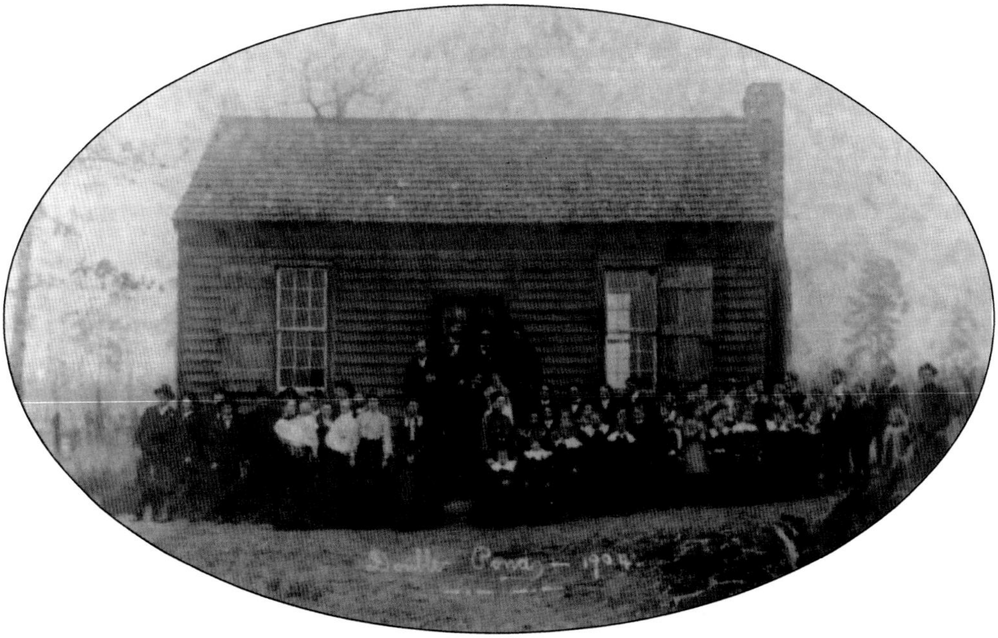

DOUBLE POND SCHOOL. Double Pond School was one of the one-room schoolhouses that served the eastern portion of Barnwell County.

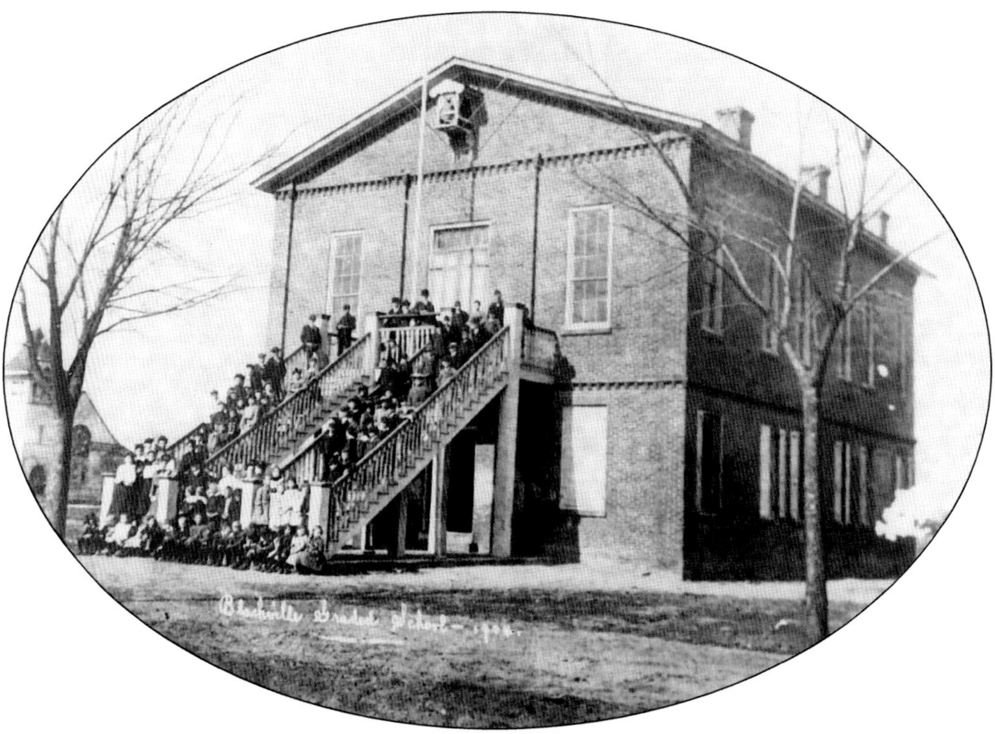

BLACKVILLE GRADED SCHOOL. This 1904 portrait of the Blackville Graded School and its occupants was one of a series of school portraits taken that year. Note the Baptist church in the background at left.

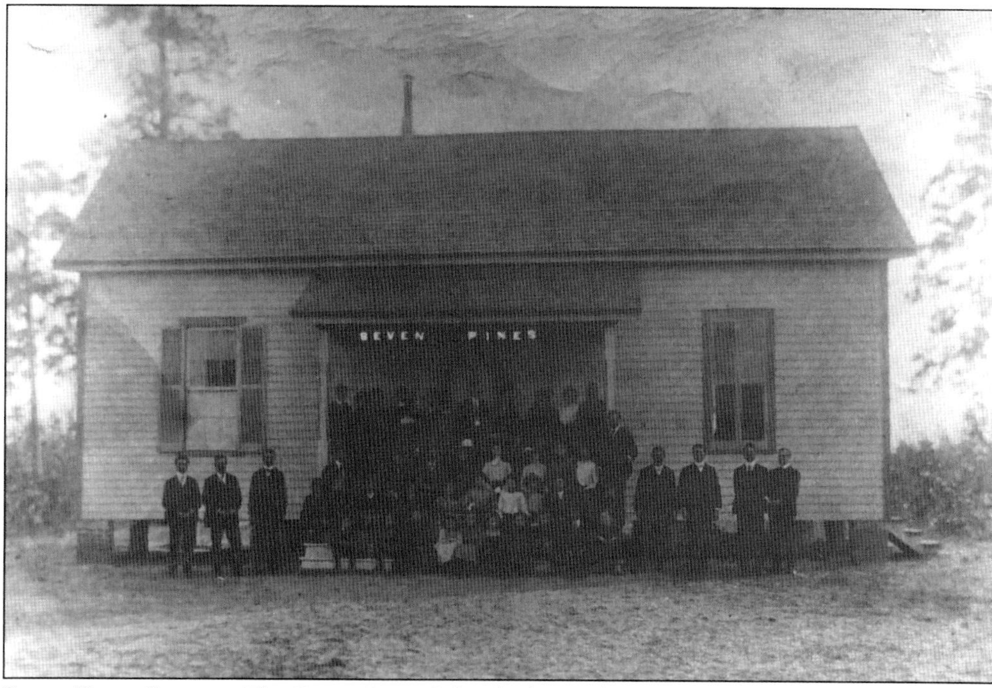

Seven Pines School. The Seven Pines School educated quite a number of age groups, as can be seen in this formal portrait of the student body.

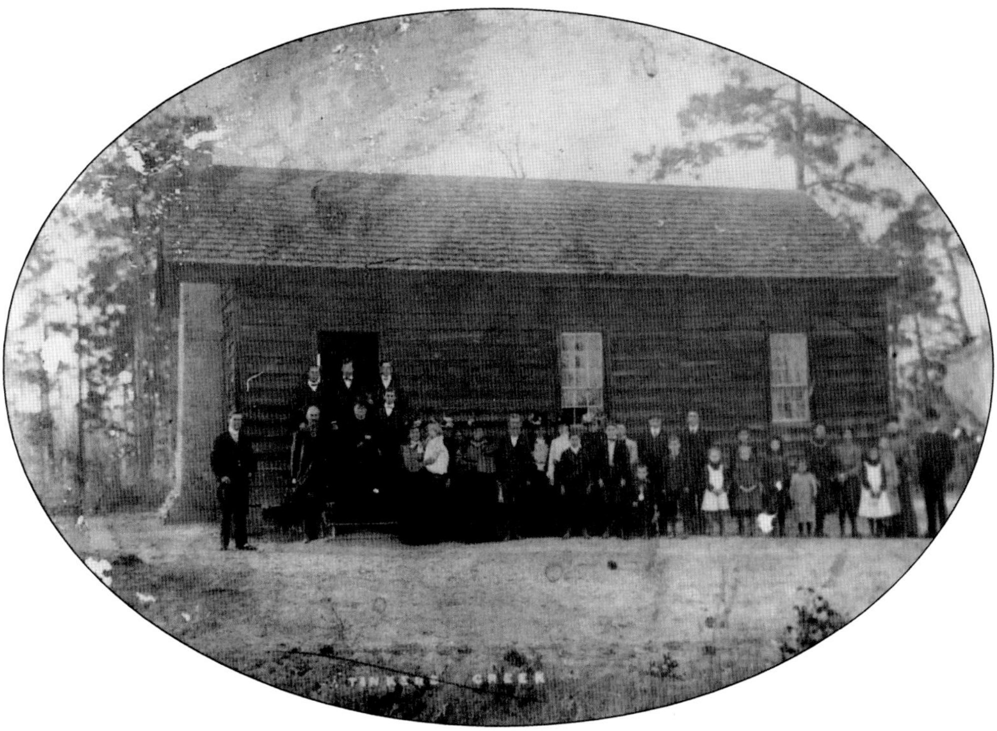

Tinker Creek School. Located between Williston and Barnwell, the Tinker Creek School also served a variety of older students.

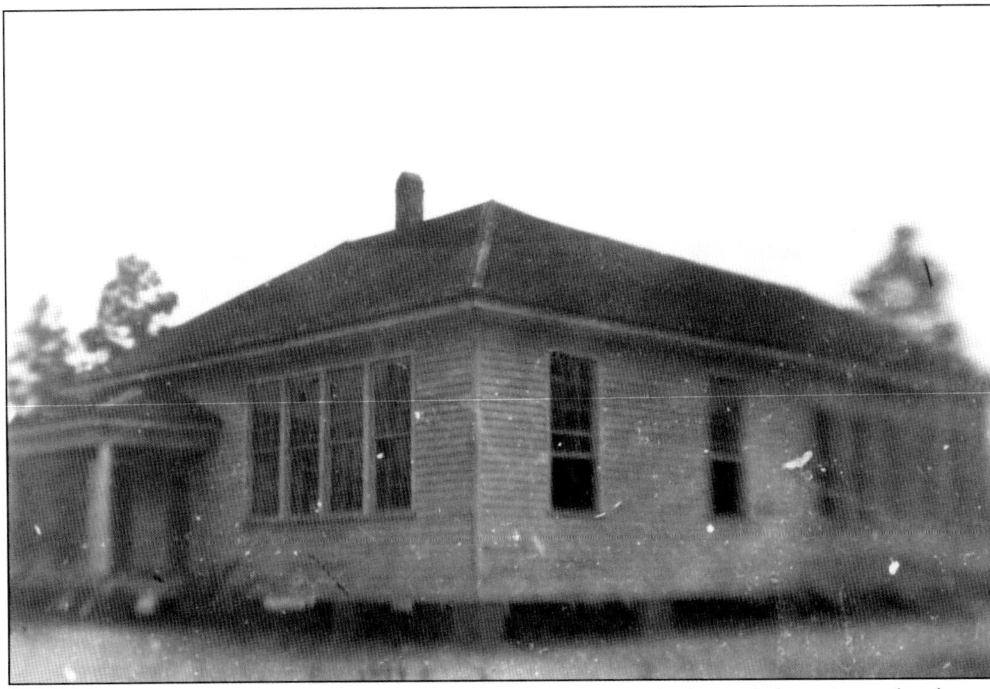

Morris School (White and Black). An examination of plots of the Morris land near Hurricane Branch reveals that 1 acre of land was given by Mrs. W.P. Morris for a schoolhouse. The building was one of a series of small schools dotting the countryside all around the county. When it ceased to be used by the white population, the structure was used for black pupils until the black schools in the town of Barnwell became available. The school was located approximately halfway between Barnwell and Kline.

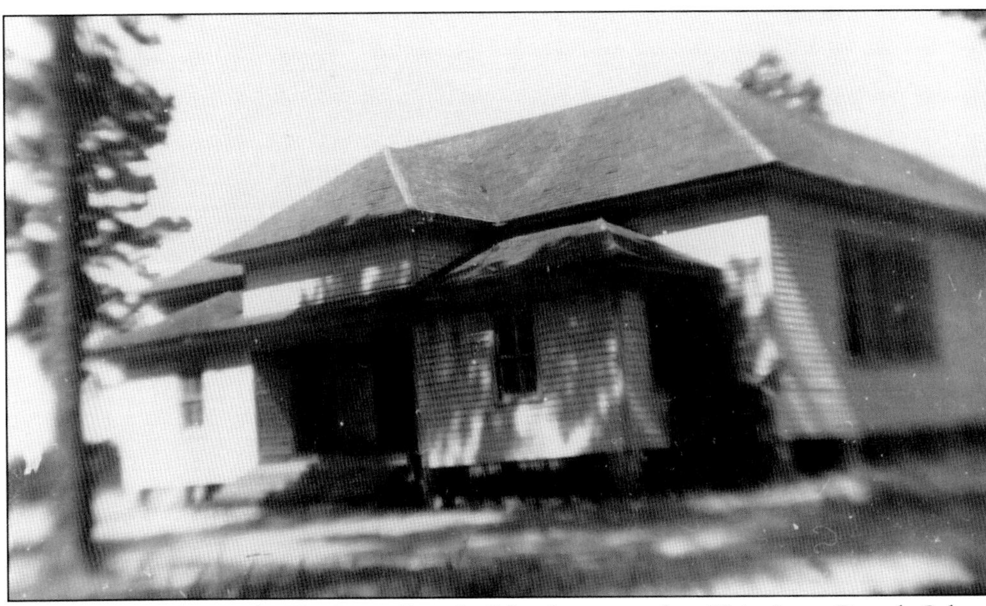

Long Branch (White). The Long Branch School was number 57 in Long Branch School District #8.

Thirteen

Treasures from the Dumpster

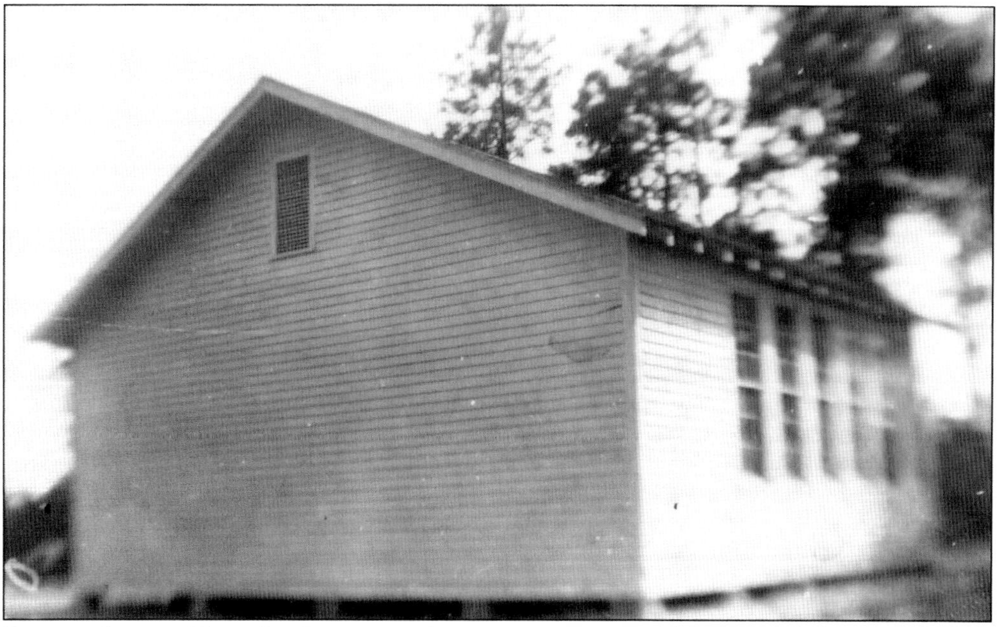

Rescued Images. The school images in this section were rescued from a trash dumpster in Elko by Jennings Rountree when he was a teenager. Most likely, these photographs were taken by Horace Crouch, the county superintendent of schools for many years, and discarded after his death. They are especially valuable because most of the negatives were stapled together and identified. Although some negatives were stuck together and portions of the emulsion missing, this group of photographs records the legacy of the days before consolidation became the norm for both white and black schools in the area. The image on this page was not identified . . . does anyone out there recognize this one?

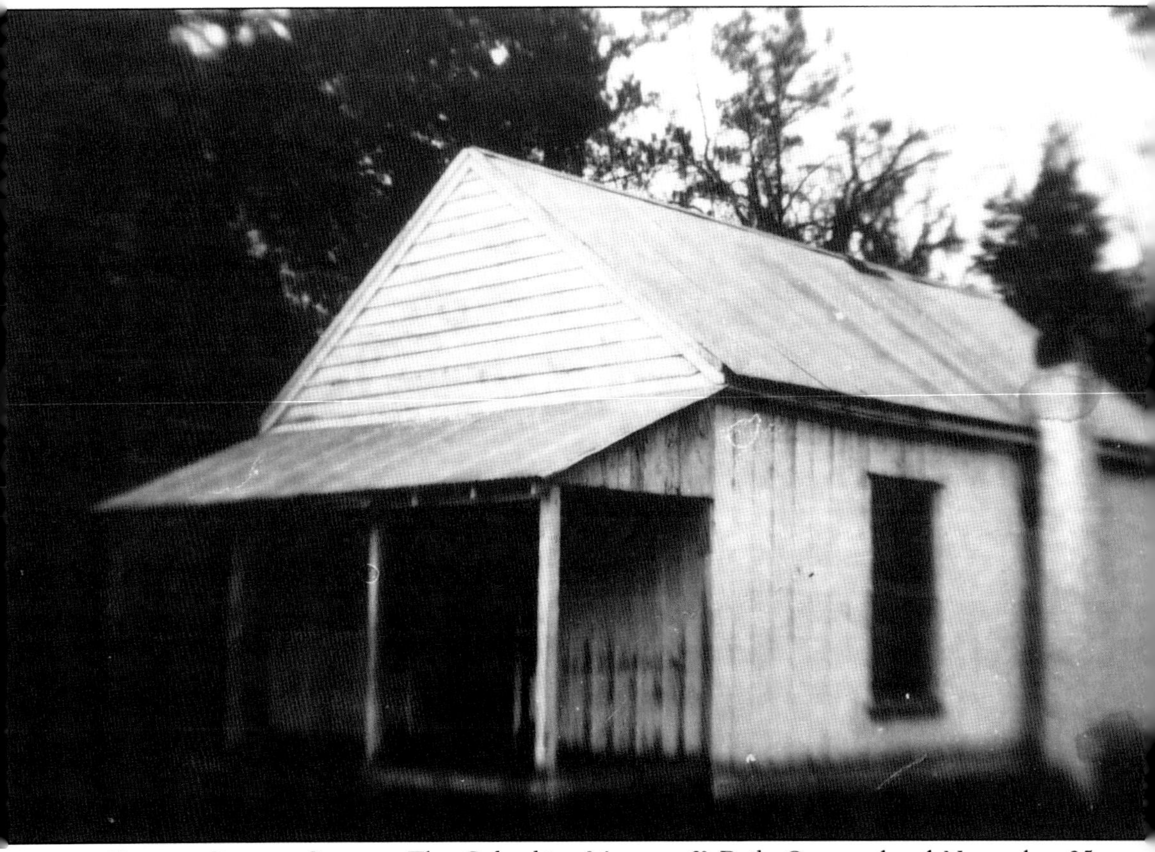

Boiling Springs School. The *Columbian Museum & Daily Gazette* dated November 25, 1820, posted the following announcement: "Teachers will be wanted to take charge of this academy on the first day of January next. The situation of the Boiling Spring is about 7 miles from Savannah River, in South Carolina; 8 miles from the village of Barnwell; and about 25 miles below Augusta. The water is equal to any on this side of the mountains. It is supposed the spring emits daily two hundred hogsheads of water which is pure, cold, and pleasant; the situation is high pine land, and has proved remarkably healthy for several years past. The salary of the teachers has not yet been determined upon by the Board of Trustees—but there is no doubt that they will be equal to other institutions of the kind throughout the state. The principal will be required to teach all the branches of education which are usually taught in other academies." Such is the legacy of Boiling Springs Academy, carried on in the one-room schoolhouse pictured here.

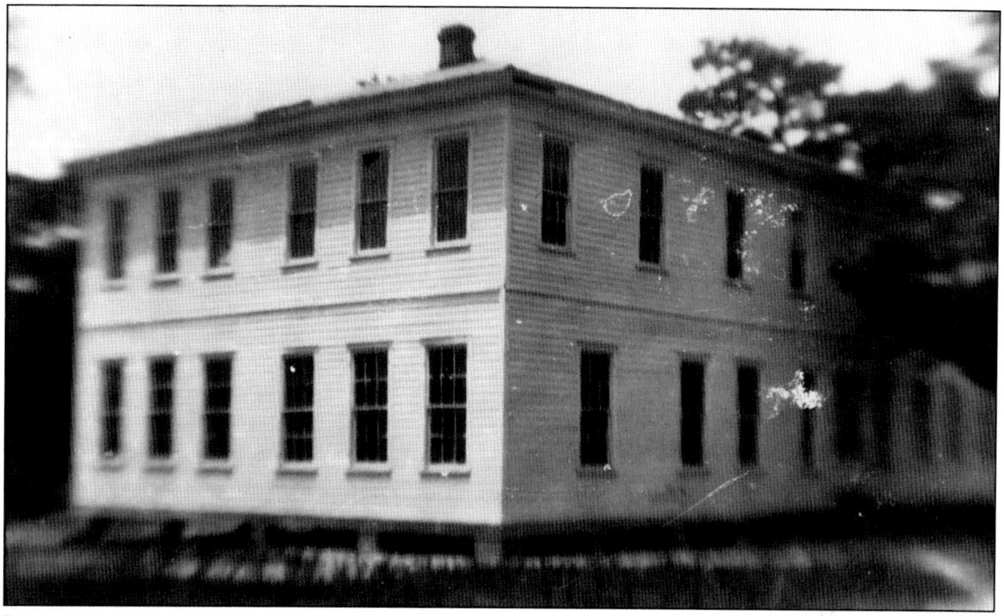

Barnwell Elementary (Black). The schools that served the black population in the early part of this century were located in the northeast section of town. The elementary school for black children was listed as school number 70.

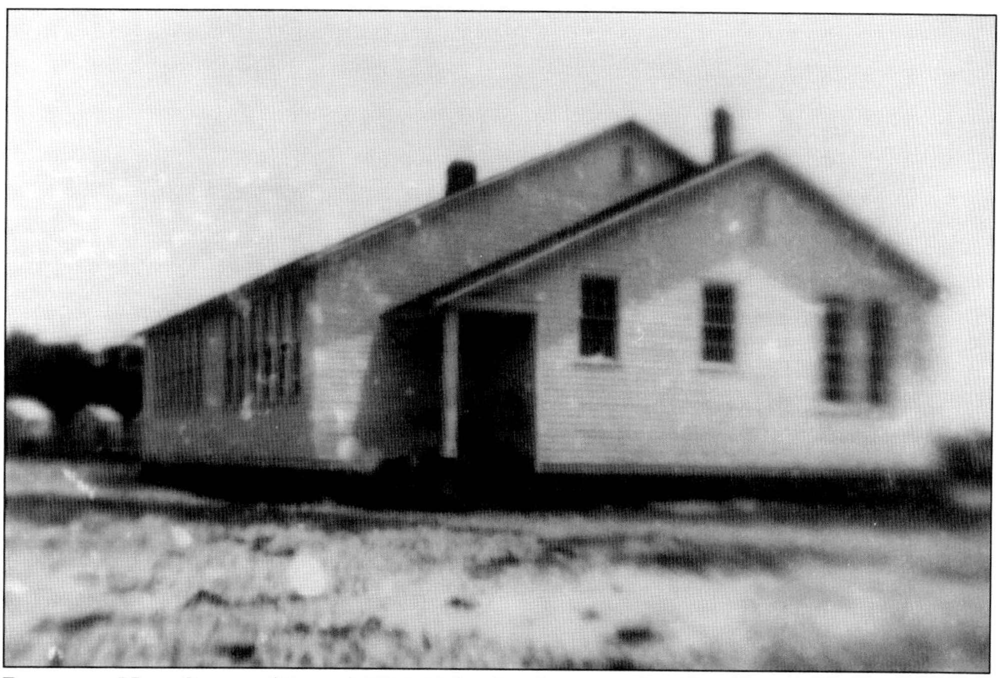

Barnwell High School (Black). This high school was number 71 in Barnwell School District 45. In the early 1950s, a modern school, Butler High, was designed and built near this one to serve the black population of Barnwell.

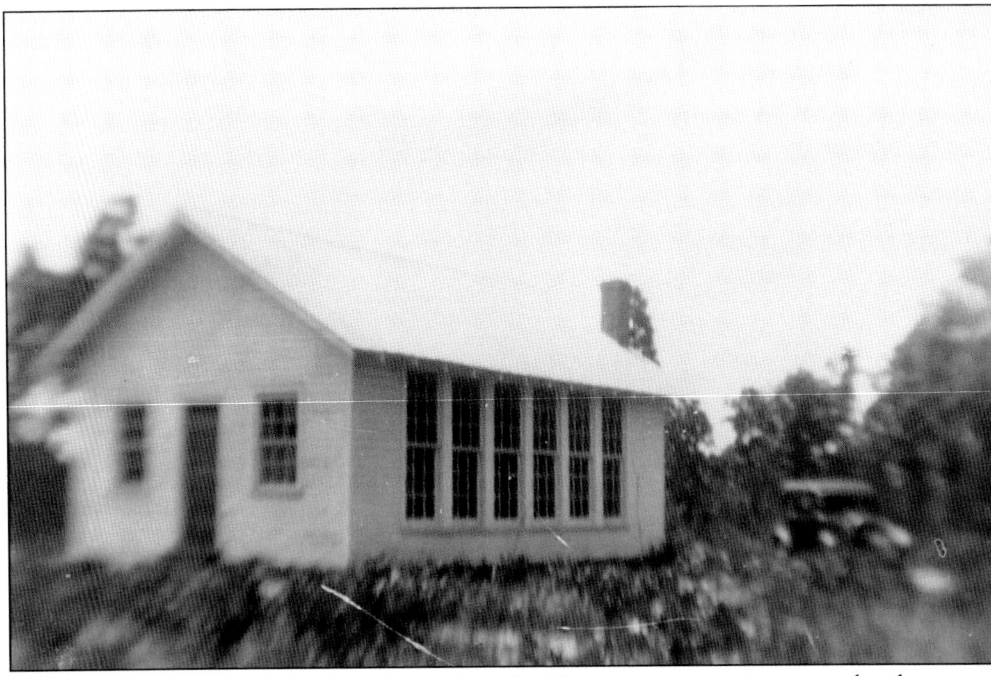

Friendship. Friendship School was located in the Sleytown community, several miles east of Barnwell. The school was number 44 in District 39.

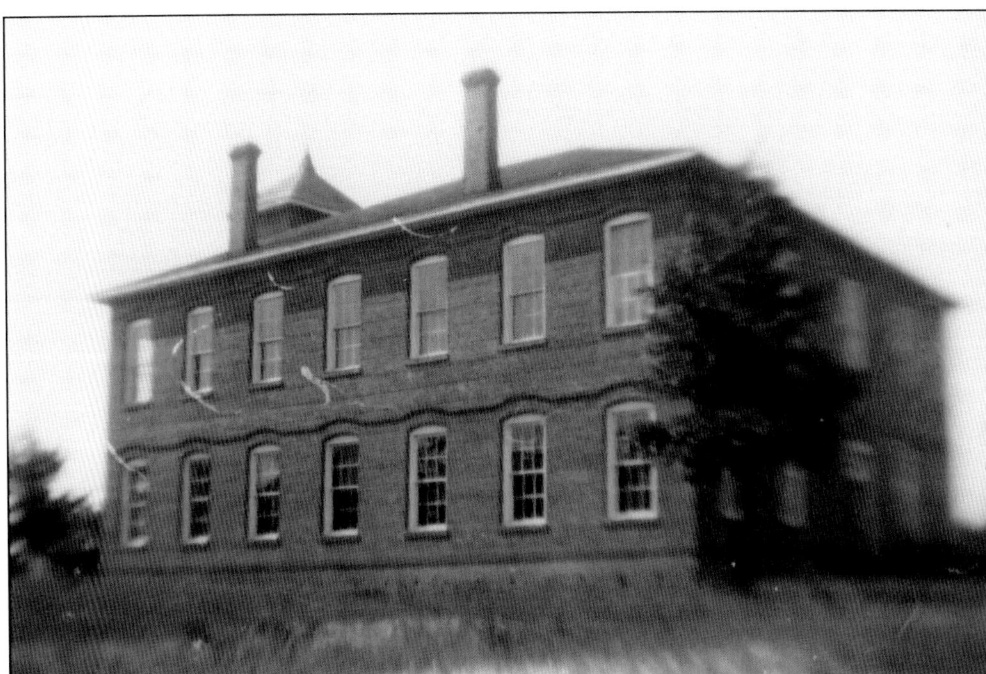

Elko. The community of Elko was large enough to support a school. This one was number 62 in Elko District 28.

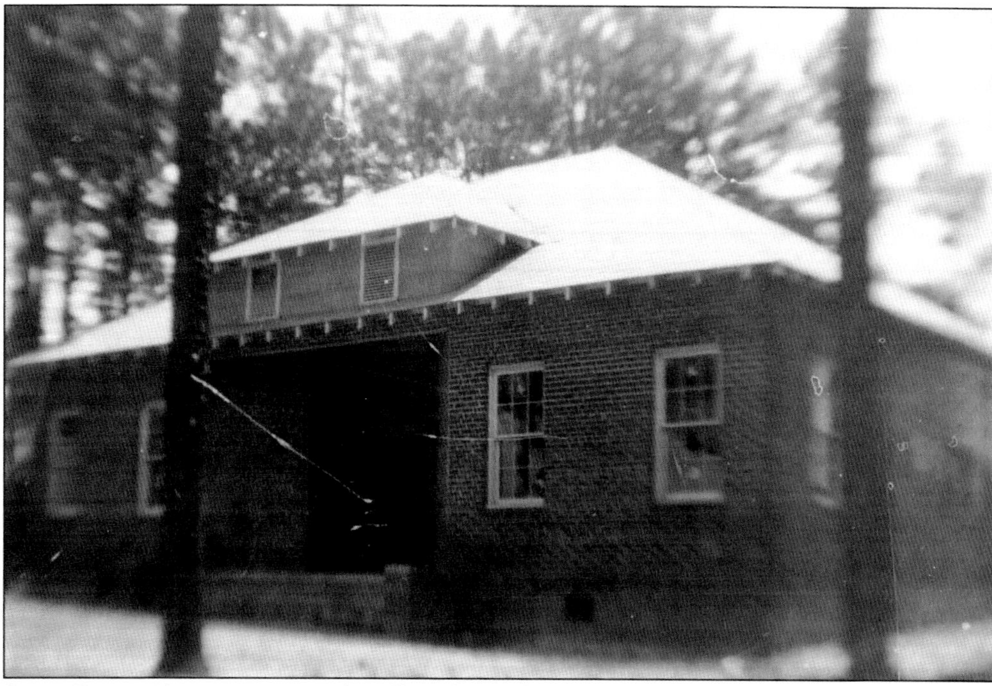

SEVEN PINES. The community of Snelling, located a few miles west of Barnwell, held classes for its youngsters in this building.

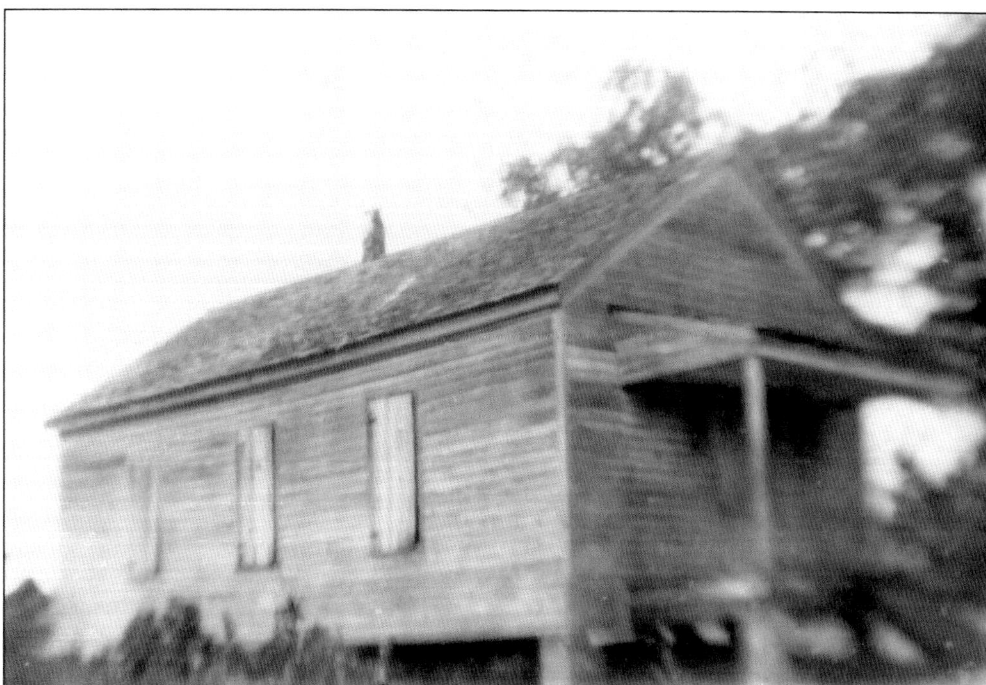

ST. PAUL'S (BLACK). The St. Paul's School for black students was school number 37 in the Seven Pines District 2.

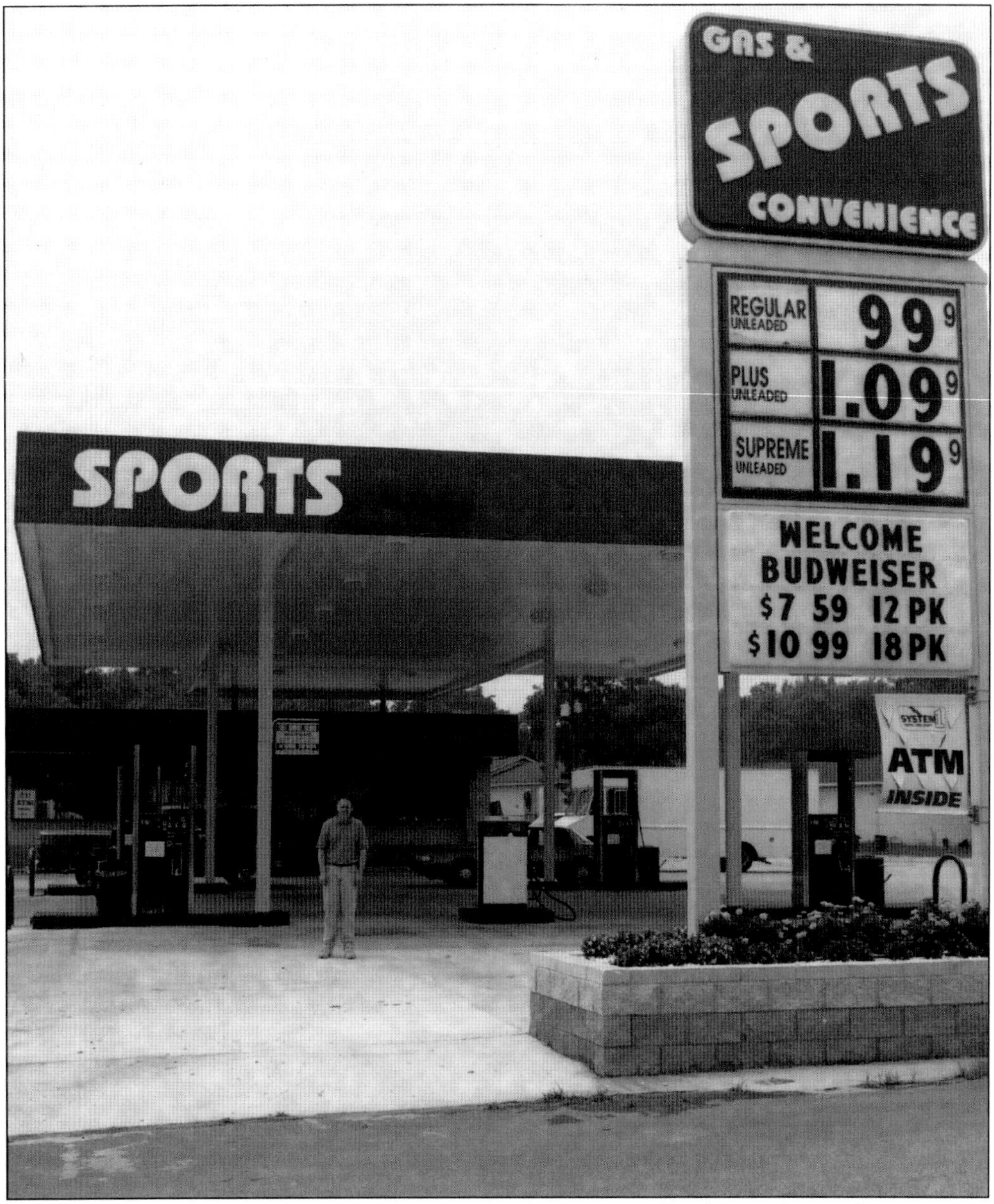

THE FUTURE OF BARNWELL COUNTY—1999. Sport Holland stands in front of his convenience store, which stands on the very spot that his father's store occupied years before (see page 36). This modern store illustrates the determination that the people of Barnwell County have to succeed and maintain the traditions that have made small-town America the backbone of our country.

As Barnwell County faces the turn of another century, we hope that its citizens will continue to rely upon our proud history to inspire and guide them as we take this county forward.